Botanical Line Drawing 1

BY

MZ CREATES

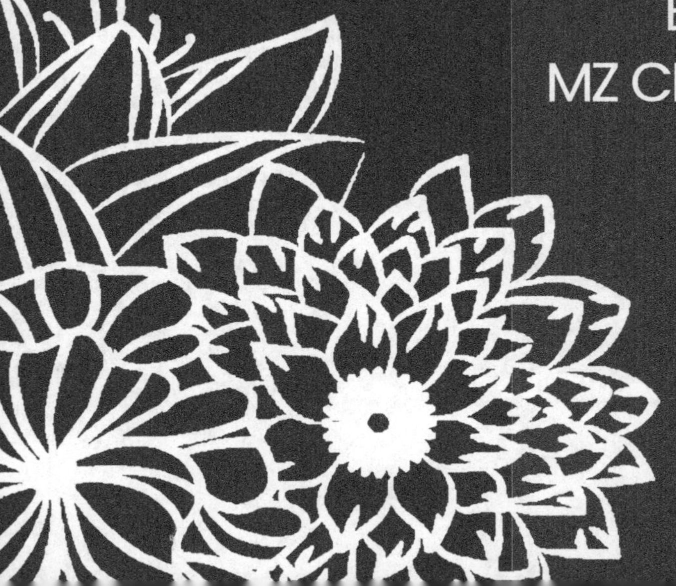

Published By:

INKTRIBE

Creativity. Empowered.

COPYRIGHTS

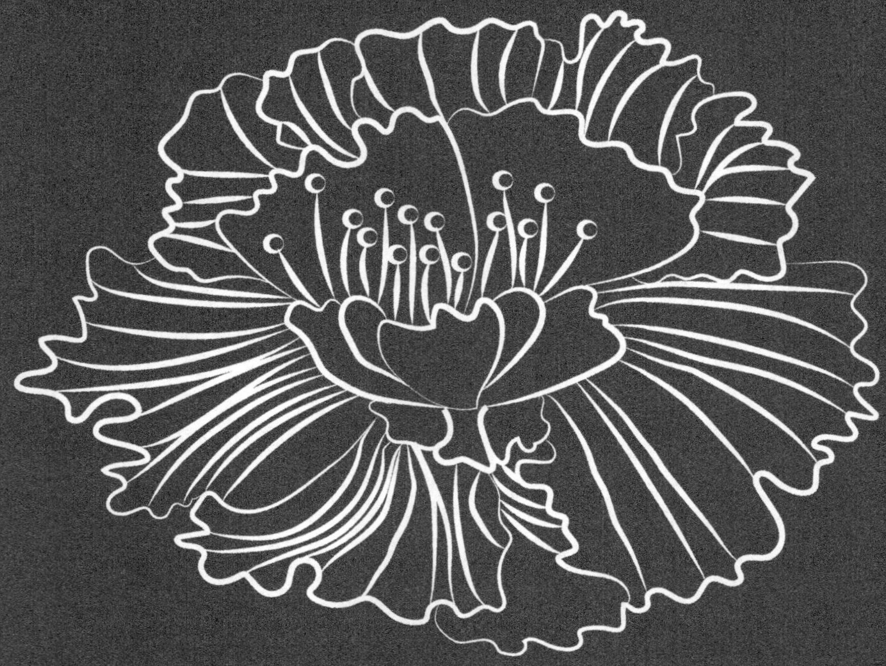

CONTENTS

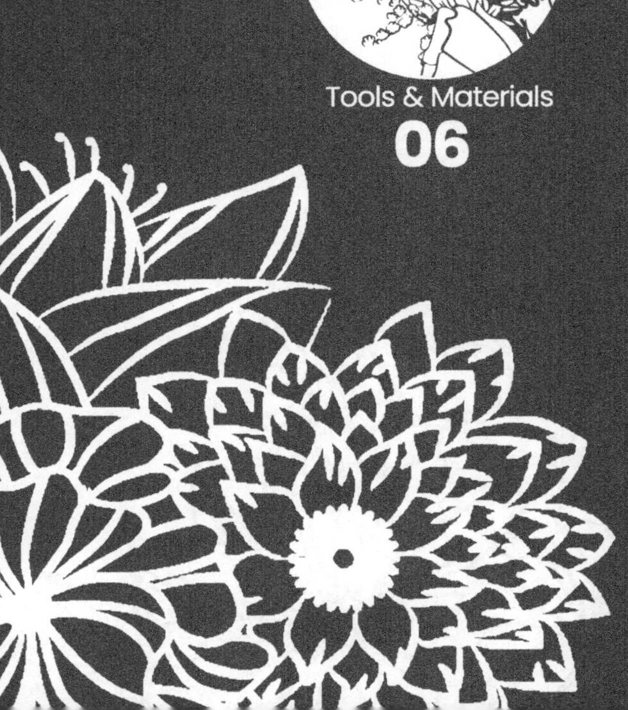

If you enjoyed this book please consider leaving a review on amazon. That helps us to bring you more drawing and art books.

If you have any questions, concerns or comments please reach out tous via ***www.mzcreates.com*** and we'll get back to you ASAP.

Search for **MZ Creates** on **amazon** for more fun, creative books and activity books!

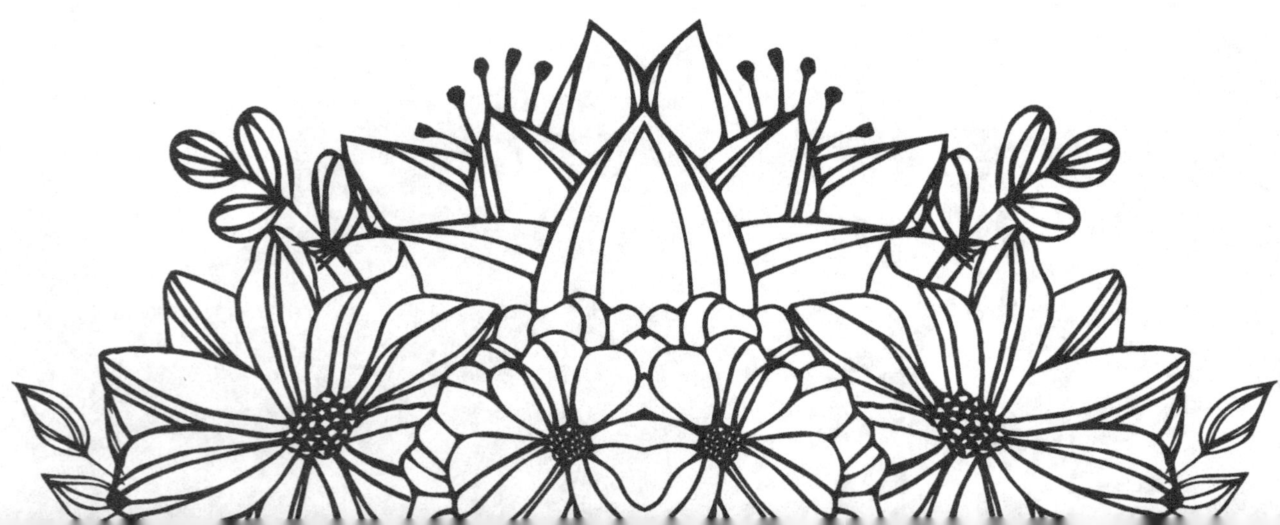

INTRODUCTION

I've always loved to doodle and draw, but I've never really had any confidence in my drawing skills. After I went to my Zentangle training and went through that three-day workshop, I came out feeling way more confident about my ability to draw.

The Zentangle method is magical because it shows you how powerful a few strokes can be and how, by going step-by-step, you can achieve something very complex.

So armed with the knowledge that I could draw, I started venturing into botanicals. Flowers have always been and will always be my greatest love. The colors, the beautiful smells, and the lovely shapes of flowers make me feel like celebrating!

If you follow me on my blog or have read either of my Zentangle books, you probably already know that I also love to bullet journal, plan, art journal, and write. Using my new-found drawing skills, I have been able to add another dimension to my work in all of these hobbies.

Once you learn how to draw florals (you will actually get addicted; consider yourself warned) you will want to put them on everything. Journal covers, t-shirts, posters, stickers, cards, scrapbook layouts, and much more—the possibilities are truly endless.

But the most beneficial aspect of all this drawing, doodling, and linedrawing in my life has been something else. Drawing deliberately, slowly, and with concentration has really helped me with stress and anxiety.

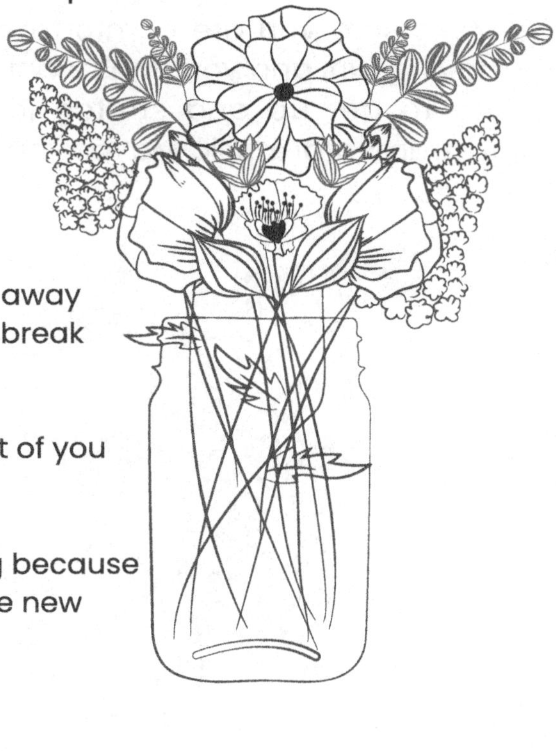

Somehow, focusing on the drawing at hand chases away other demons in your head and gives you a mental break for a little while.

Also, seeing something beautiful come to life in front of you and with your hands is a joy in itself.

So whether you want to learn botanical line drawing because you want to learn to draw, or you want to learn some new flower types, this book will serve you well.

TOOLS & MATERIALS

The tools and materials you need for line drawing are just a few. This is one of the reasons I love to draw and practice, since I can even do this on the iPad. I always have a small journal and one fine-tipped pen with me.

I would suggest you start with the following things and experiment a little:

- White Paper - Neenah is a great brand.
- Fine Tip Pens in different line weights (0.5, 0.7, and 0.1) - I recommend Sakura.
- White Pens - try Sakura white pens - they work really well for me.
- Some black paper or cardstock to experiments with white on black.
- Watercolors - if you want to add paint.
- Color Pencils - if this is the medium you prefer.
- Gold Pen - for adding some glimmer and highlights.
- Drawing surface.

Make sure you are comfortable when you're drawing. Time flies when you're having fun, and you don't want to end your drawing session with body cramps. Try to get up and stretch in the middle. I like listening to some relaxing instrumental music. Maybe you would like to try that?

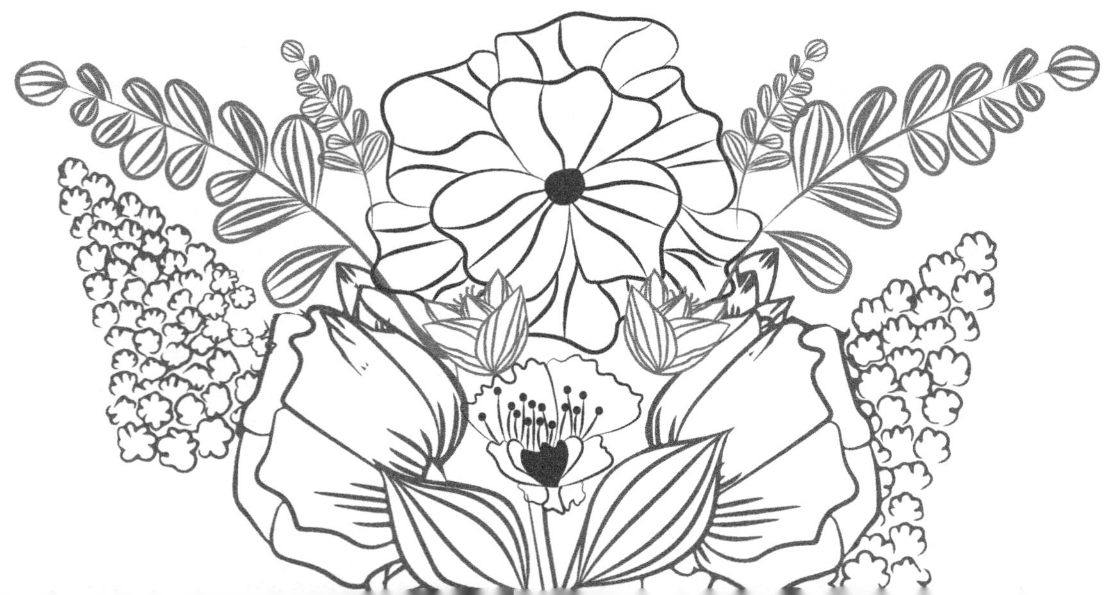

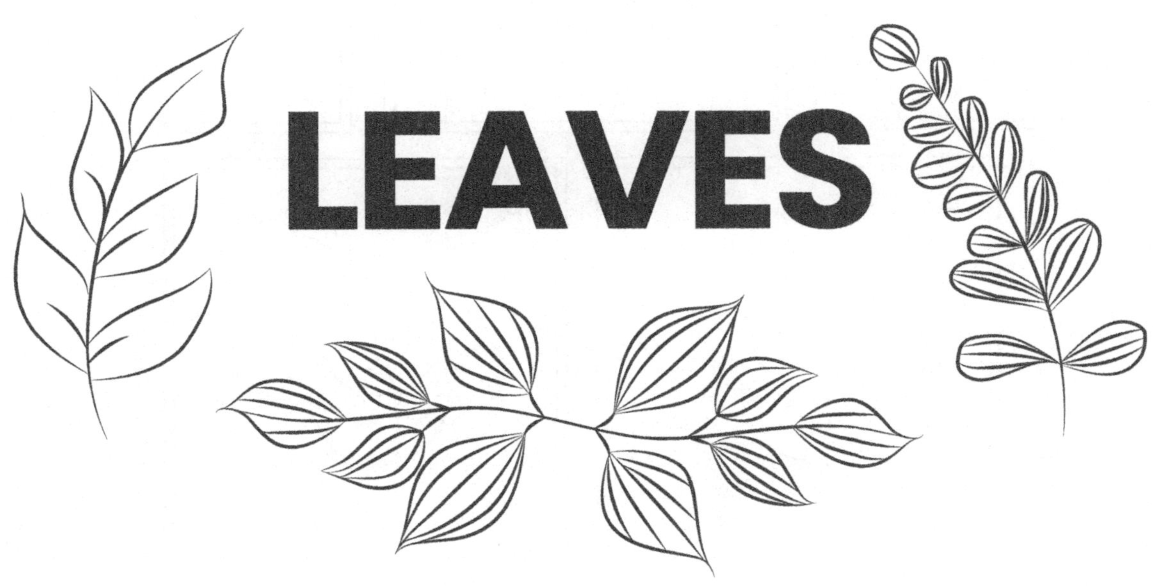
LEAVES

Botanical Line Drawing 1

Green Ash

01

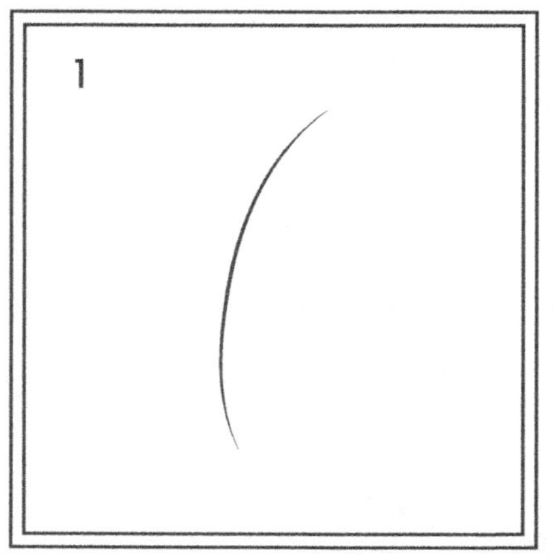

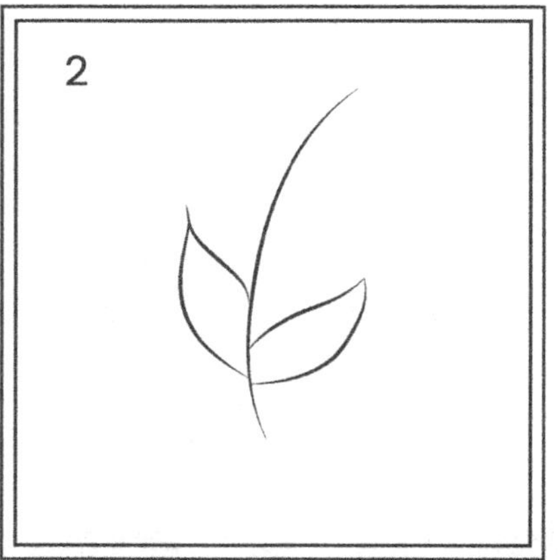

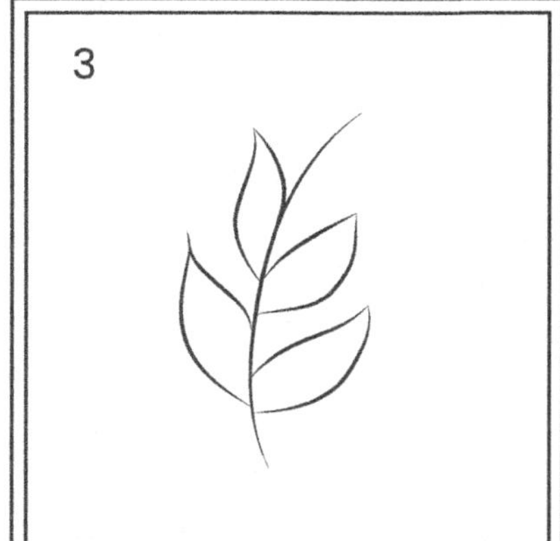

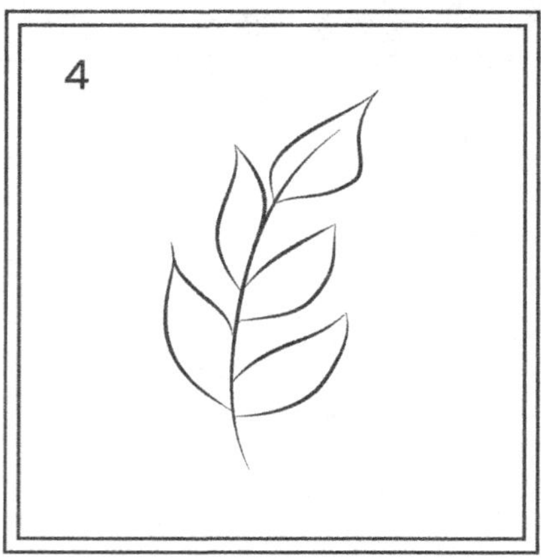

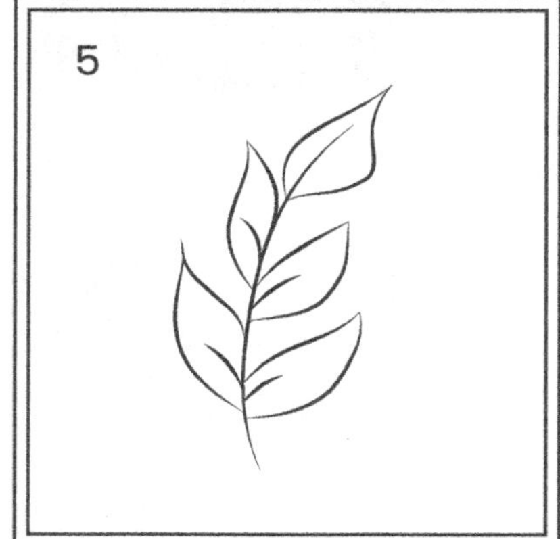

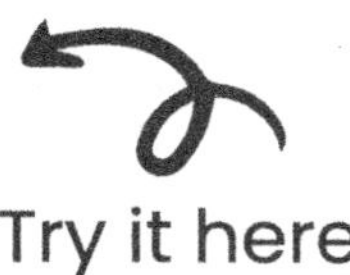

Try it here

Botanical Line Drawing 1

Red Wood

02

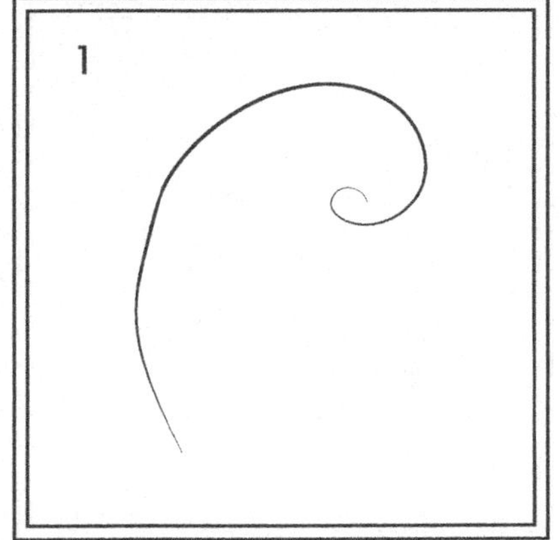

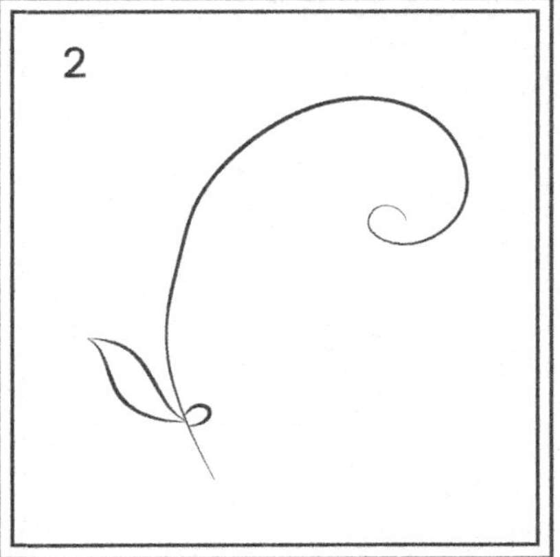

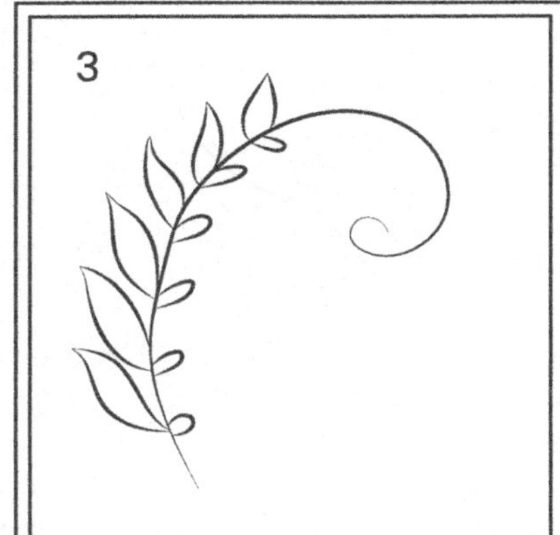

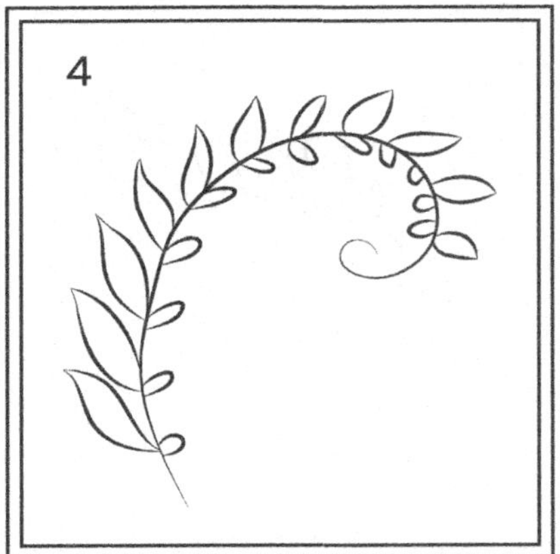

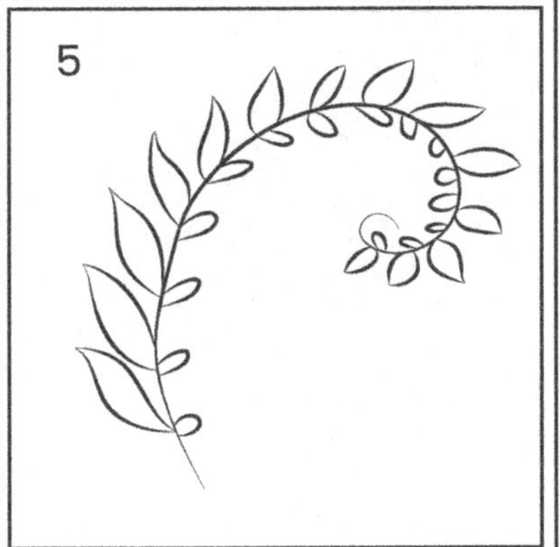

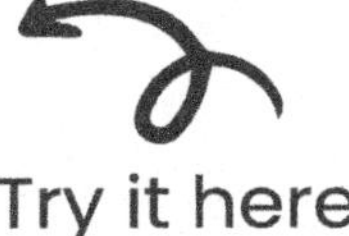

Try it here

Botanical Line Drawing 1

Fern

03

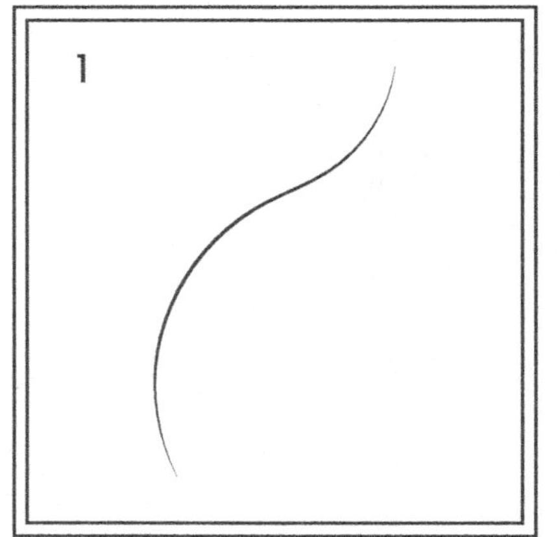

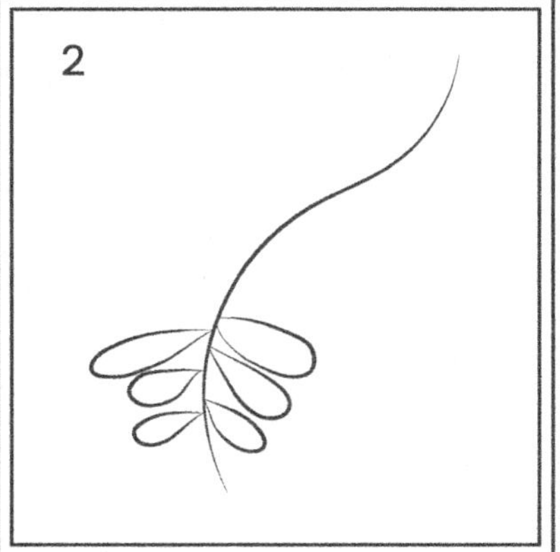

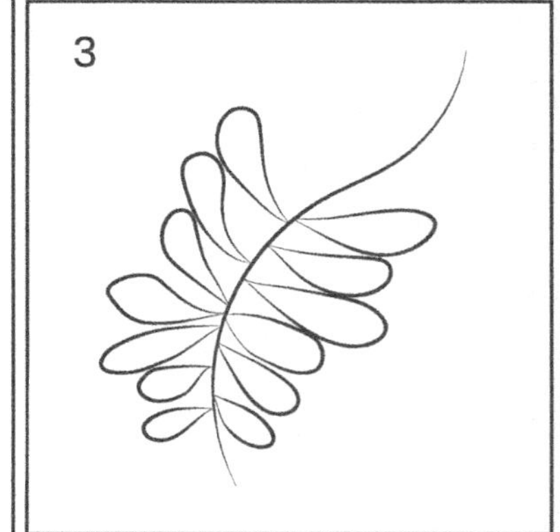

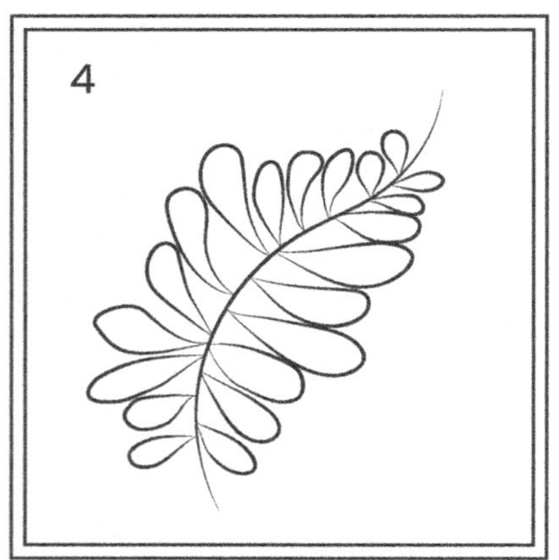

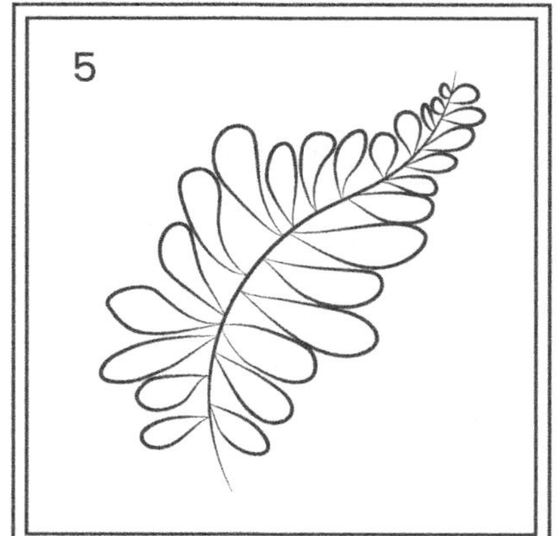

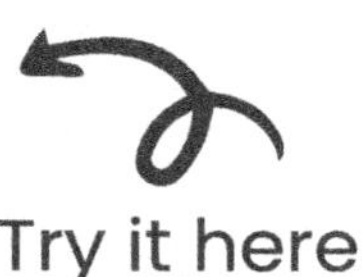

Try it here

Botanical Line Drawing 1

Pignut Hicky

04

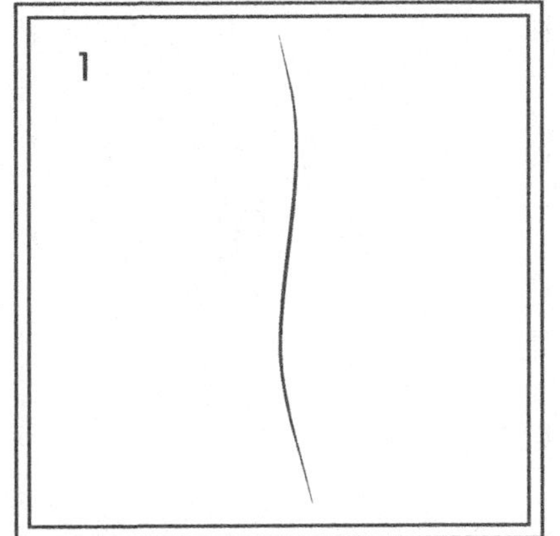

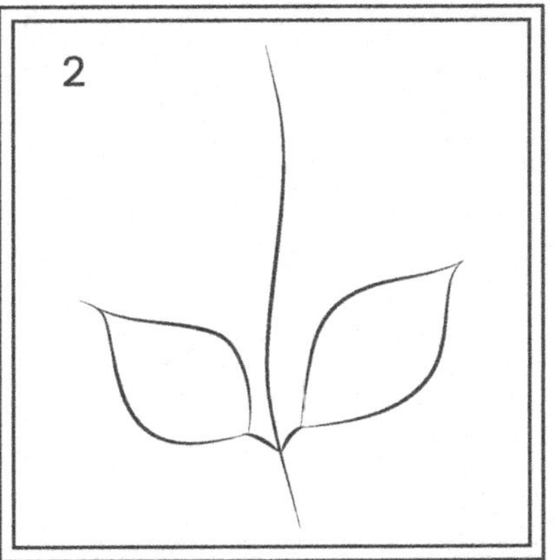

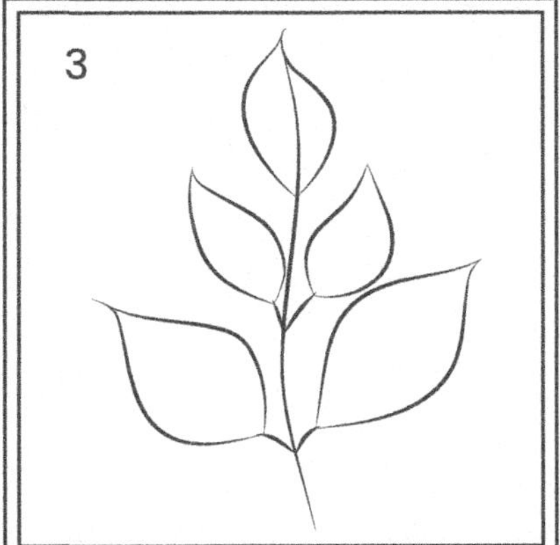

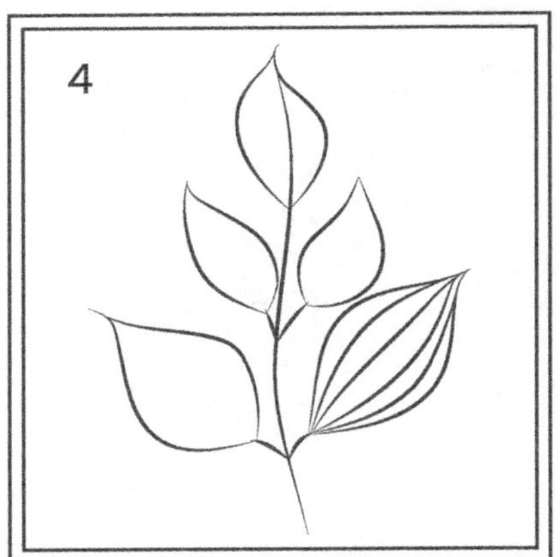

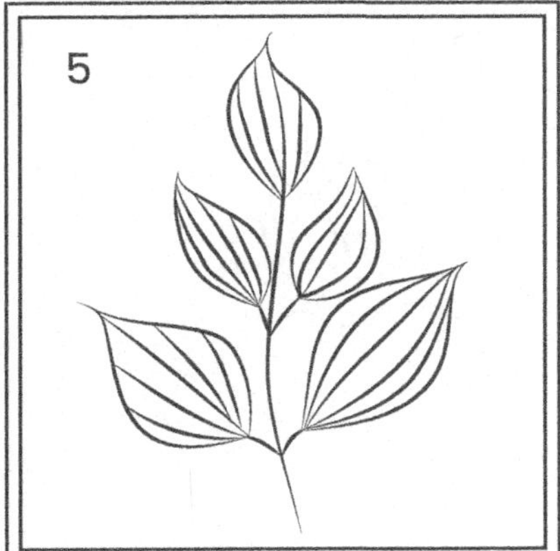

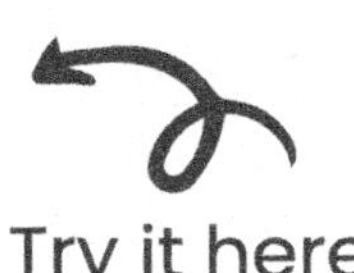

Try it here

Botanical Line Drawing 1

Wild Senna

05

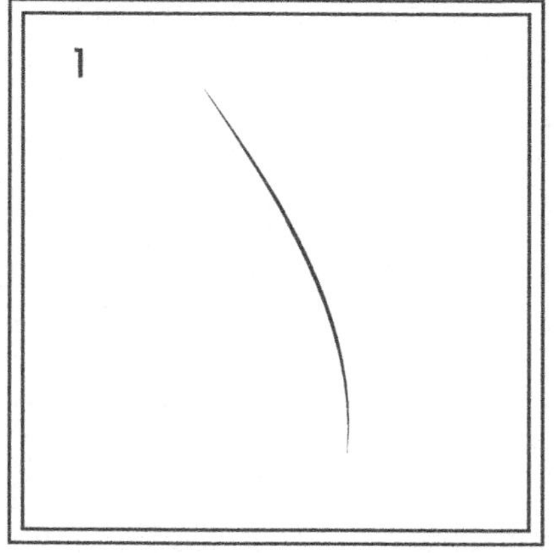

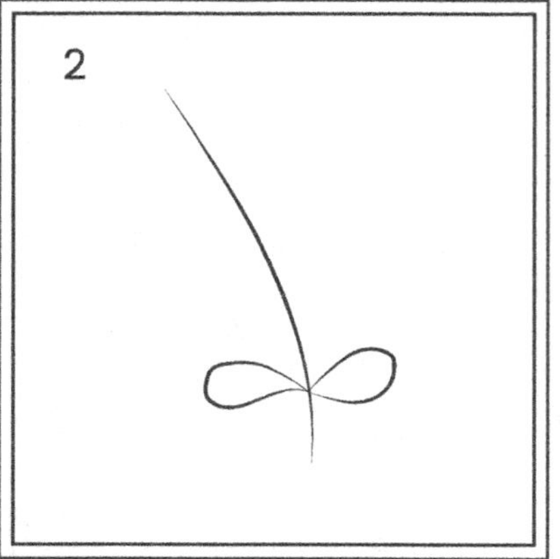

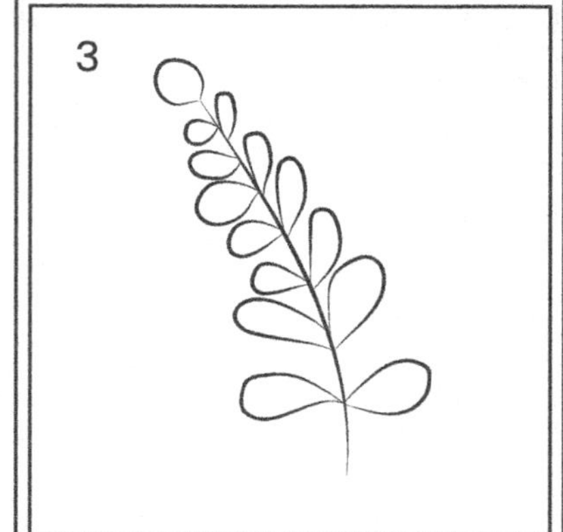

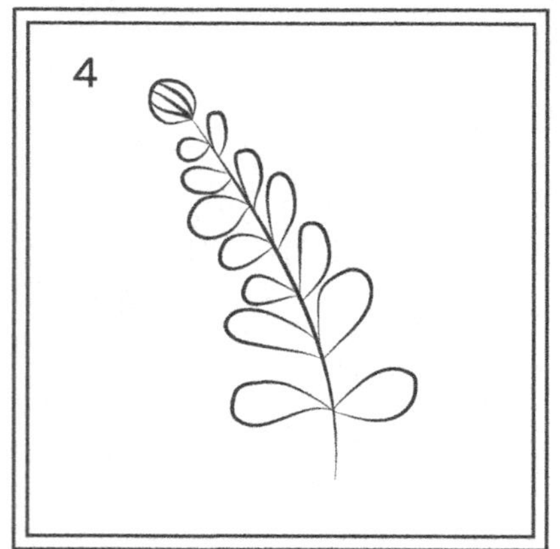

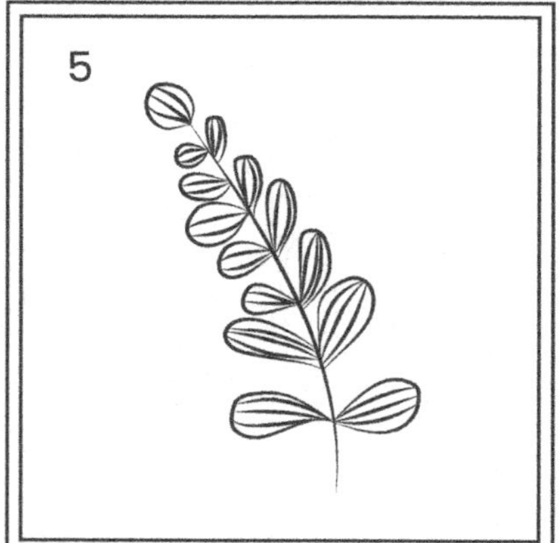

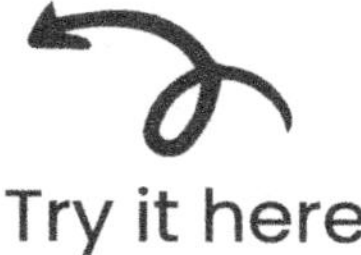

Try it here

Botanical Line Drawing 1

Black Tree

06

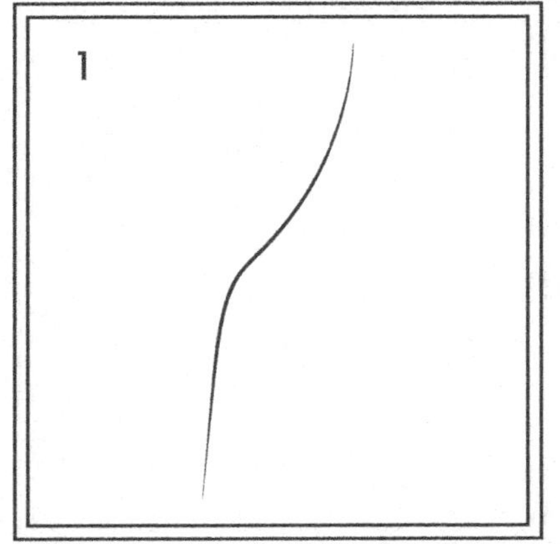

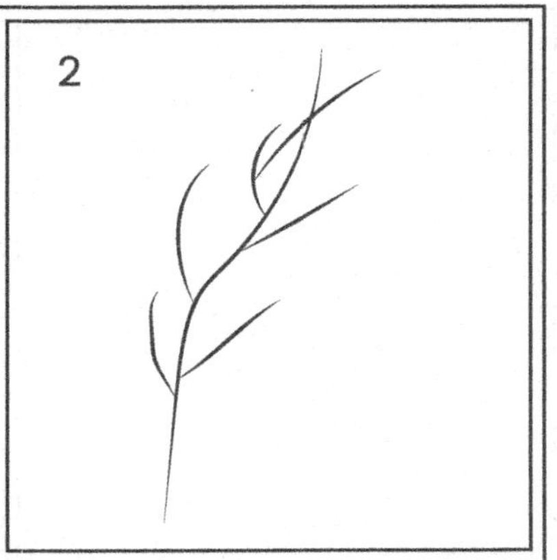

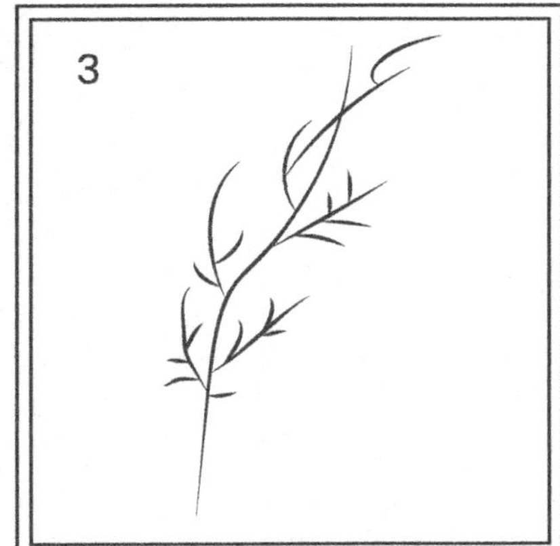

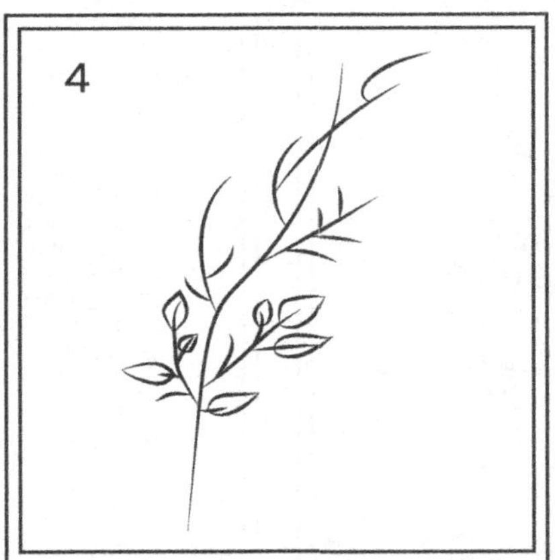

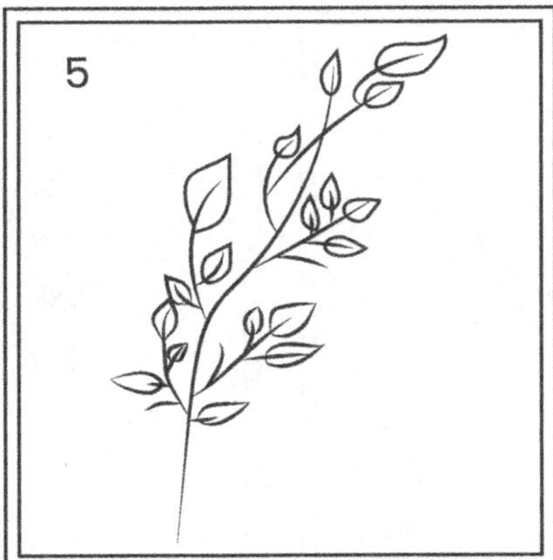

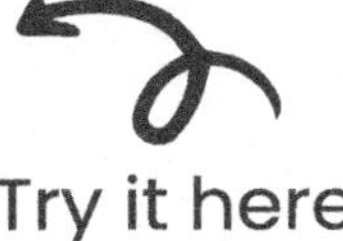

Try it here

Botanical Line Drawing 1

Olive Tree

07

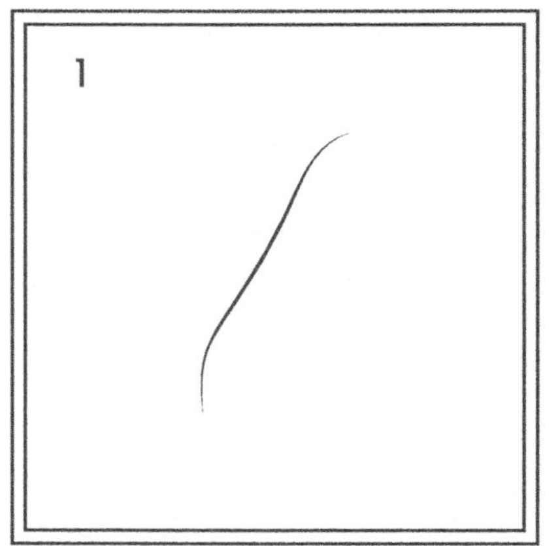

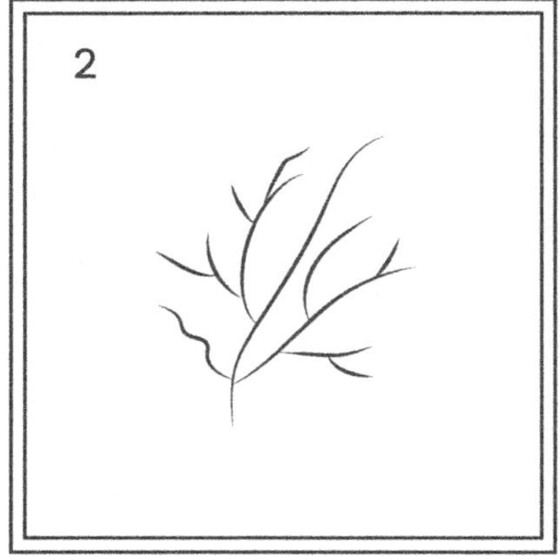

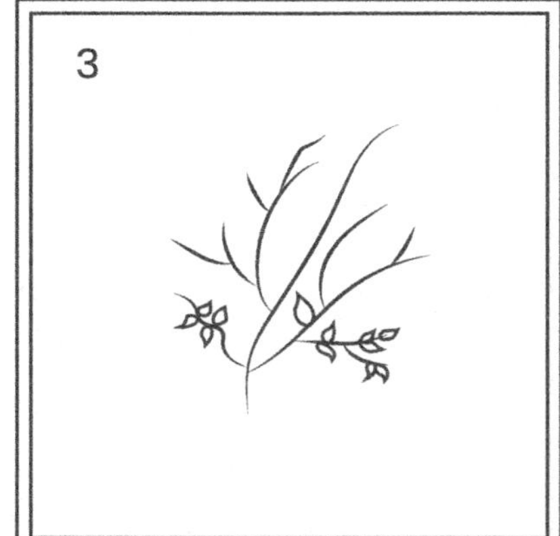

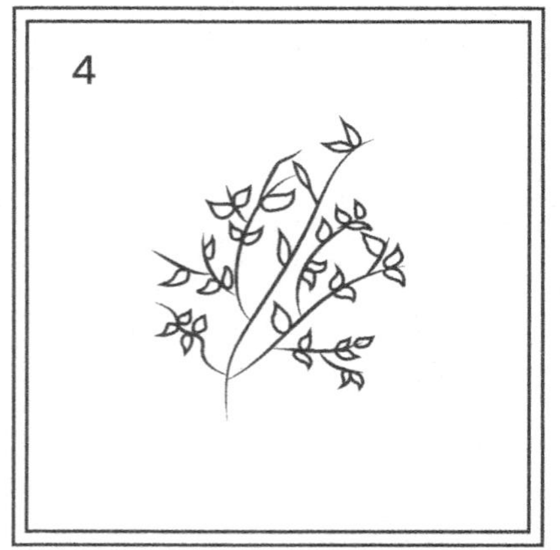

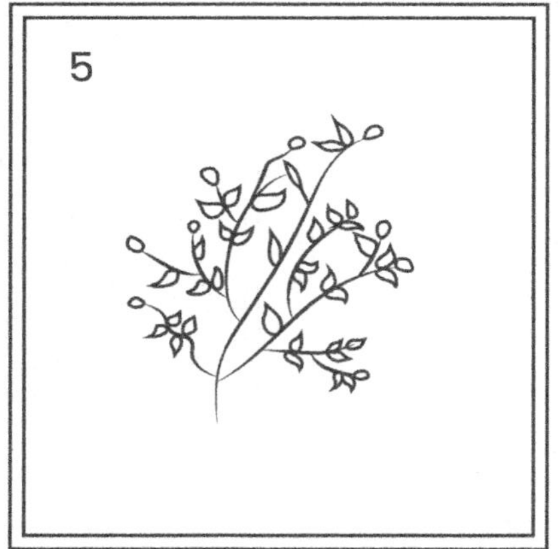

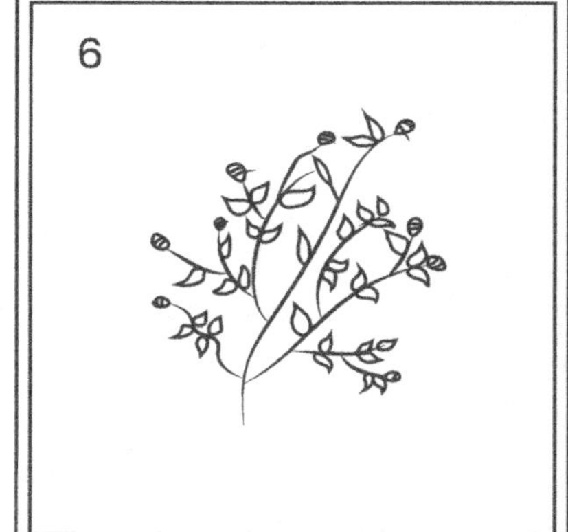

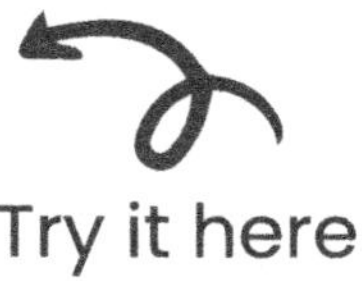

Try it here

Botanical Line Drawing 1

Palm Frond

08

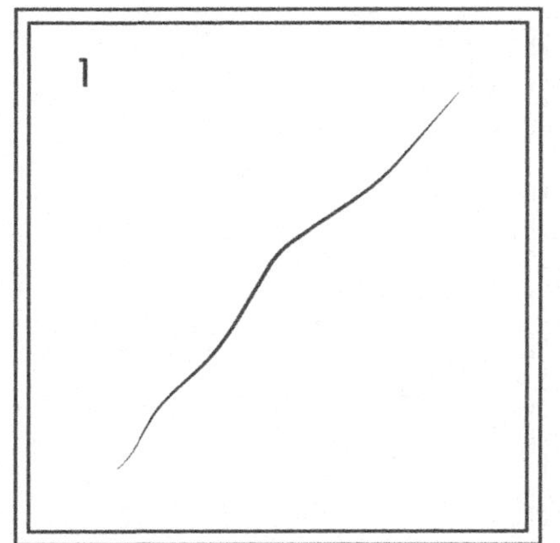

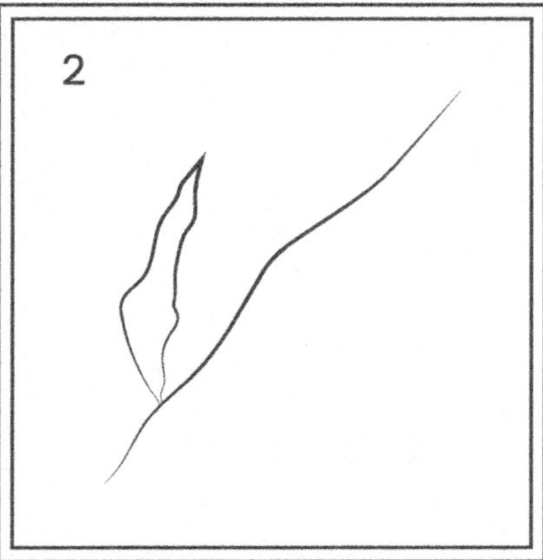

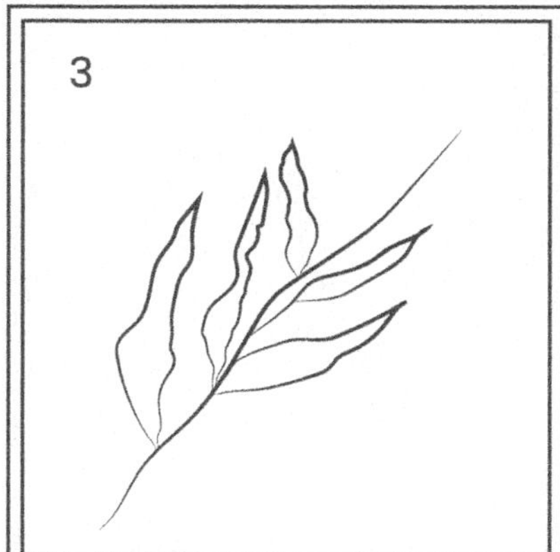

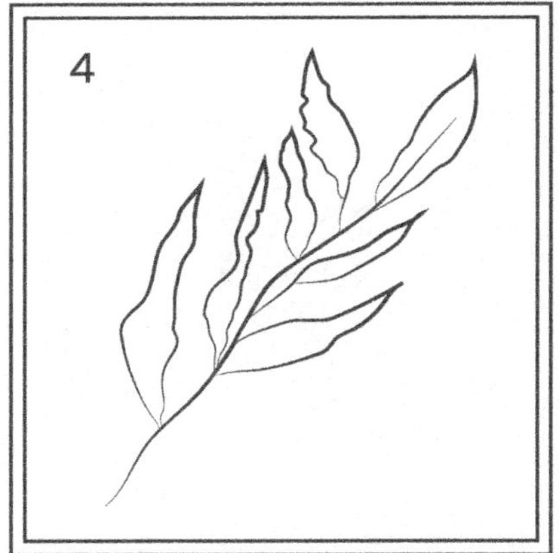

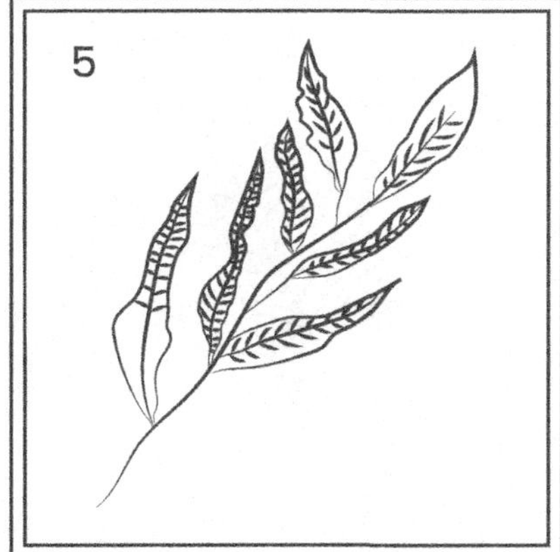

Try it here

Botanical Line Drawing 1

Redwood 2

09

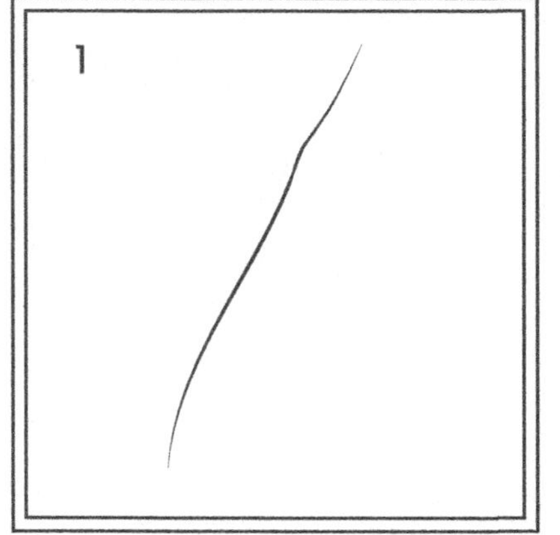

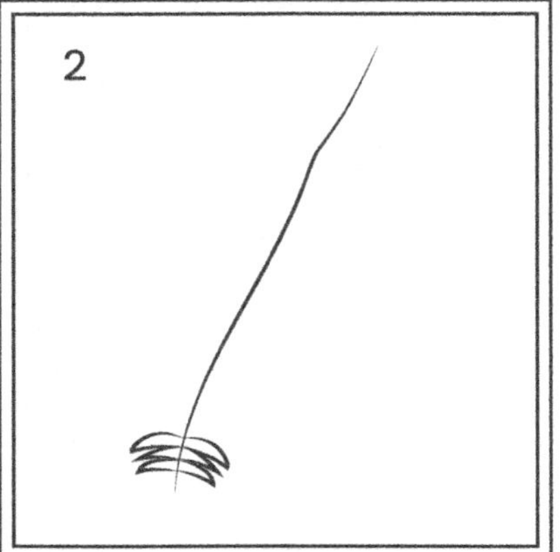

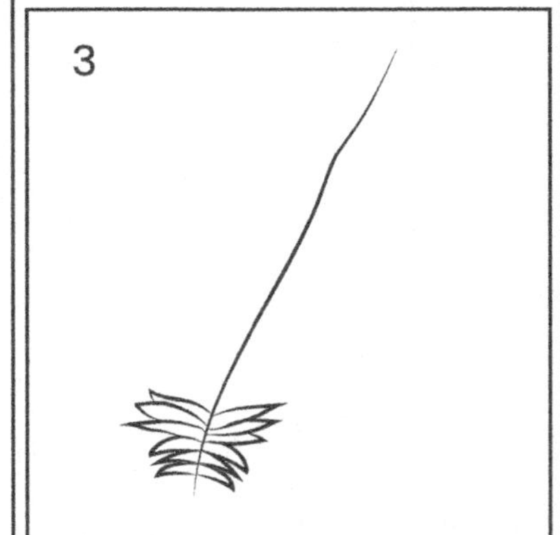

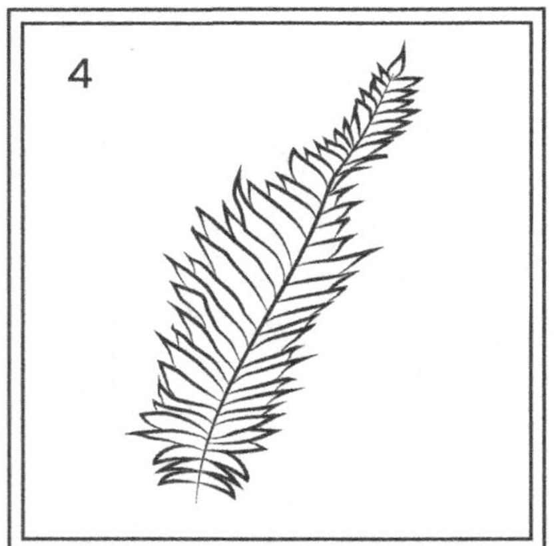

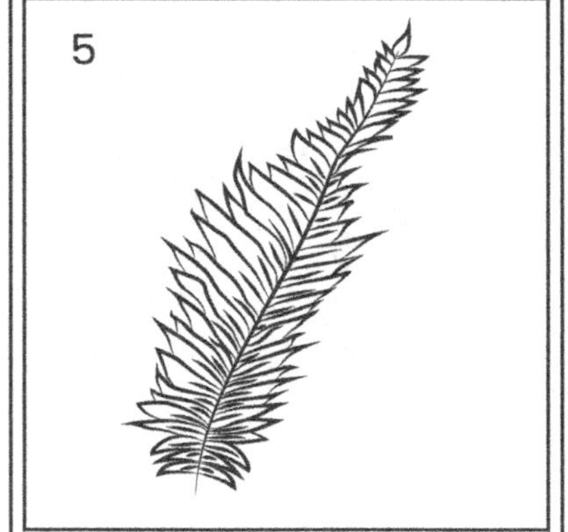

Try it here

FLOWERS

Botanical Line Drawing 1

Lotus

10

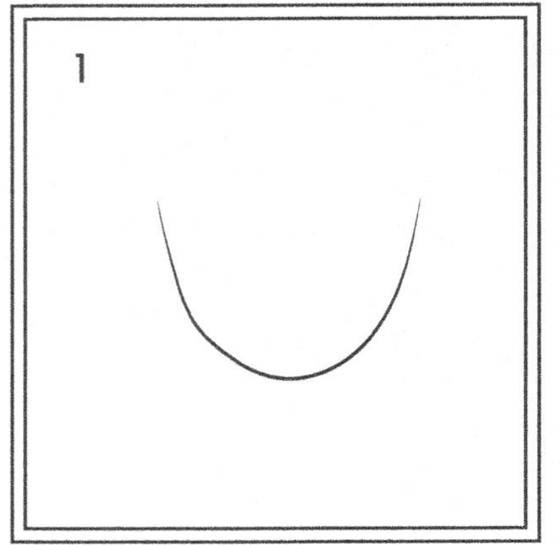

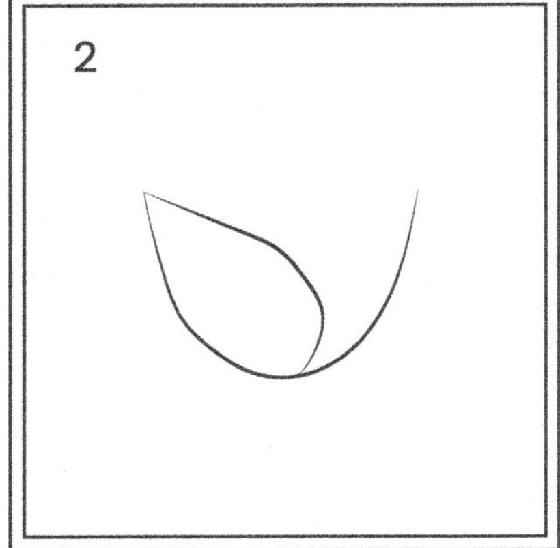

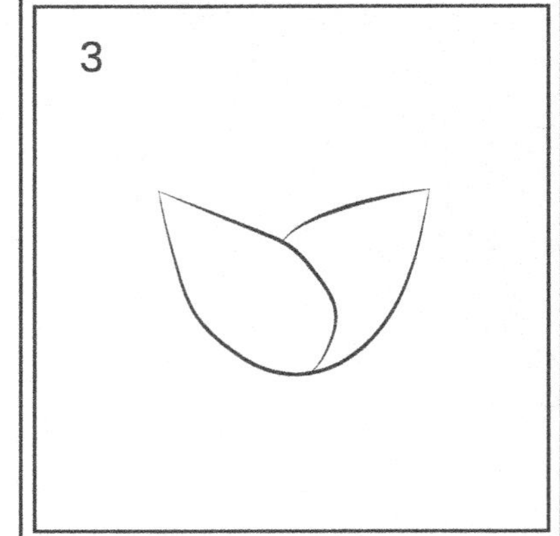

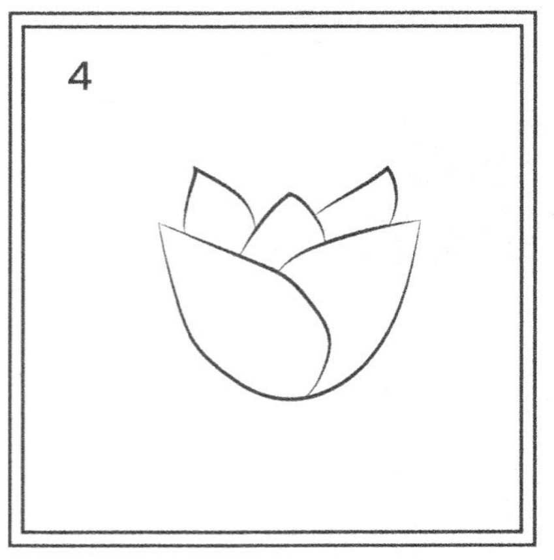

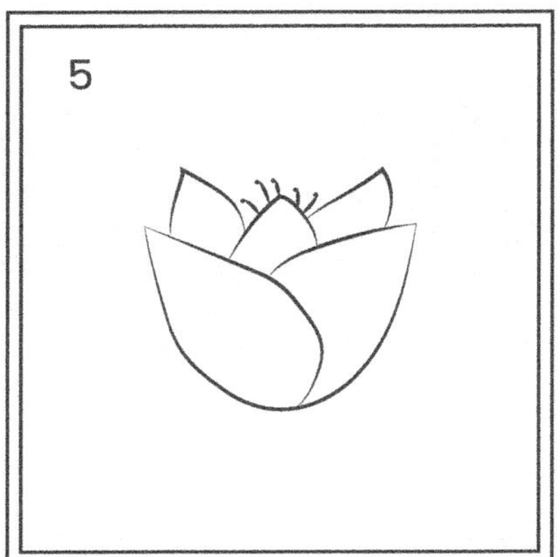

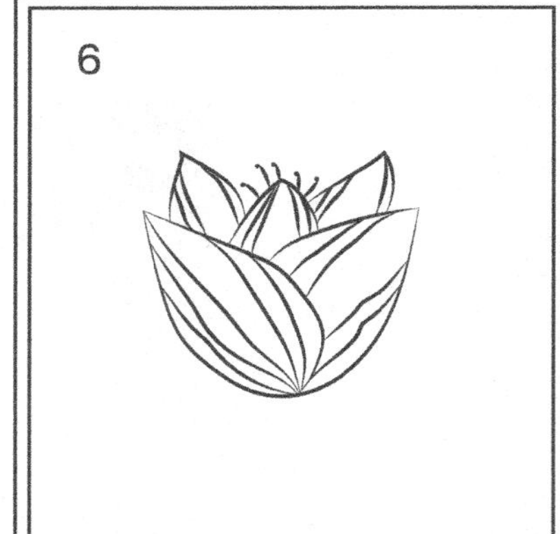

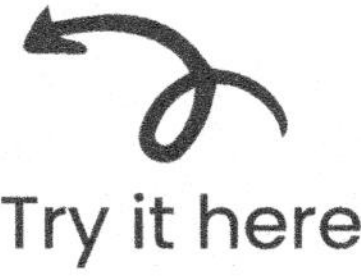

Try it here

Botanical Line Drawing 1

Pansy

11

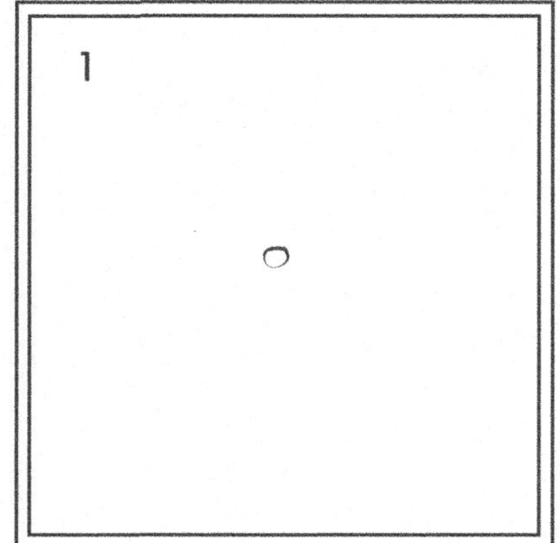

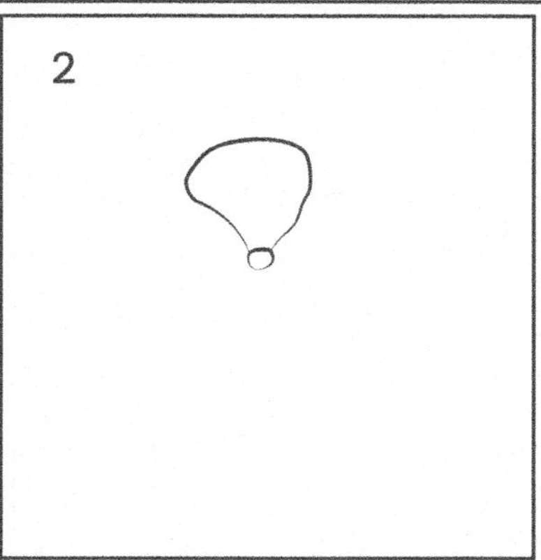

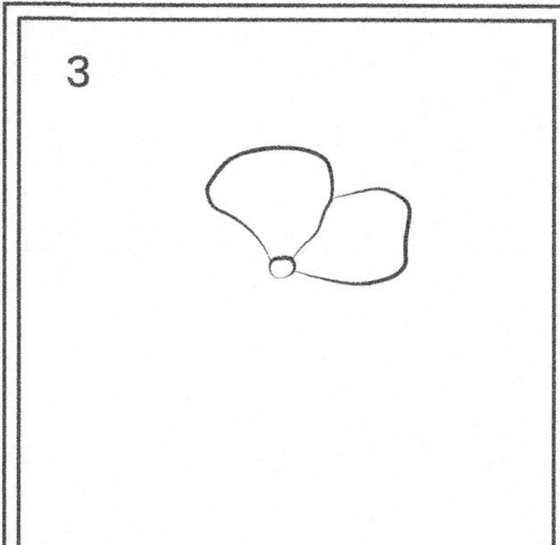

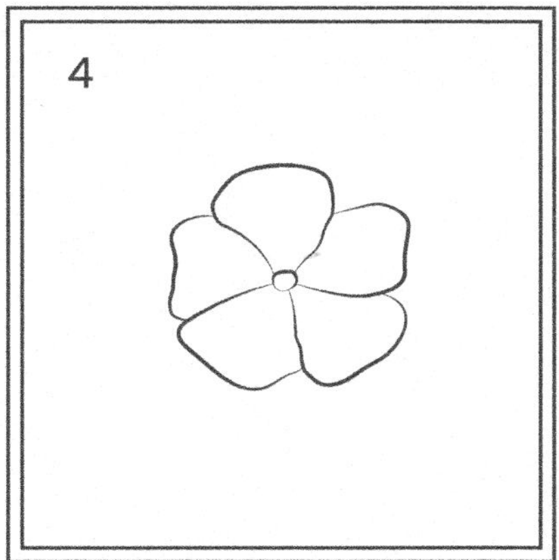

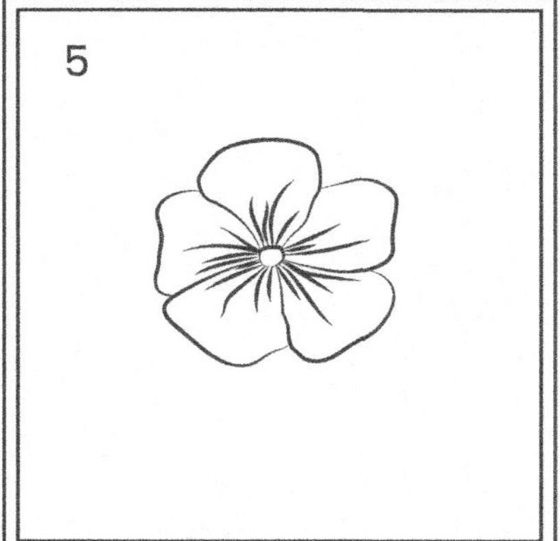

Try it here

Botanical Line Drawing 1

Sweet Pea

12

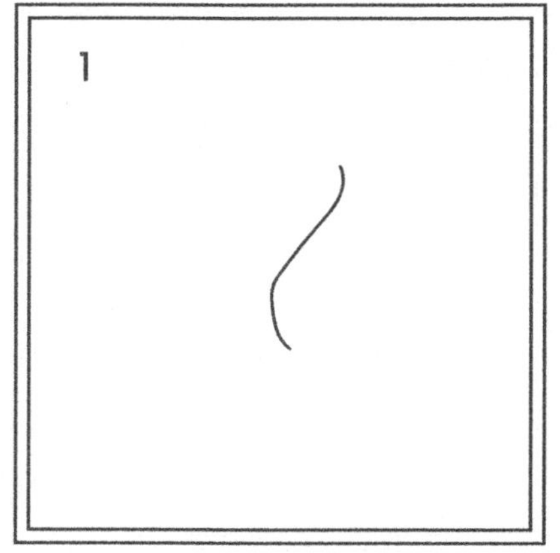

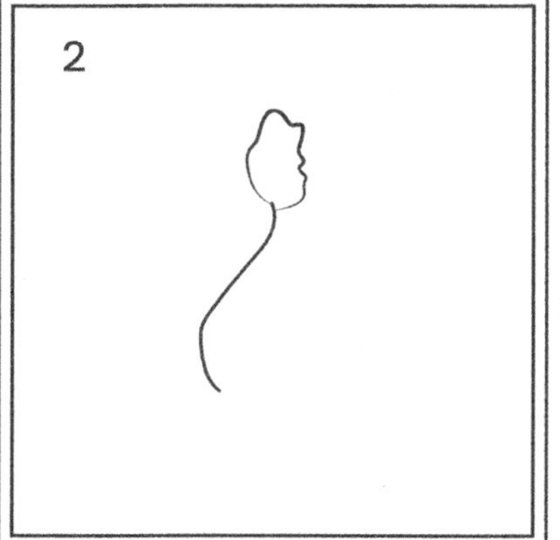

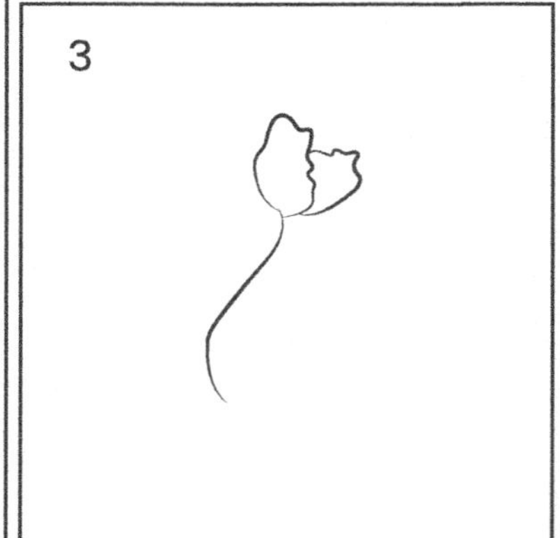

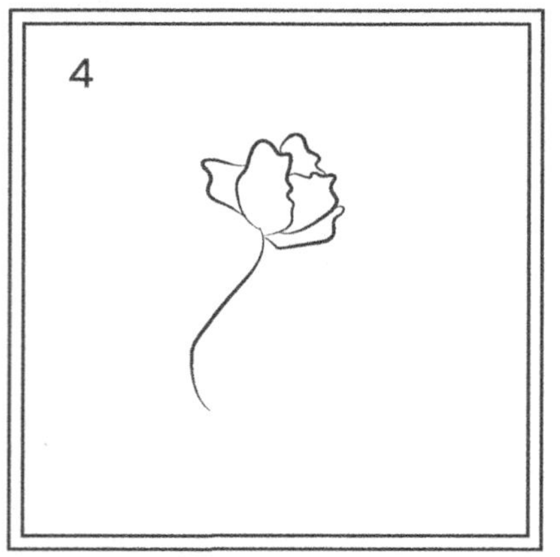

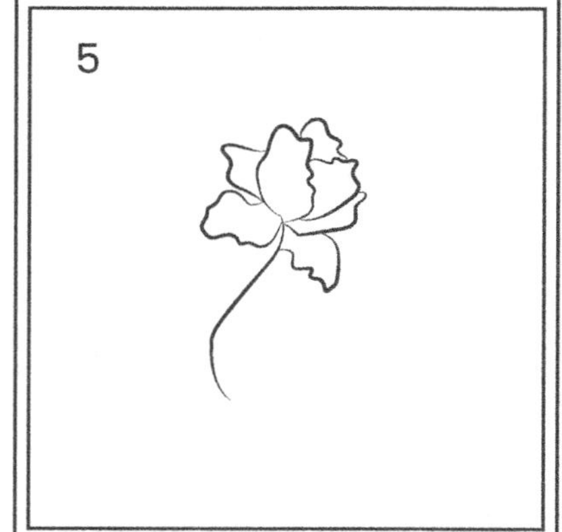

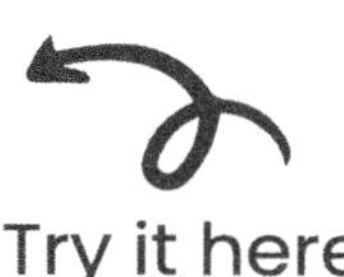

Botanical Line Drawing 1

Poppy

13

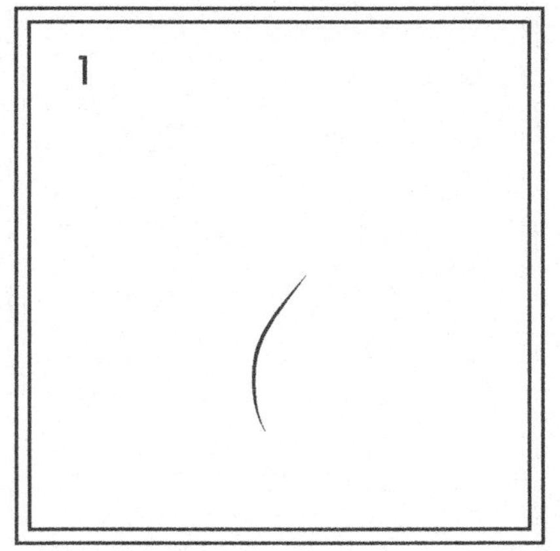

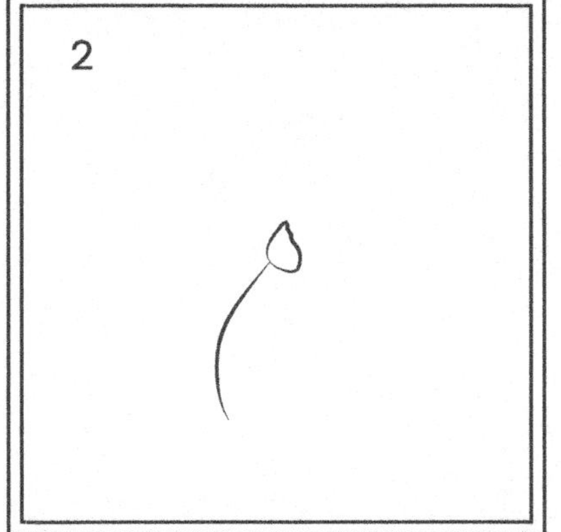

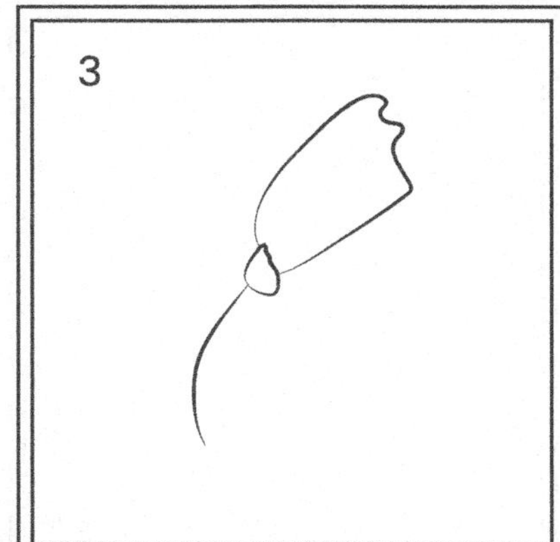

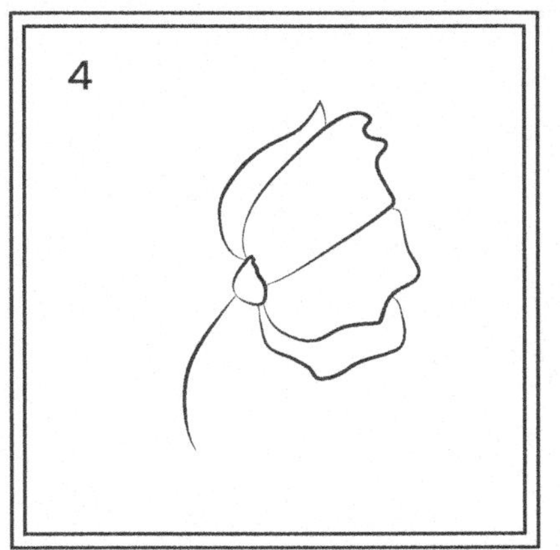

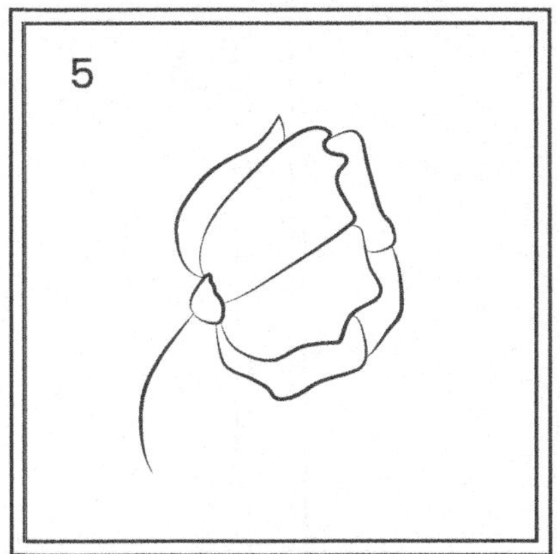

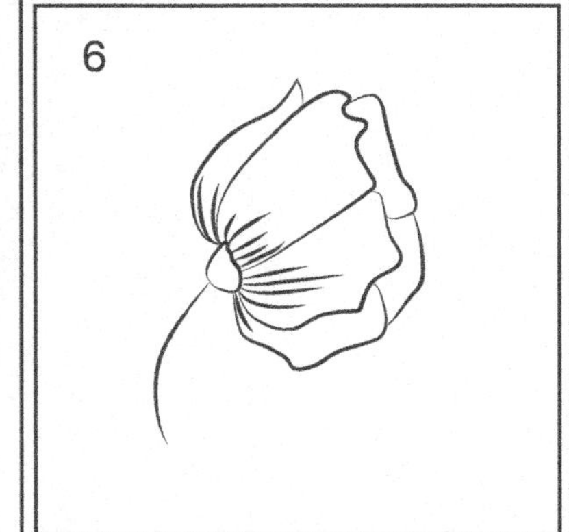

Try it here

Botanical Line Drawing 1

Rose

14

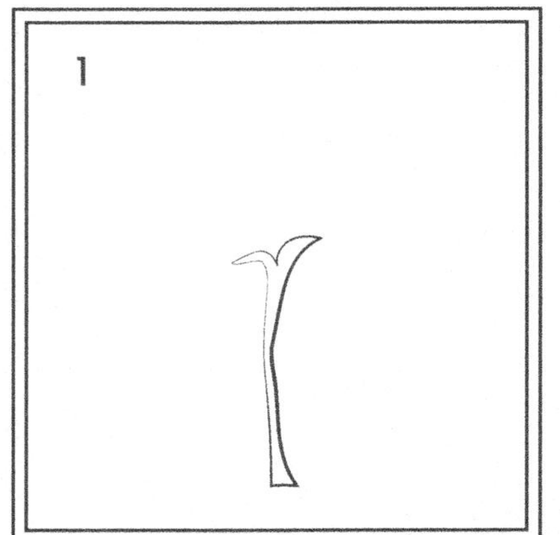

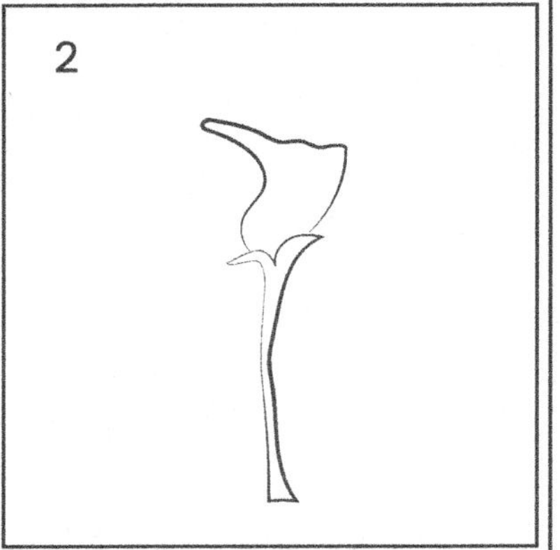

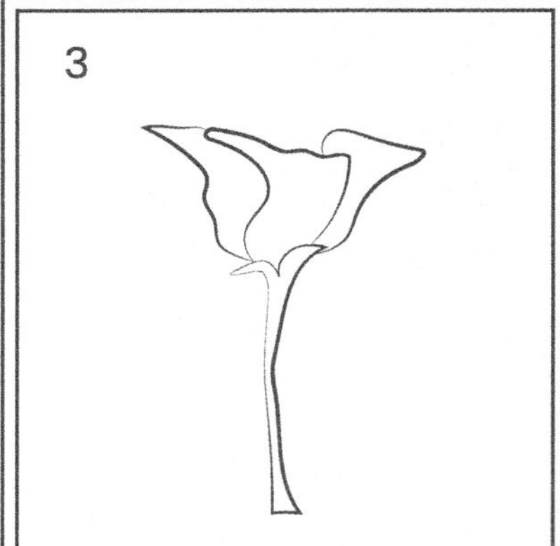

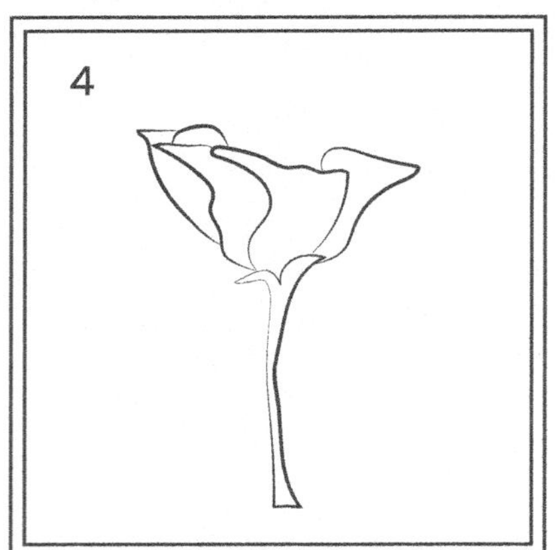

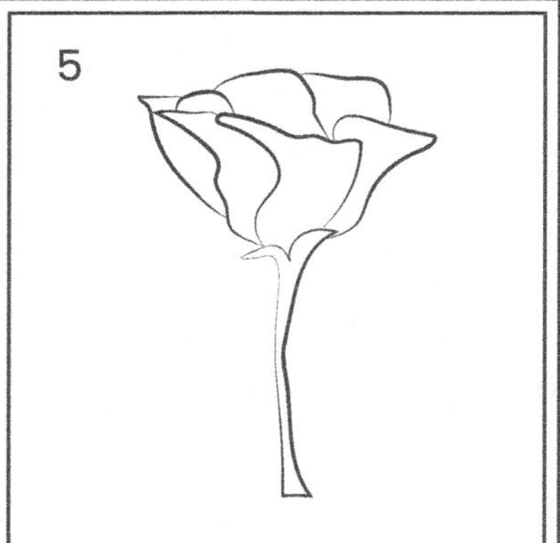

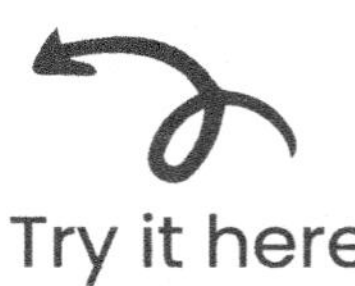

Try it here

Botanical Line Drawing 1

Bluebonnet

15

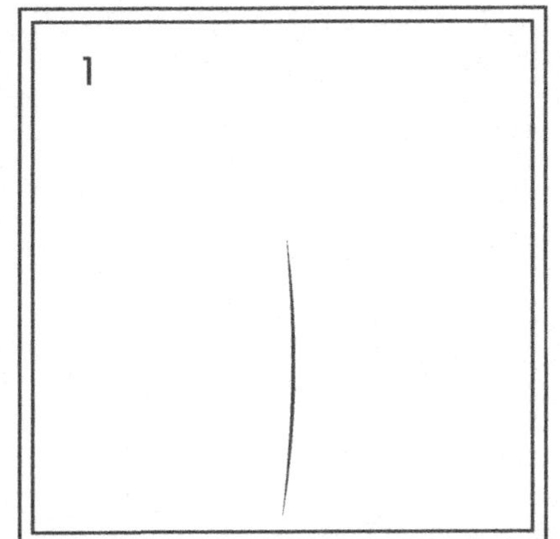

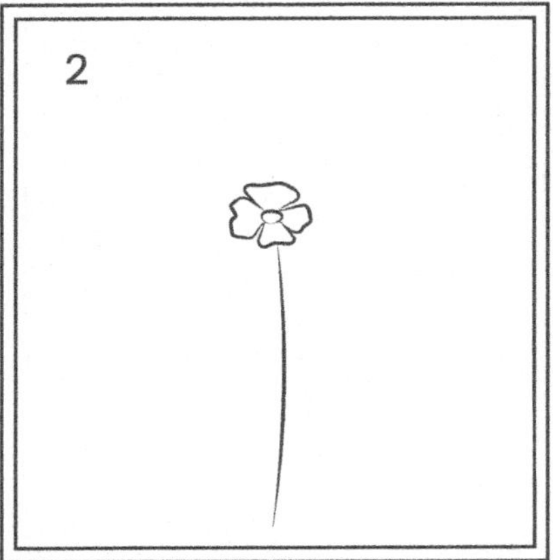

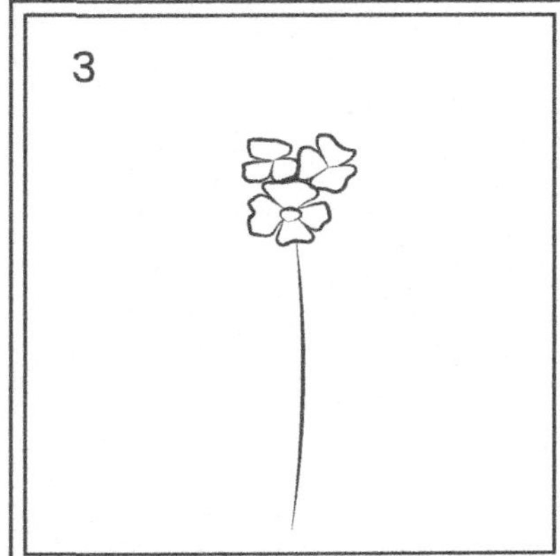

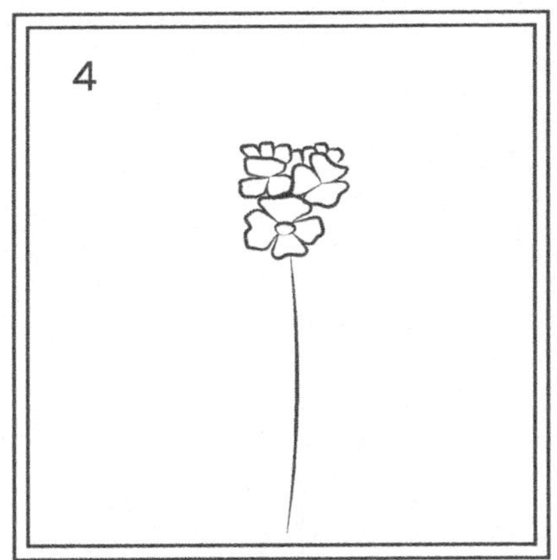

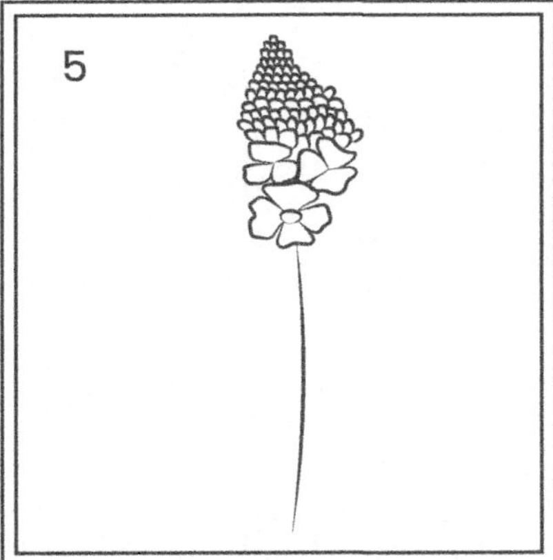

Try it here

Botanical Line Drawing 1

Hyacinth

16

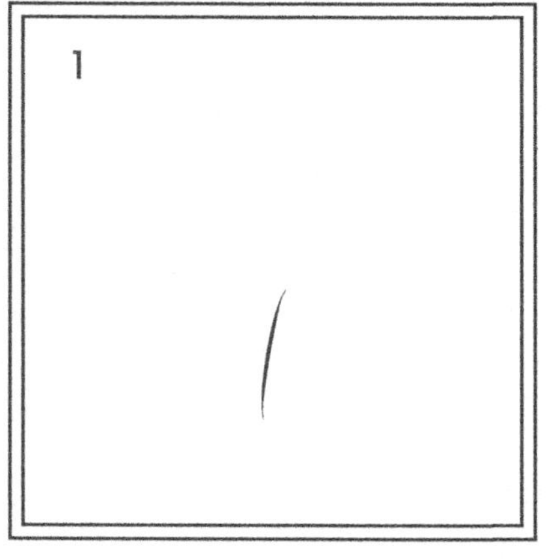

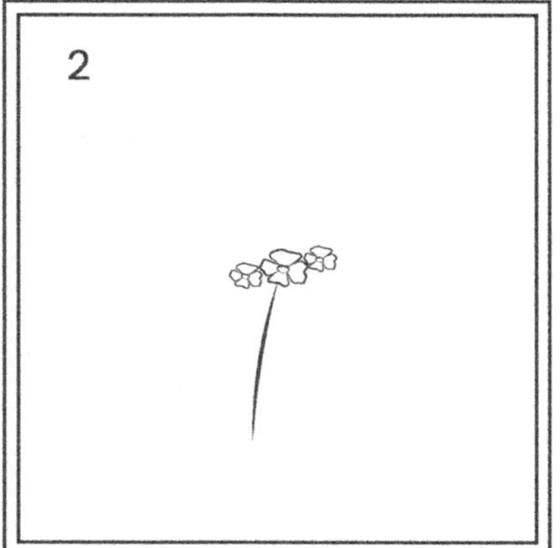

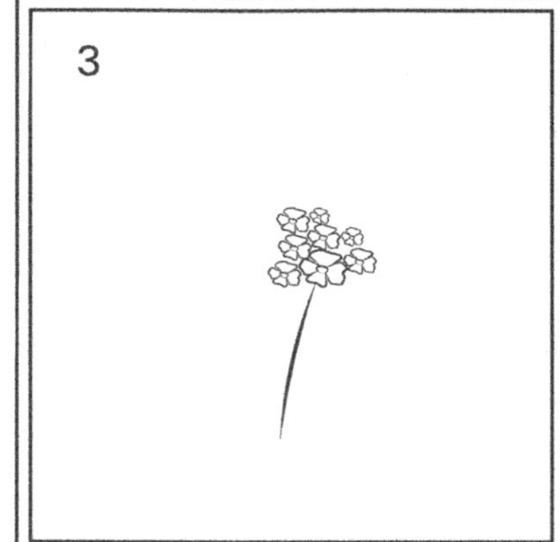

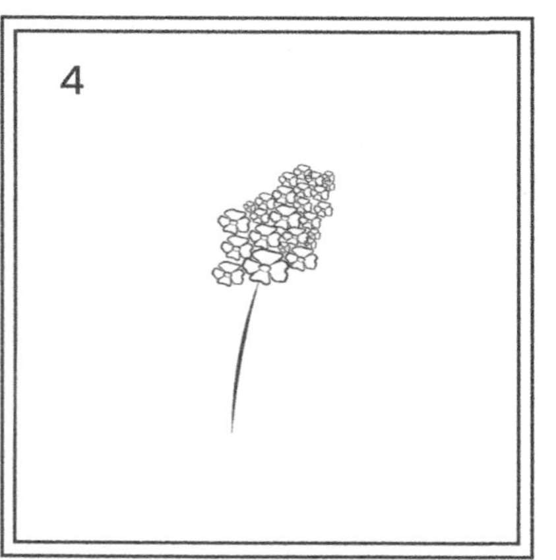

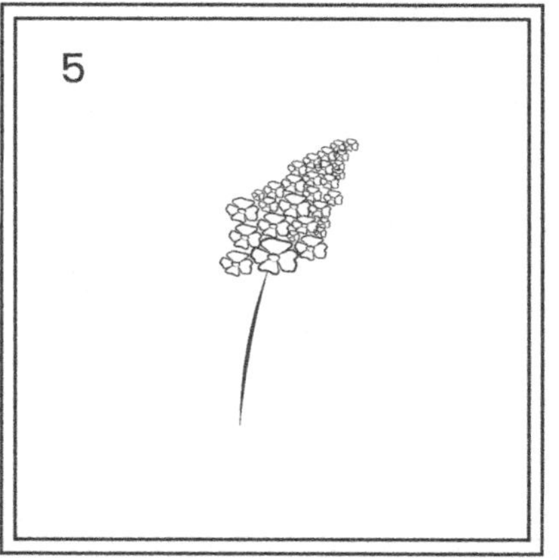

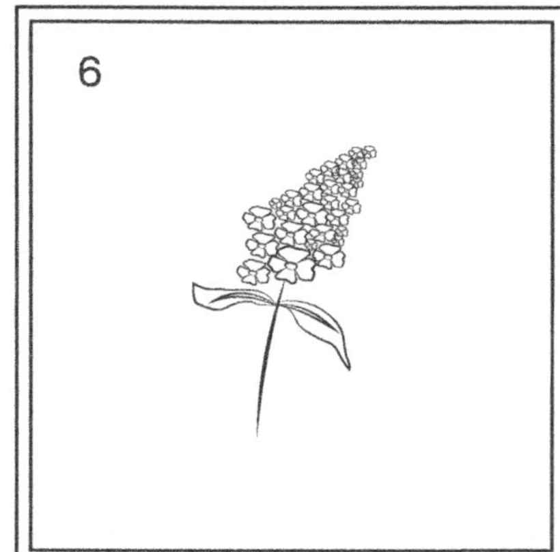

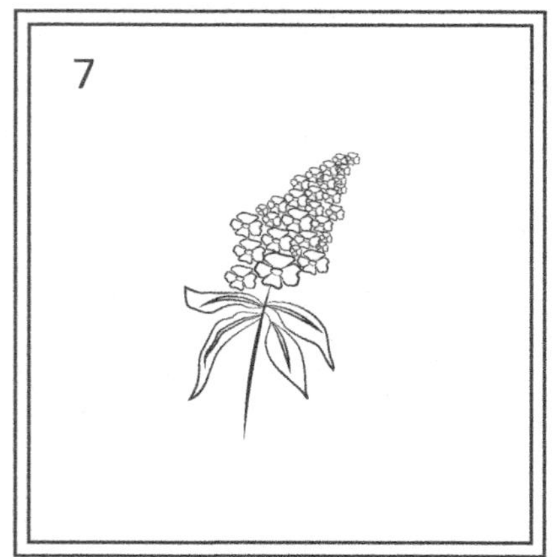

Botanical Line Drawing 1

Lily

17

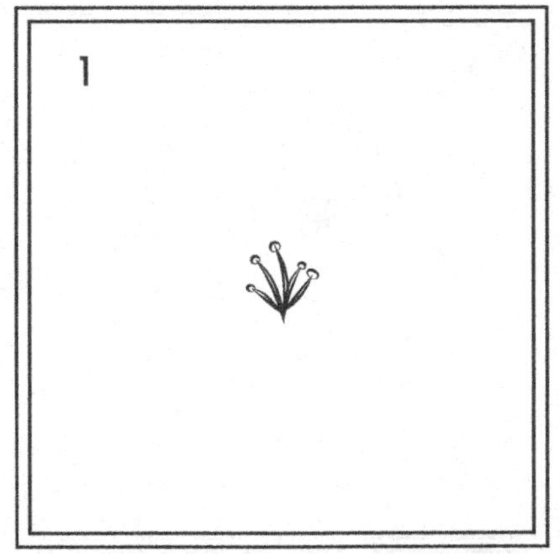

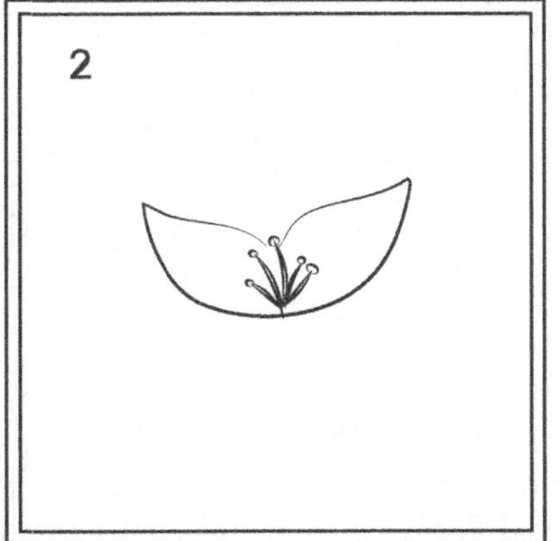

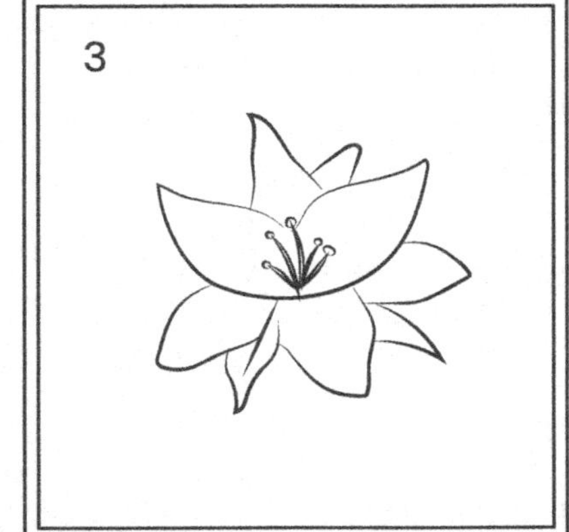

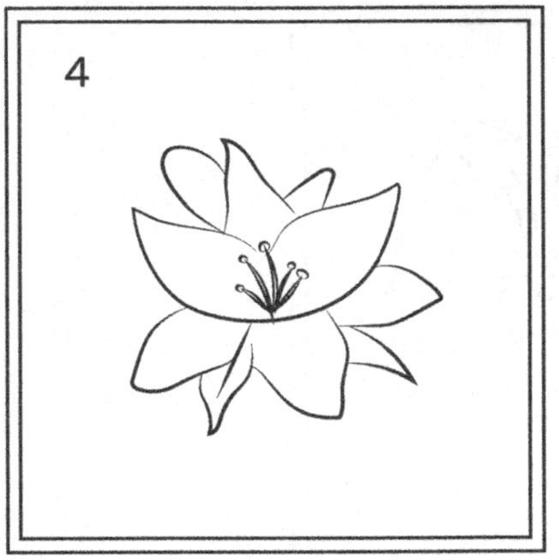

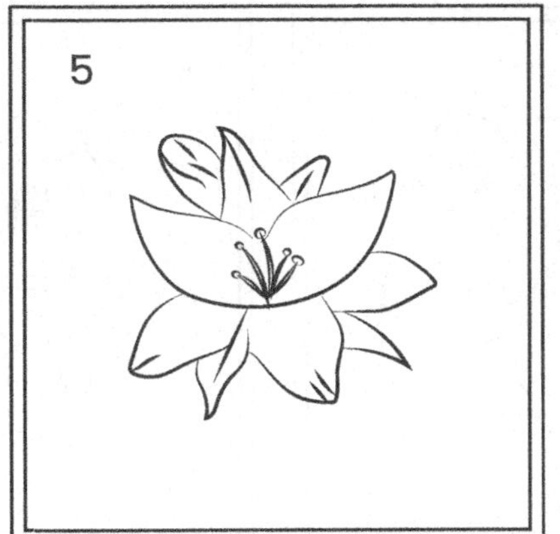

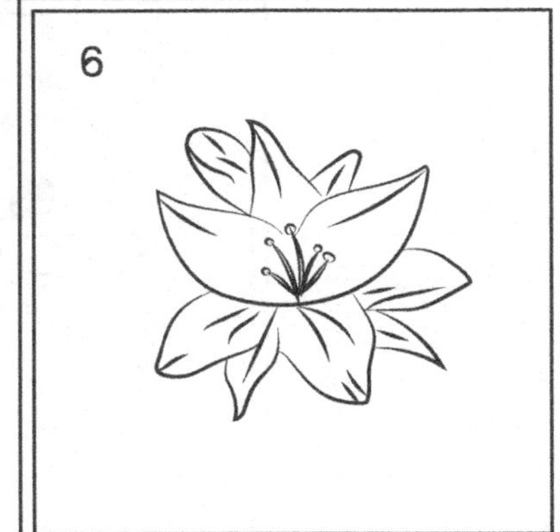

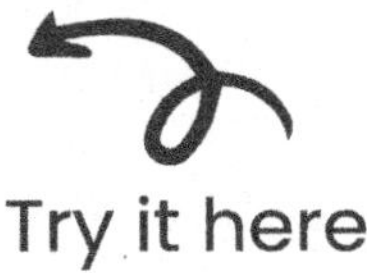

Try it here

Botanical Line Drawing 1

Hibiscus

18

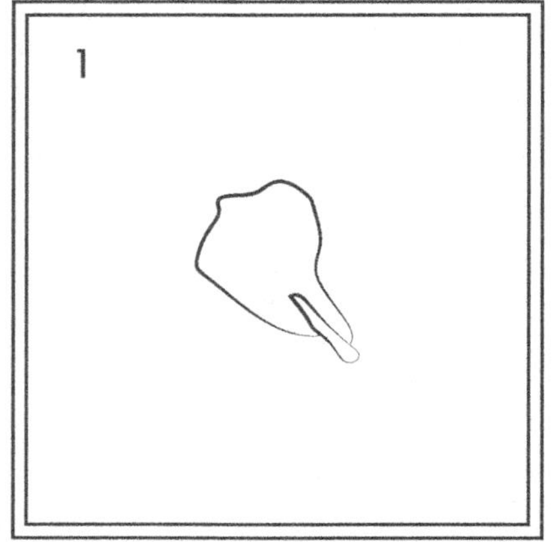

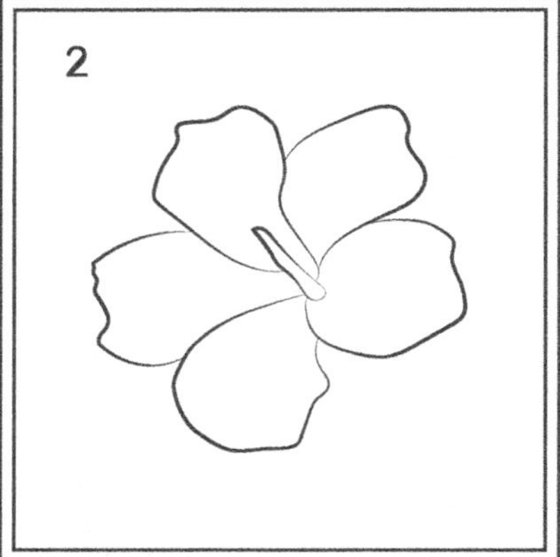

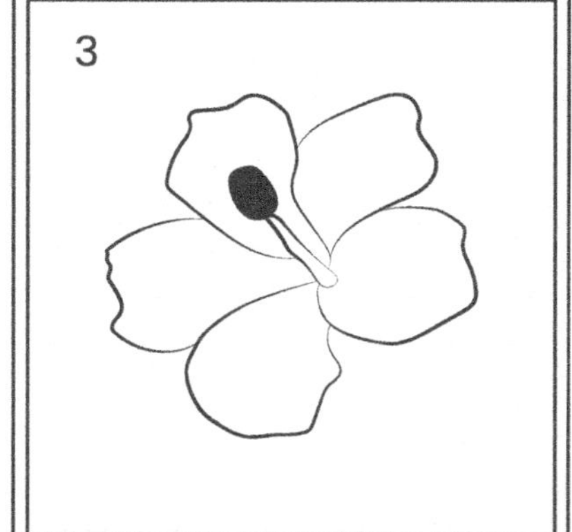

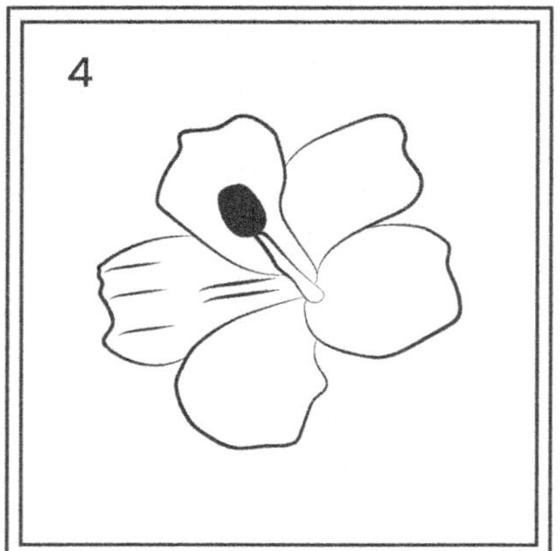

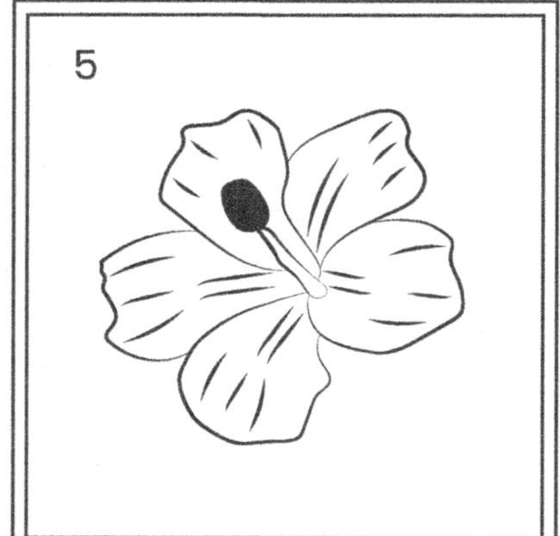

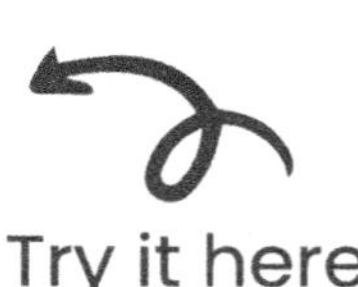

Try it here

Botanical Line Drawing 1

Succulent

19

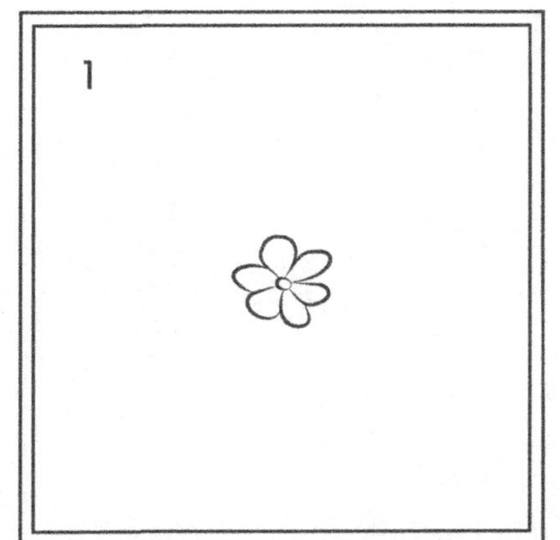

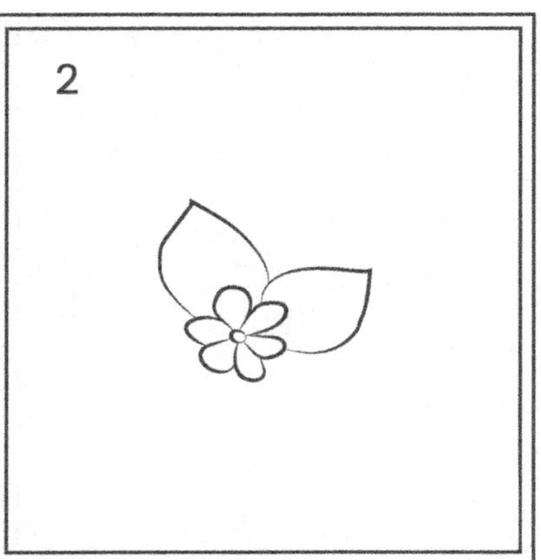

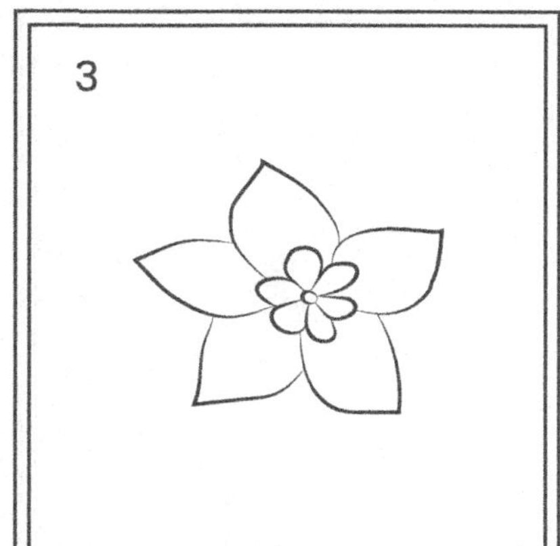

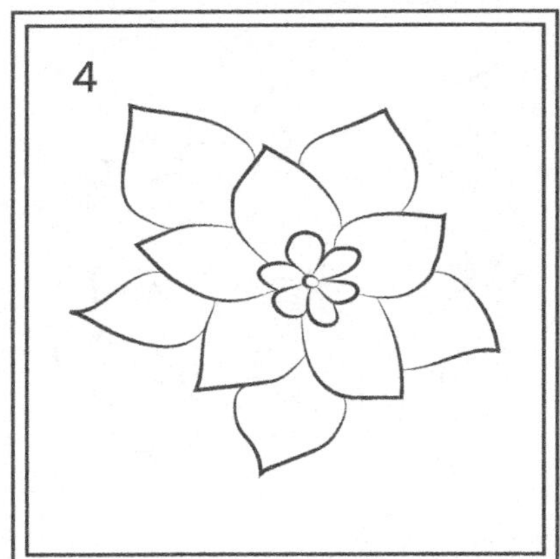

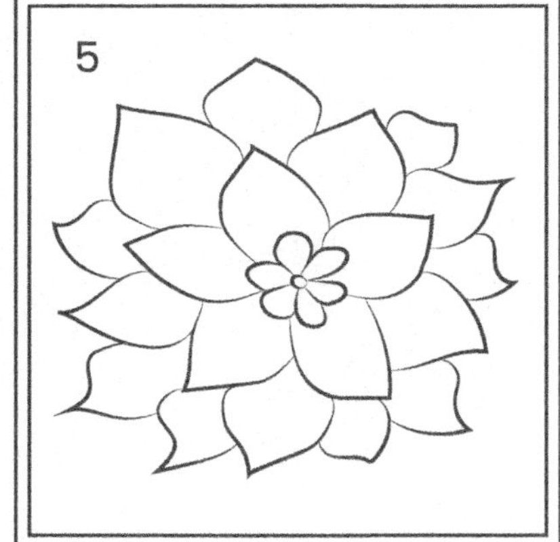

Try it here

Botanical Line Drawing 1

Carnation

20

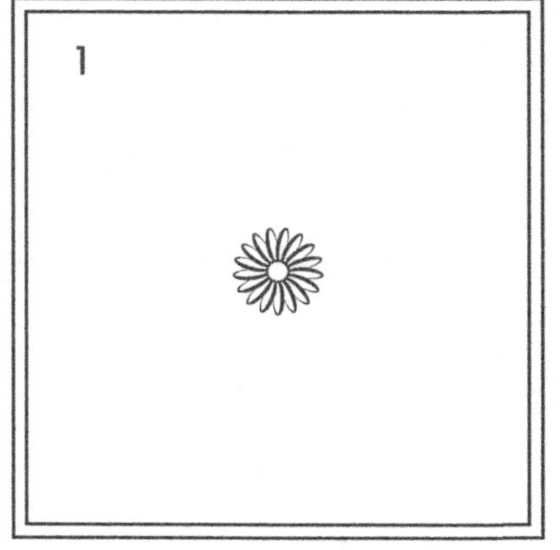

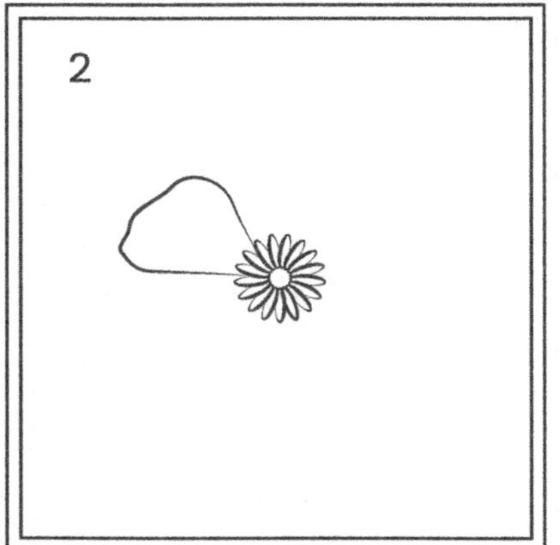

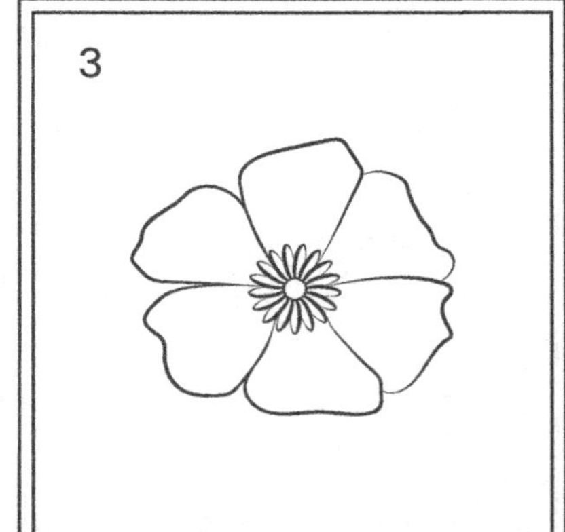

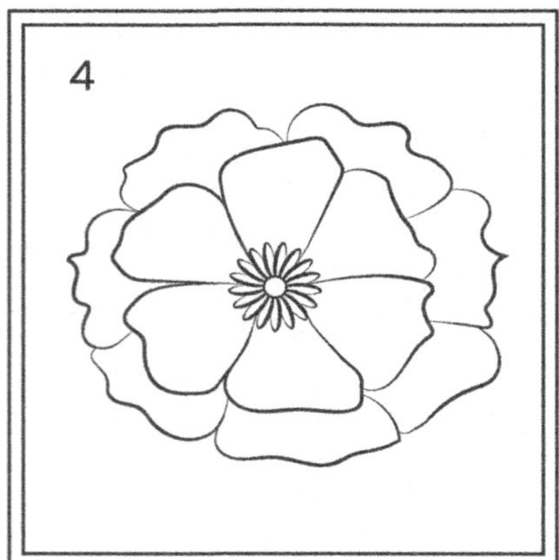

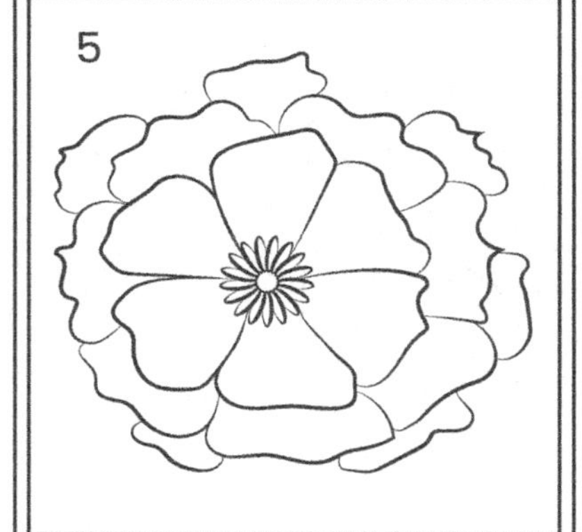

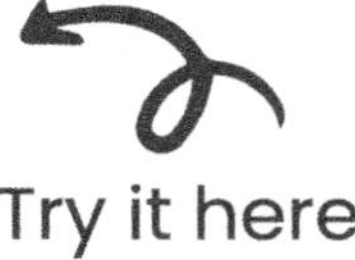

Try it here

Botanical Line Drawing 1

Rose 2

21

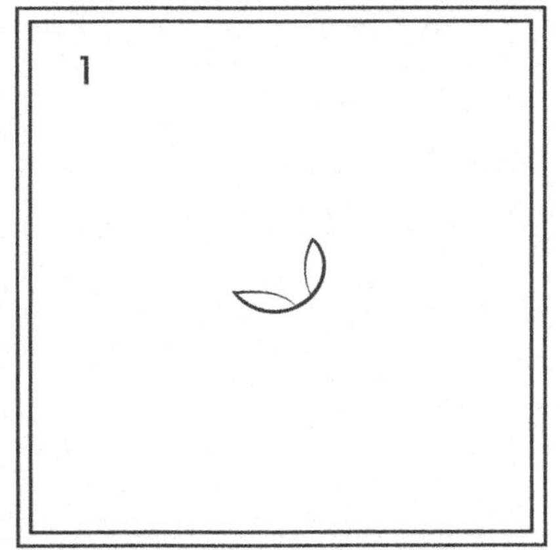

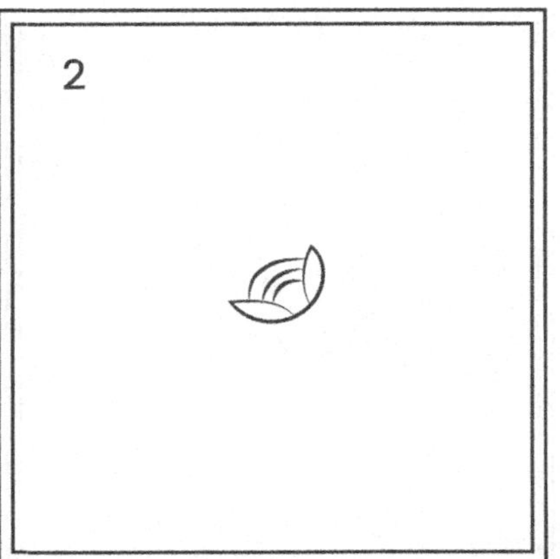

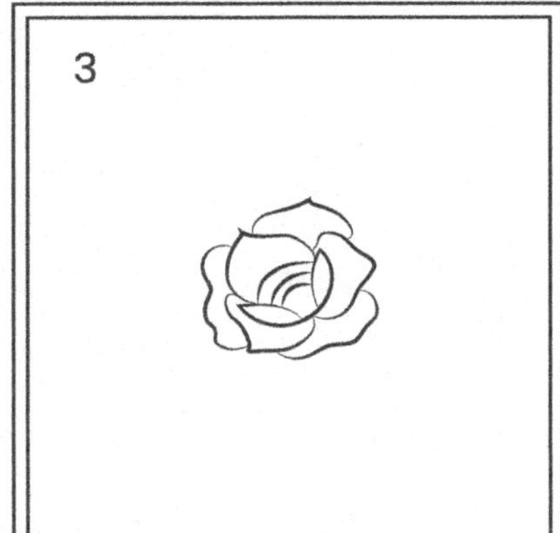

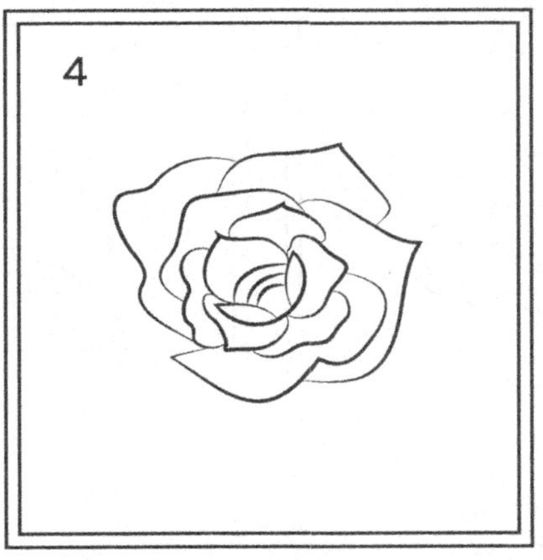

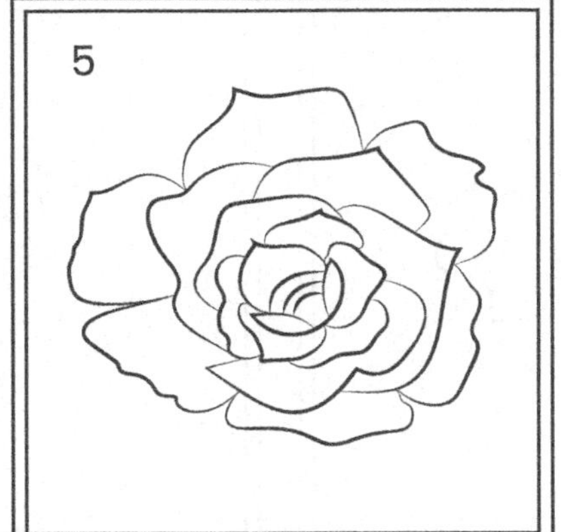

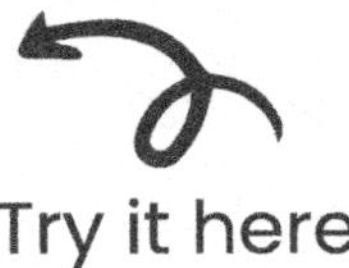

Try it here

Botanical Line Drawing 1

Zinnia

22

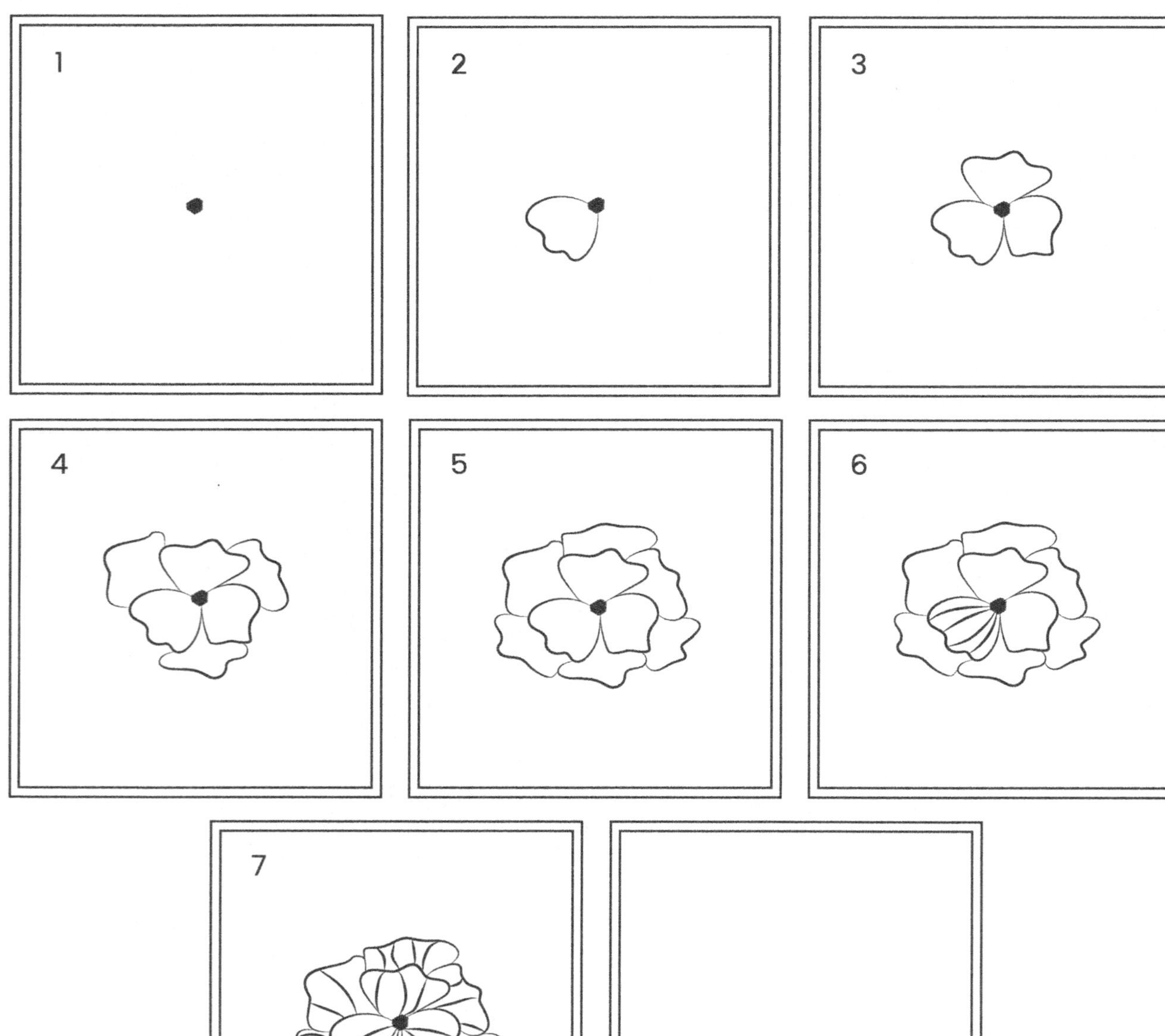

Botanical Line Drawing 1

Dahlia

23

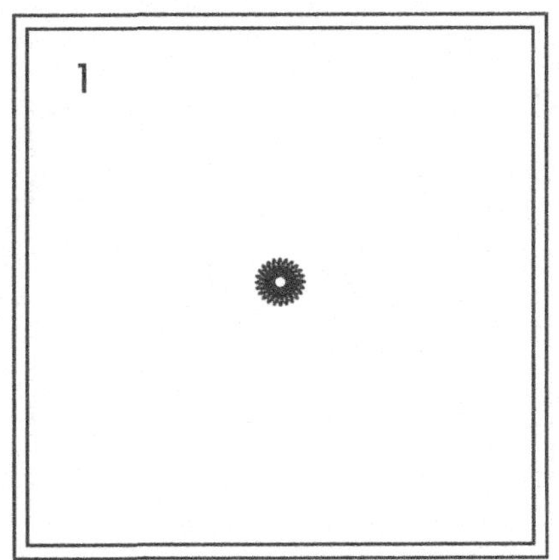

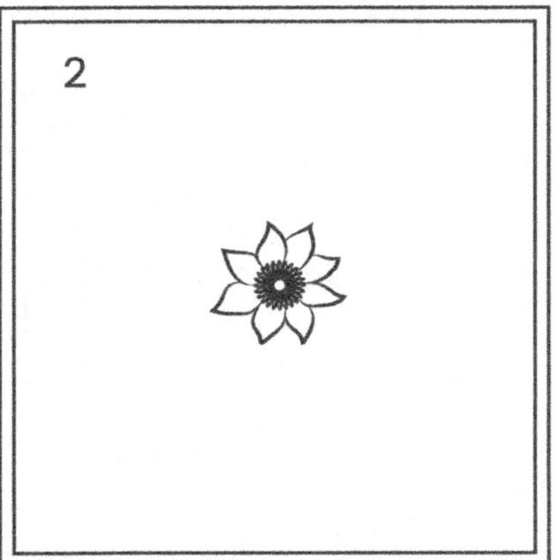

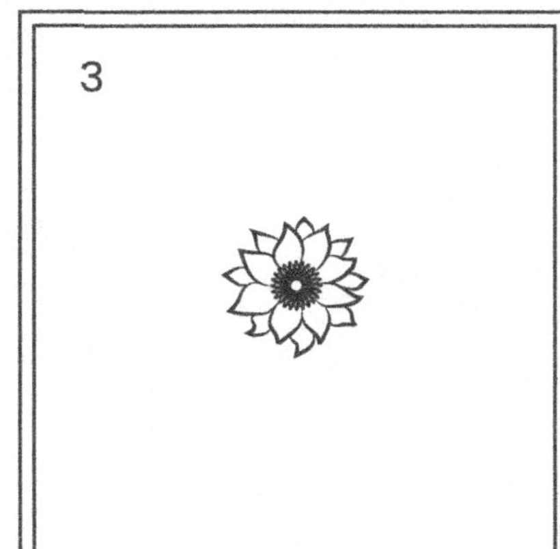

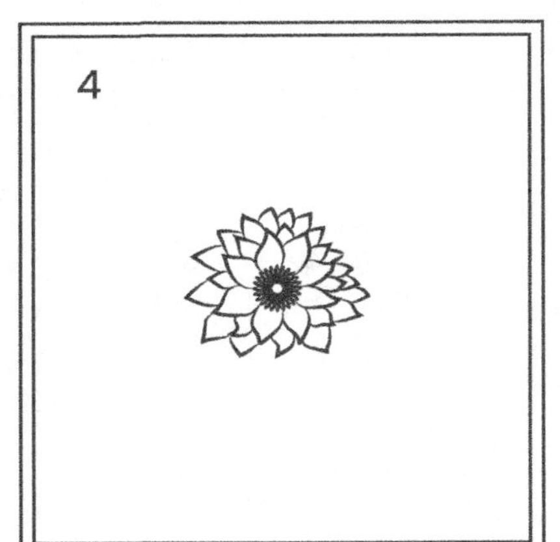

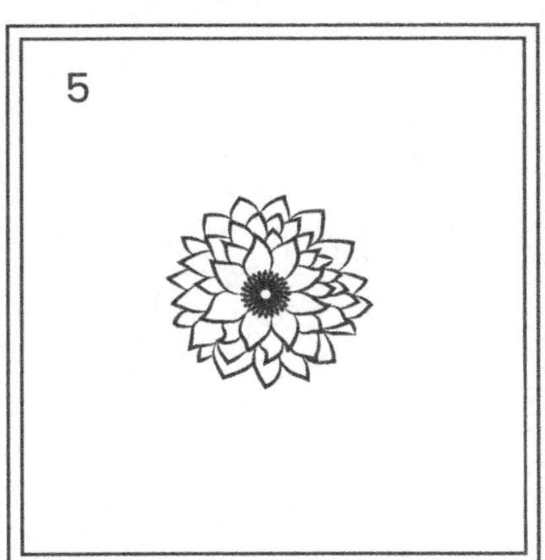

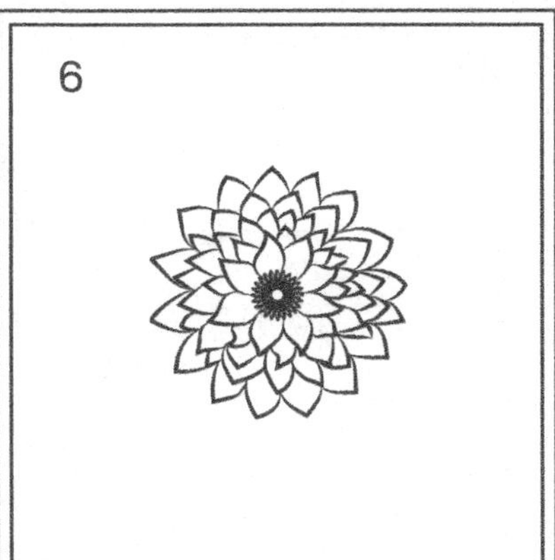

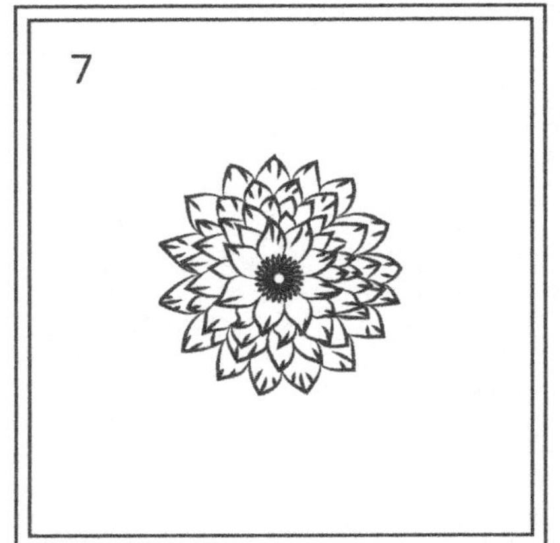

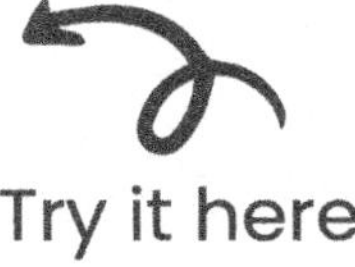

Try it here

Botanical Line Drawing 1

Peony

24

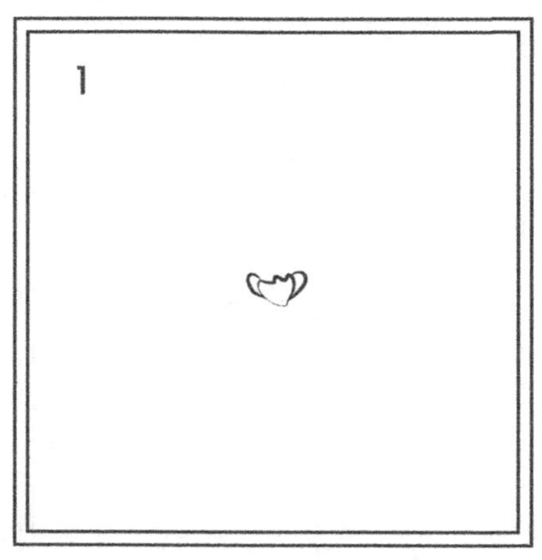

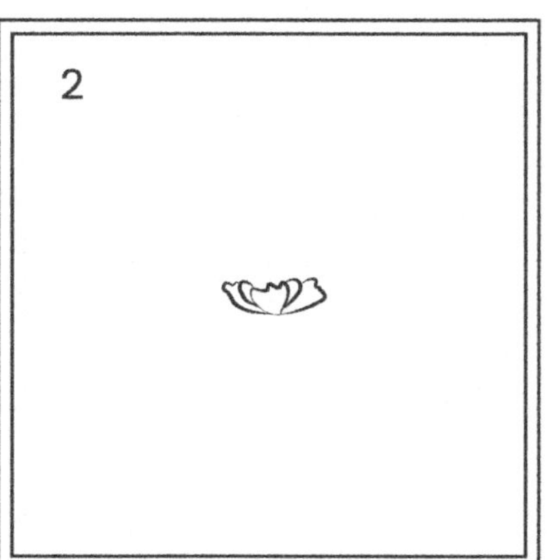

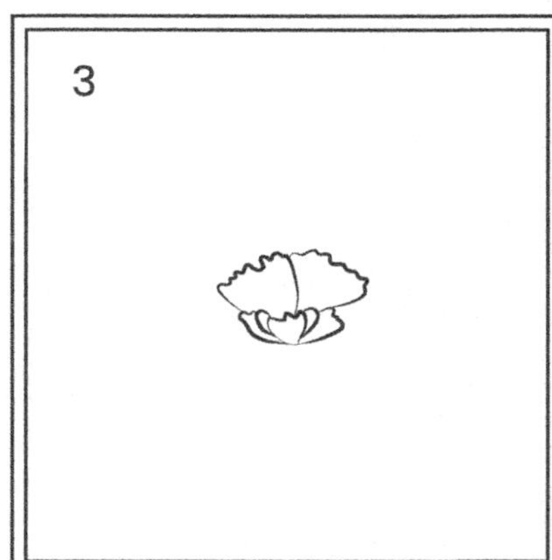

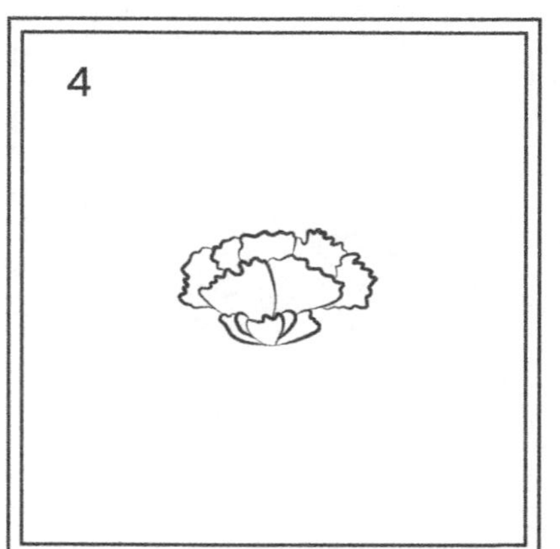

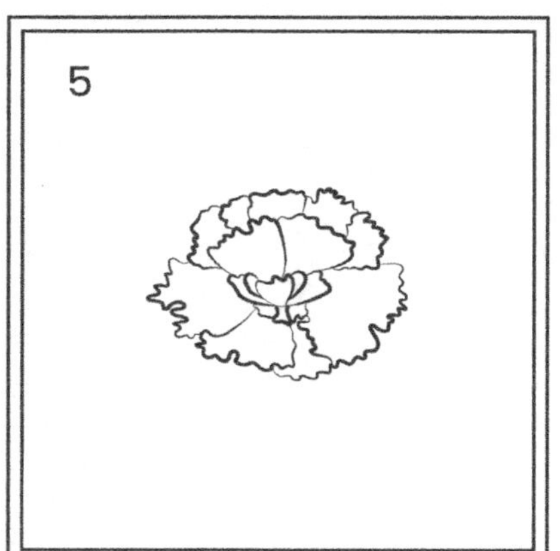

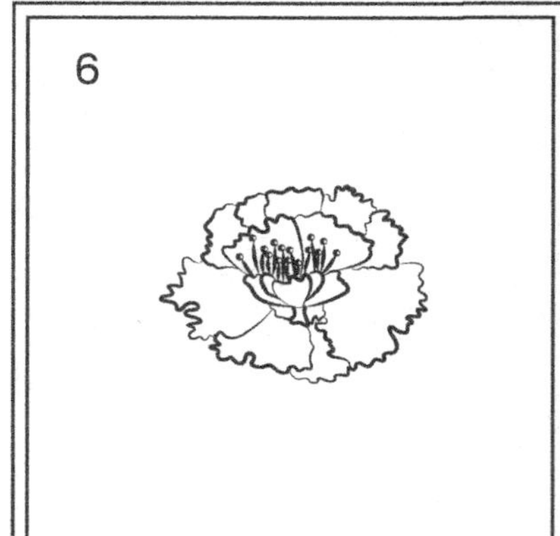

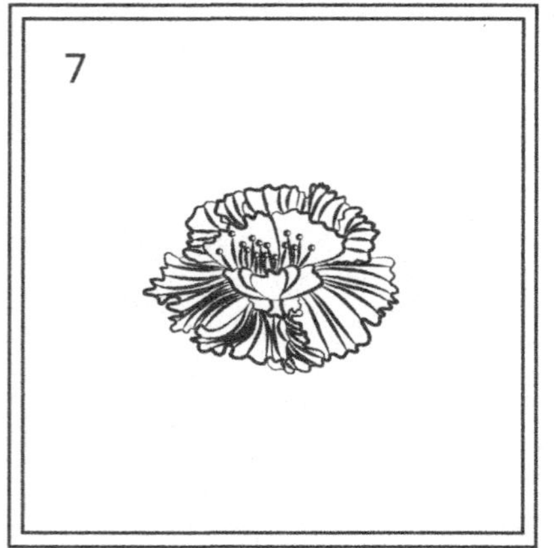

Try it here

Botanical Line Drawing 1

Kanzan Sakura

25

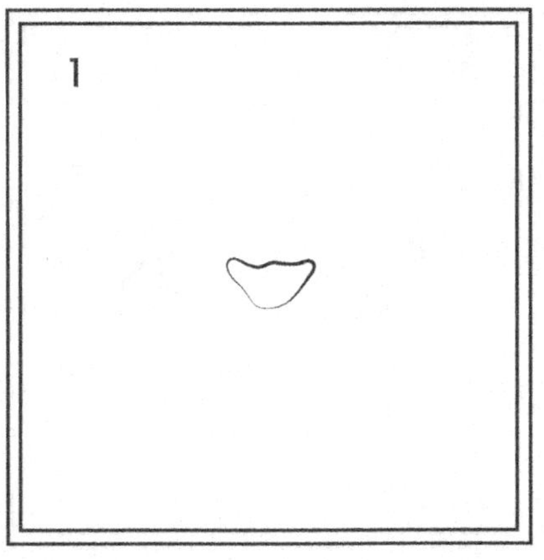

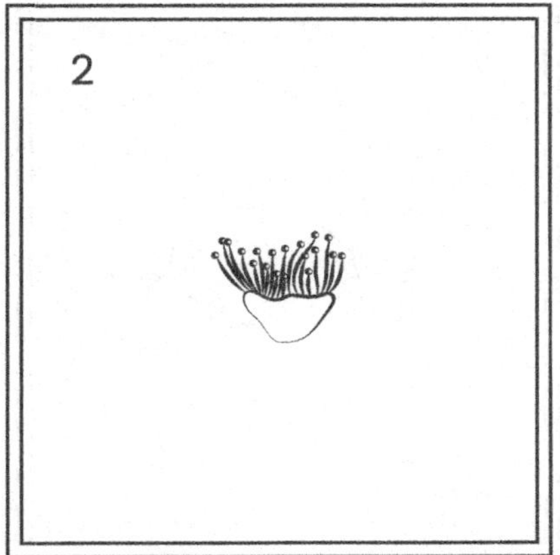

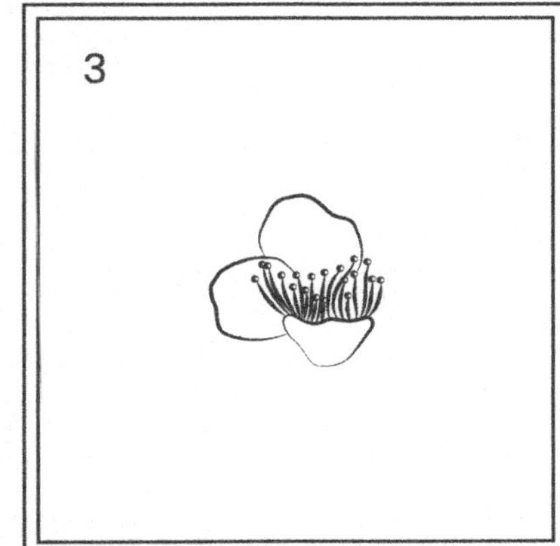

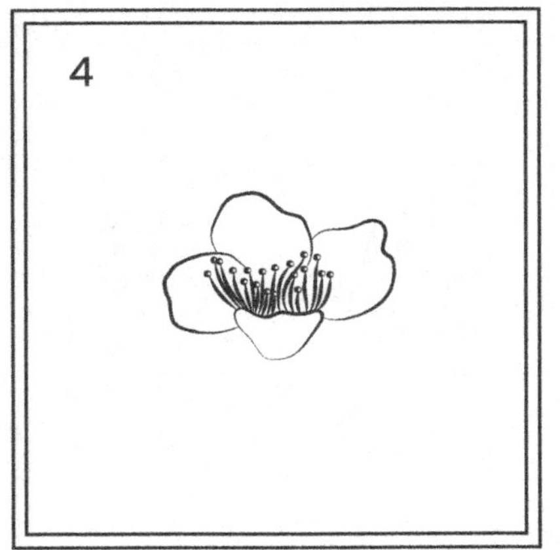

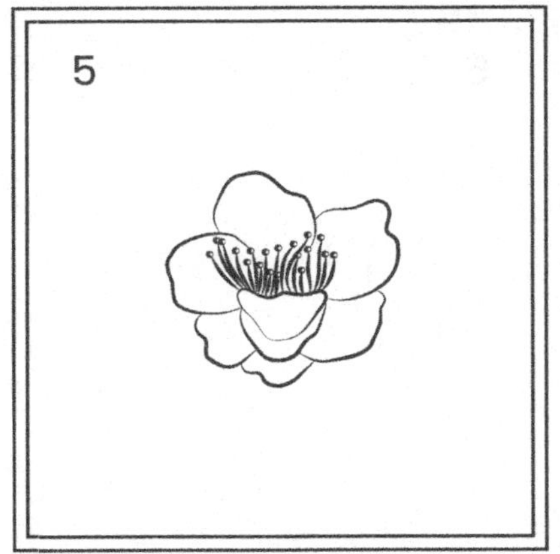

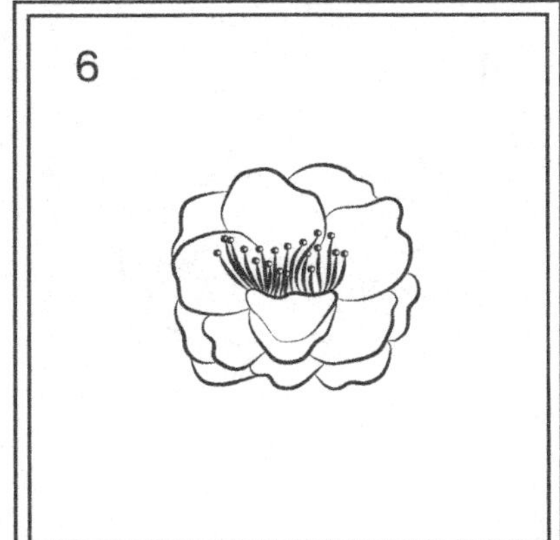

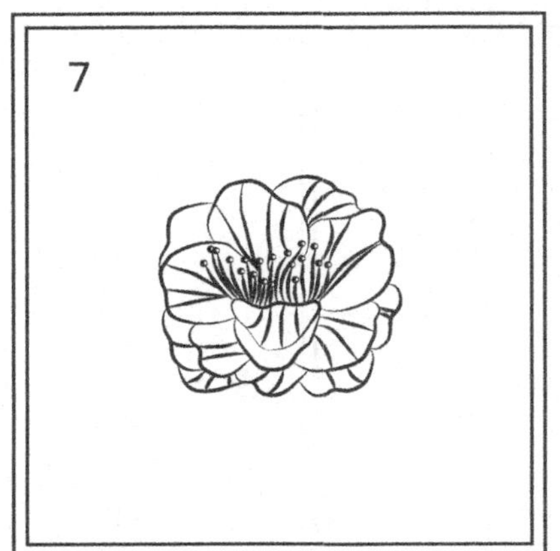

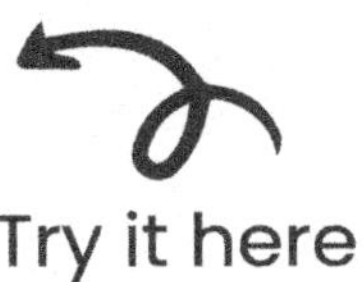

Try it here

Botanical Line Drawing 1

Pansy 2

26

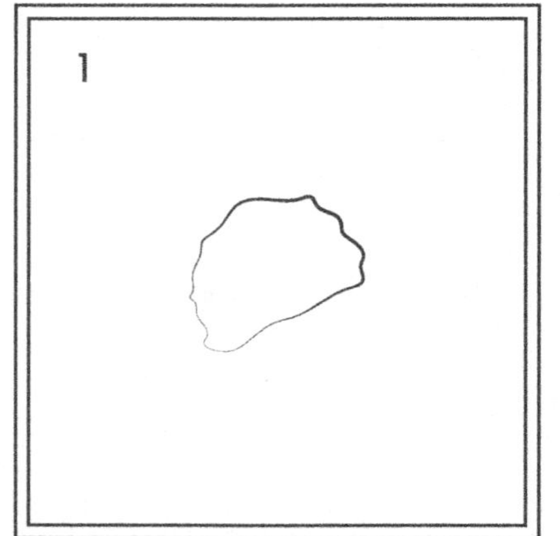

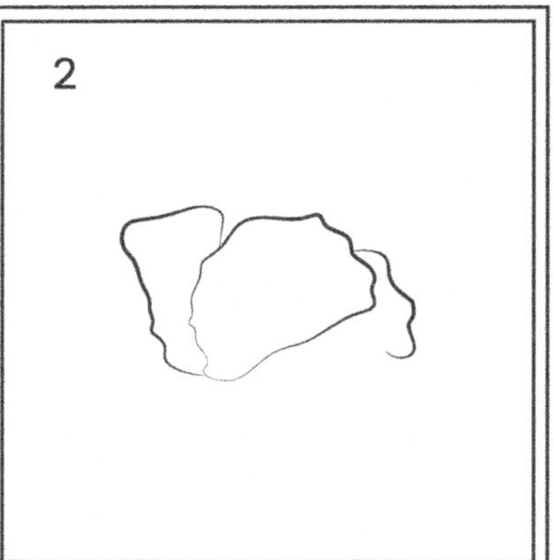

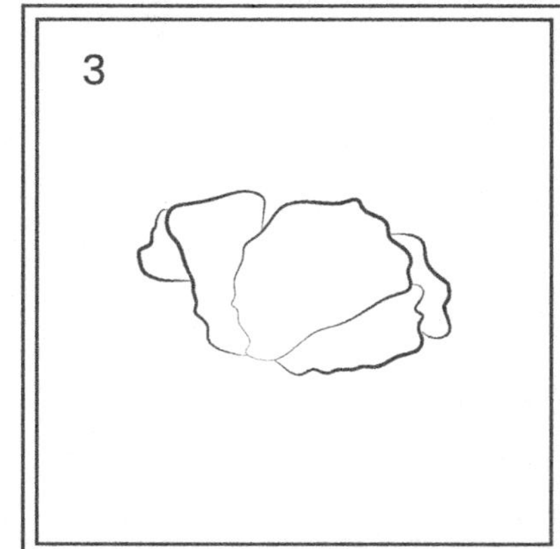

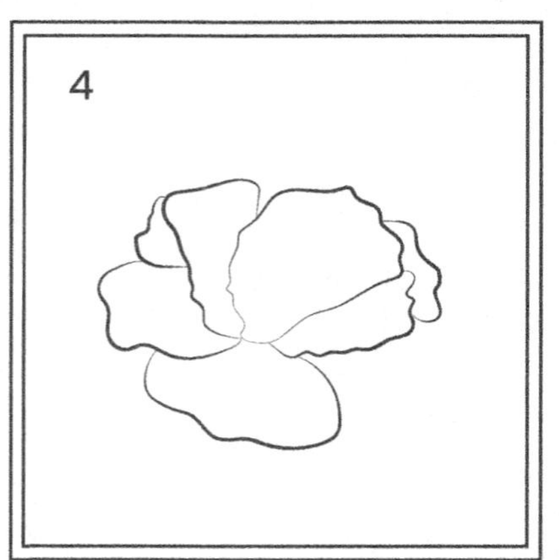

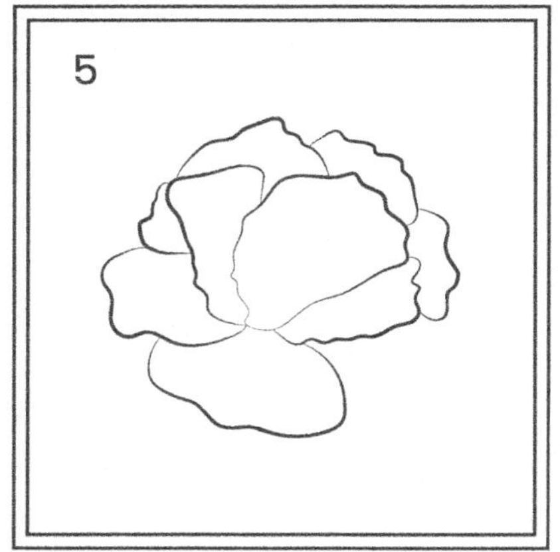

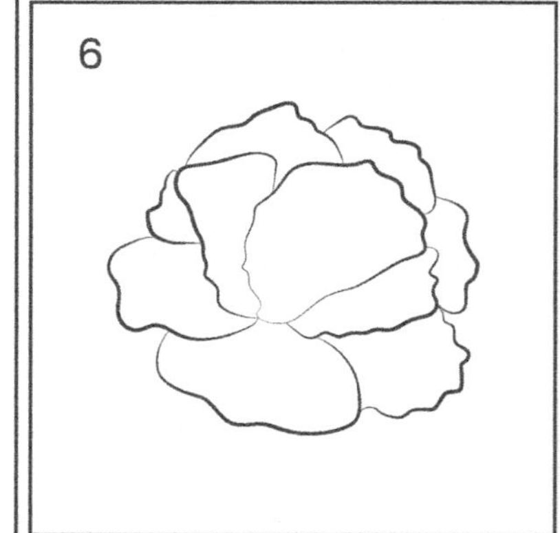

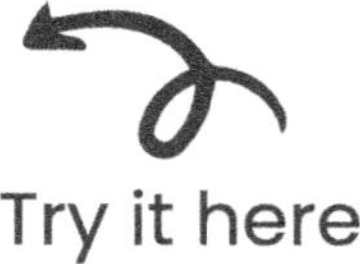

Botanical Line Drawing 1

Poppy 2

27

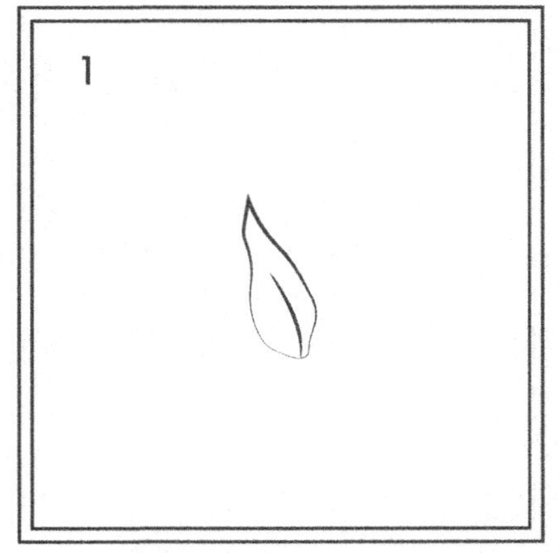

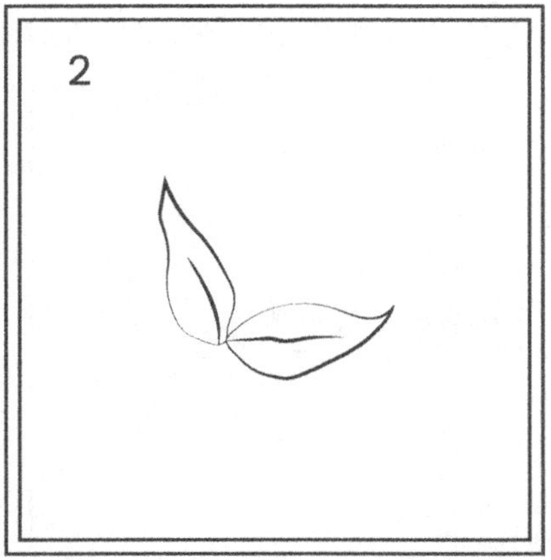

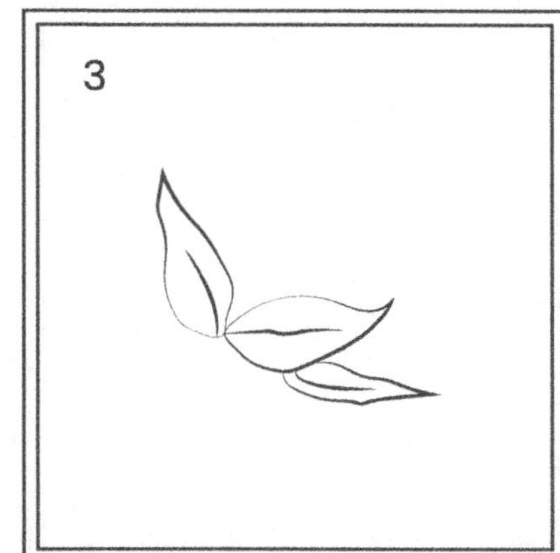

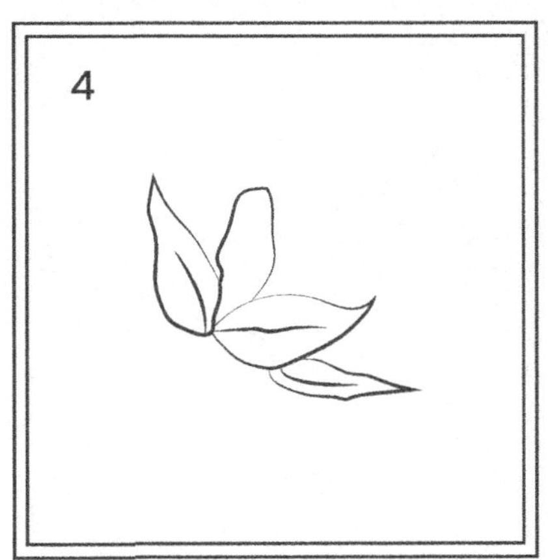

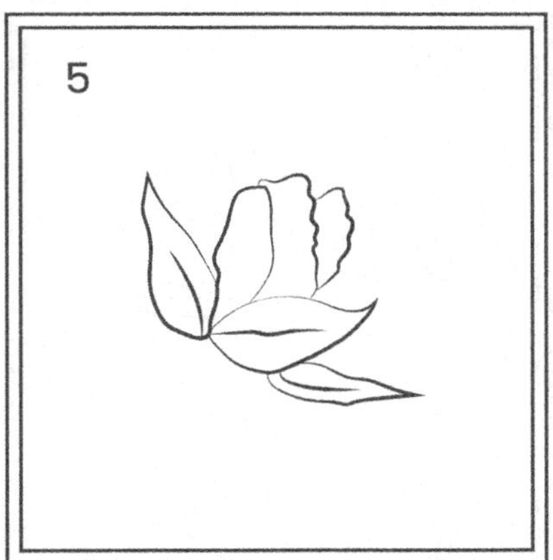

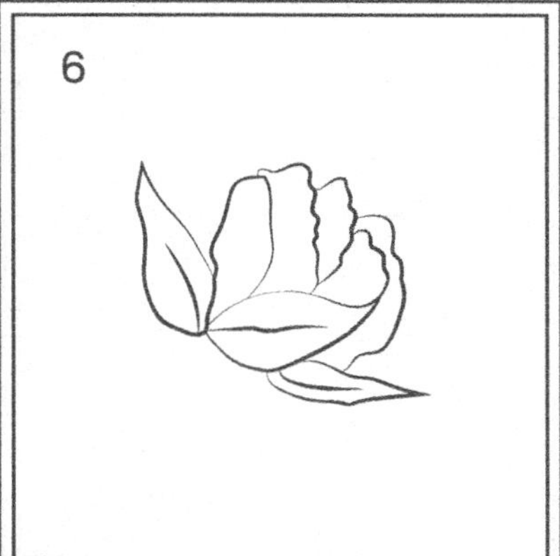

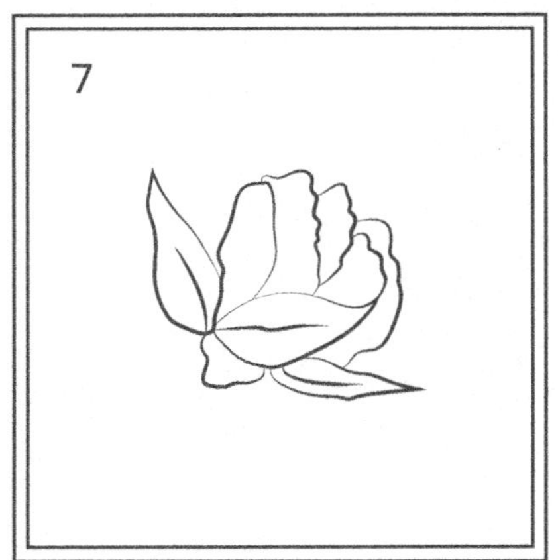

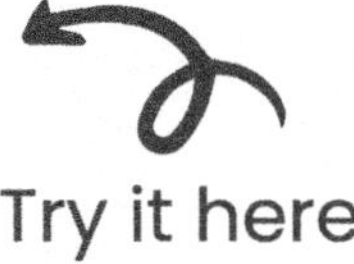

Try it here

Botanical Line Drawing 1

Peony Bud

28

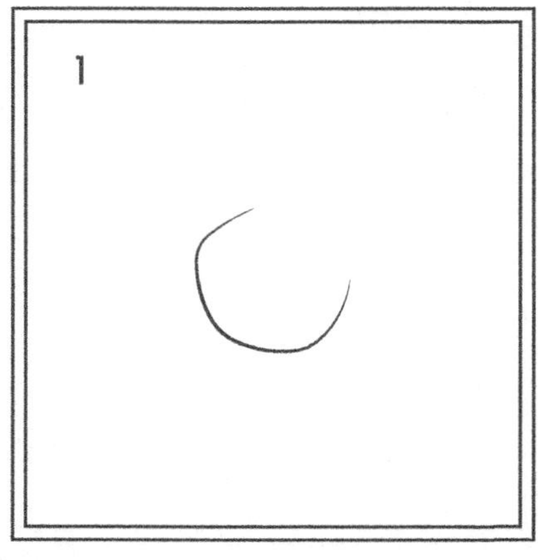

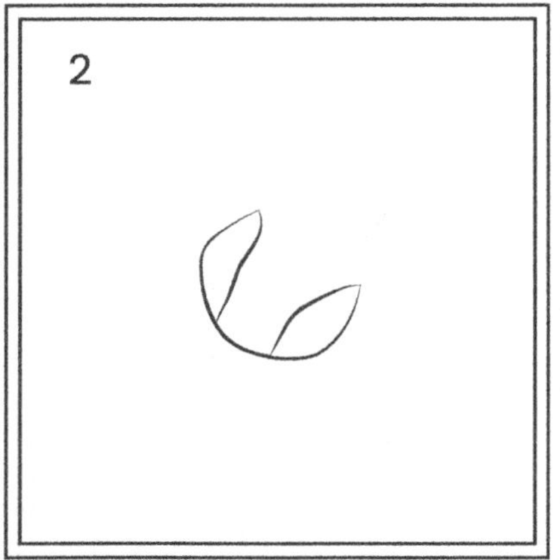

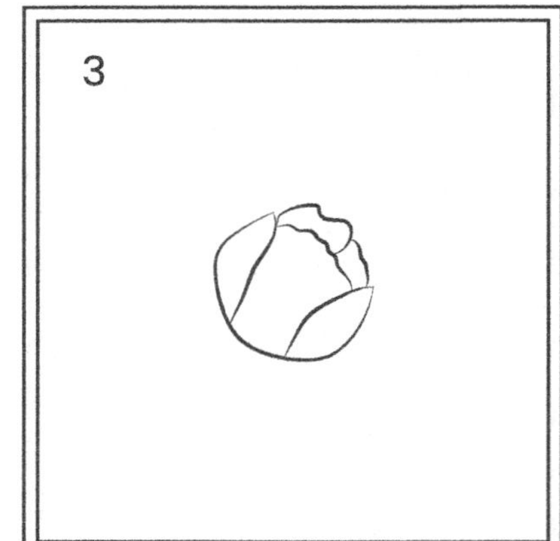

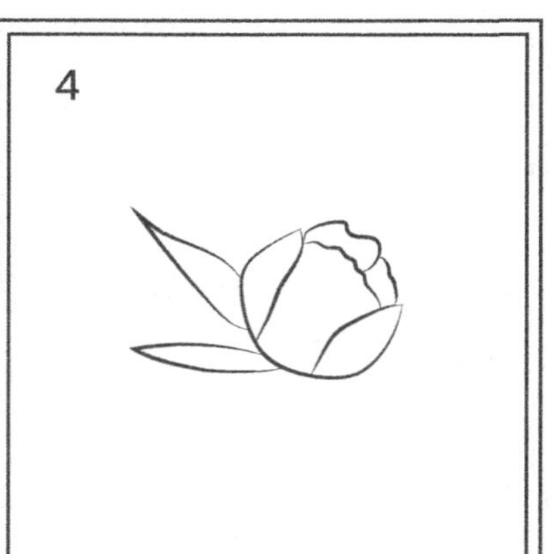

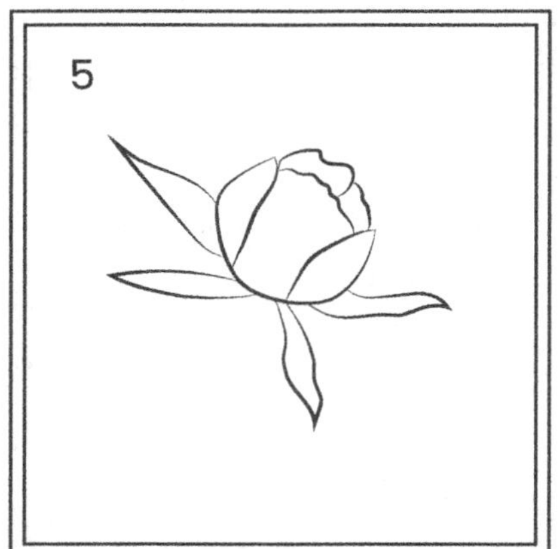

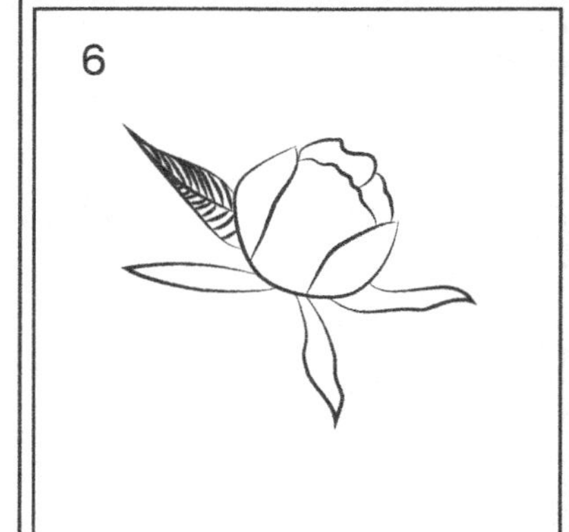

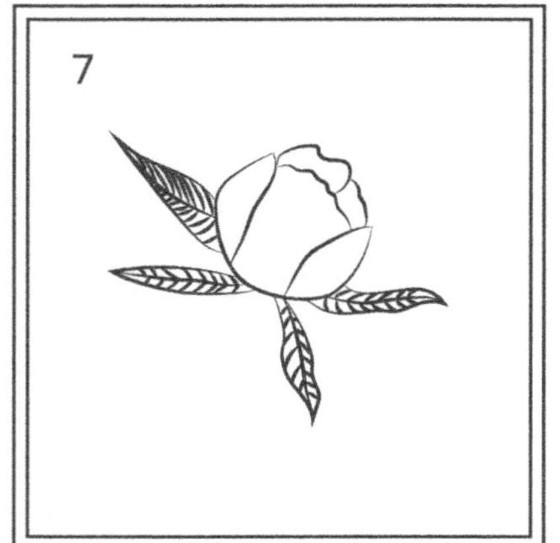

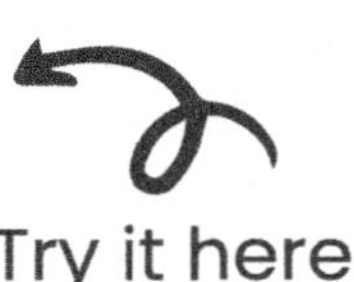

Try it here

Botanical Line Drawing 1

Carnation 2

29

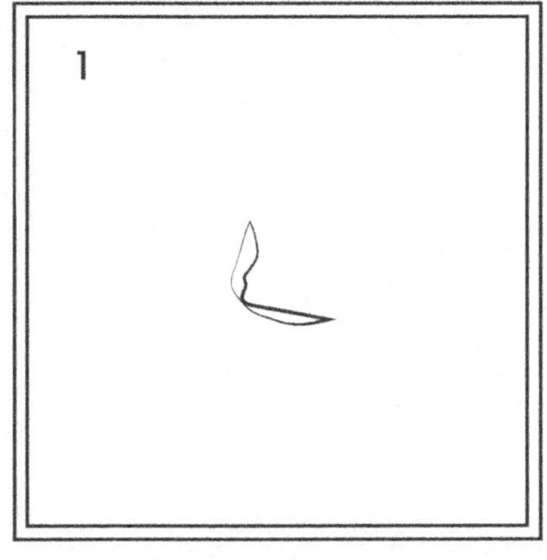

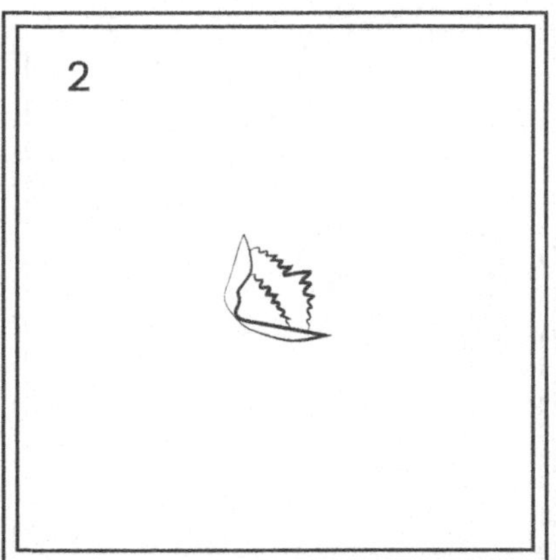

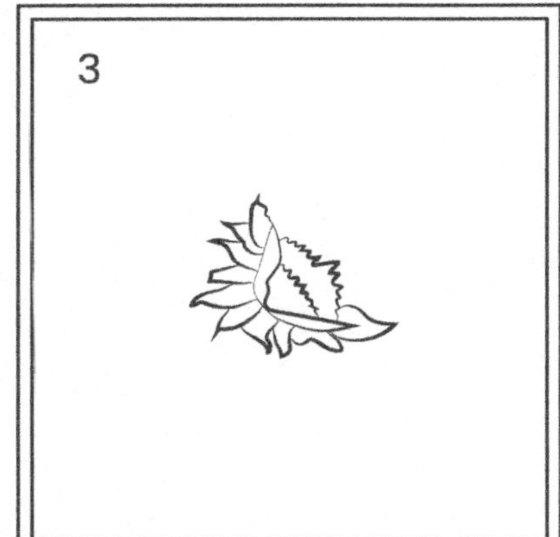

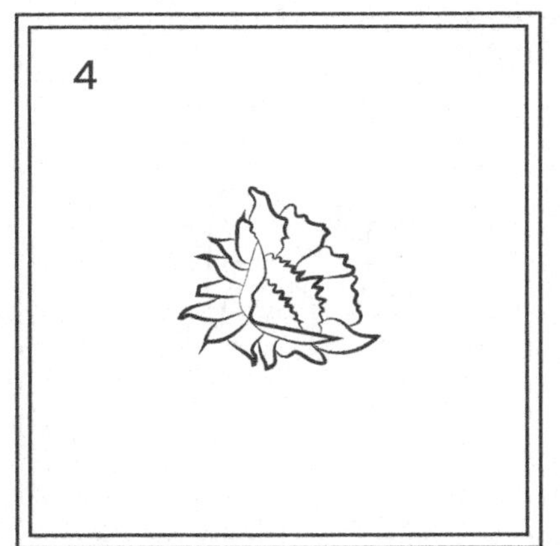

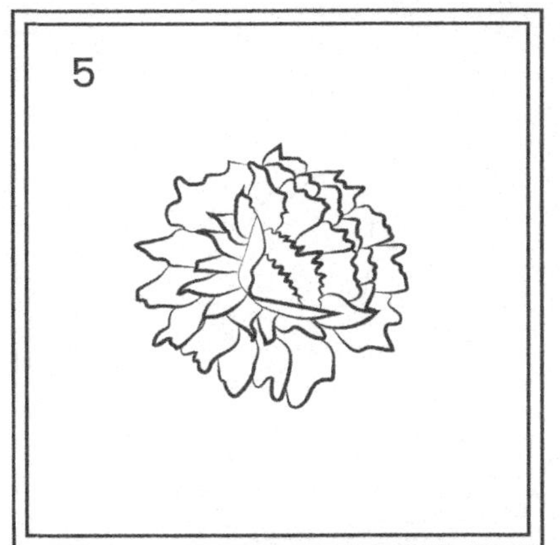

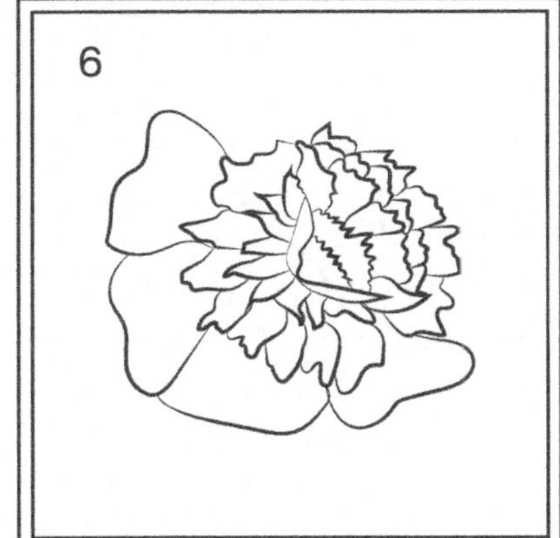

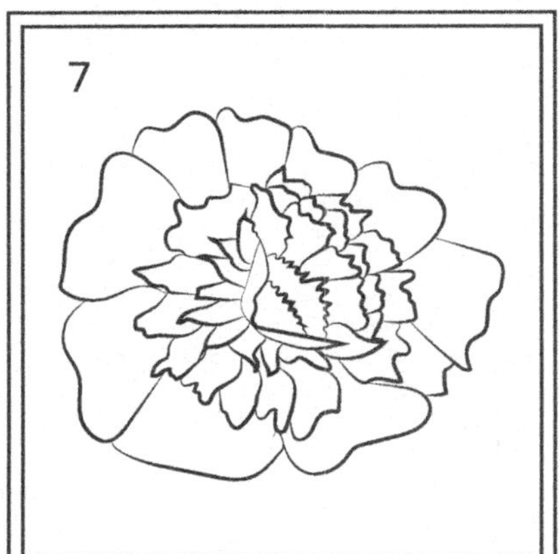

Try it here

Botanical Line Drawing 1

Lotus

30

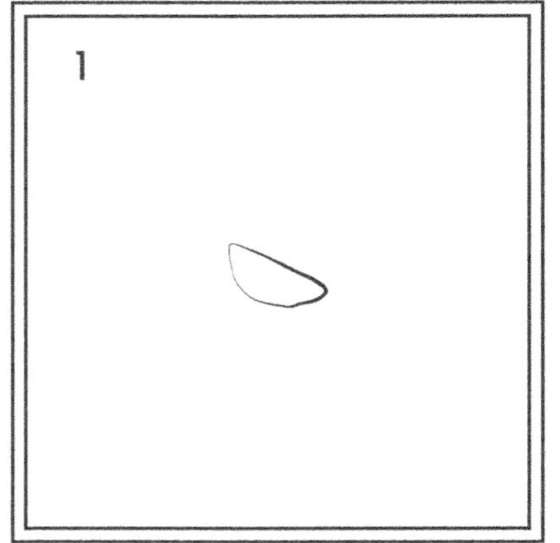

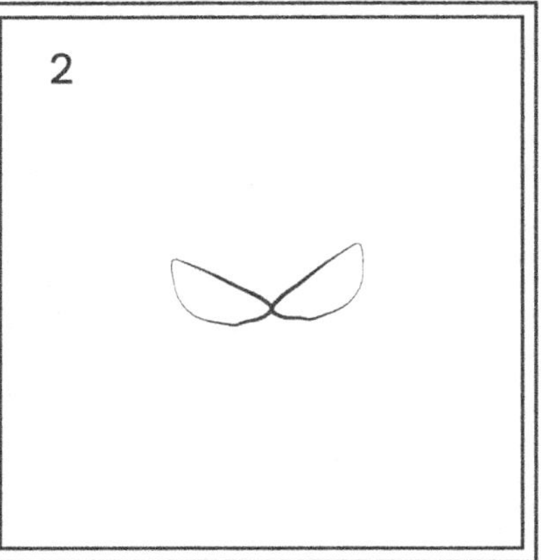

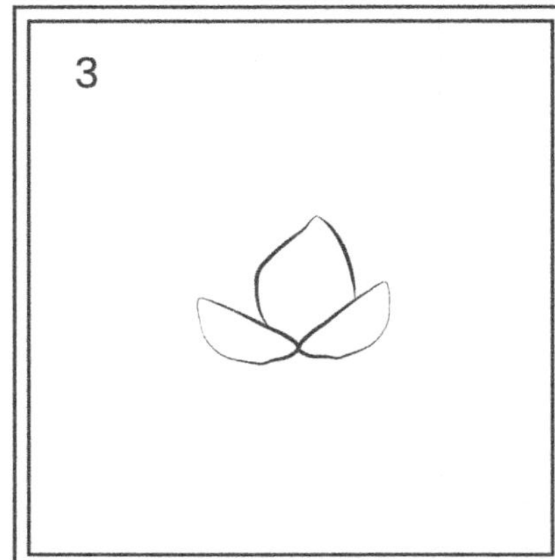

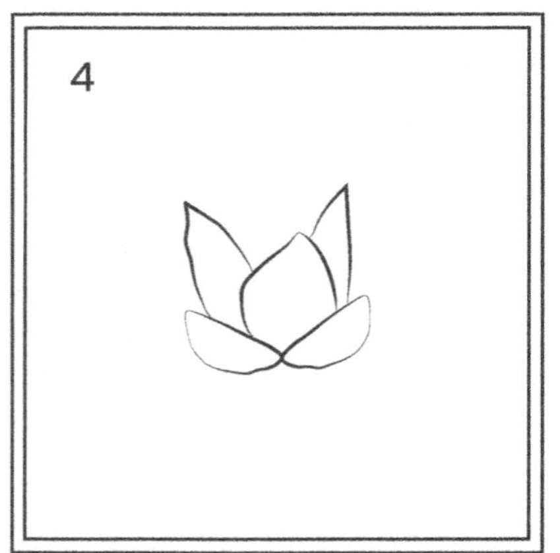

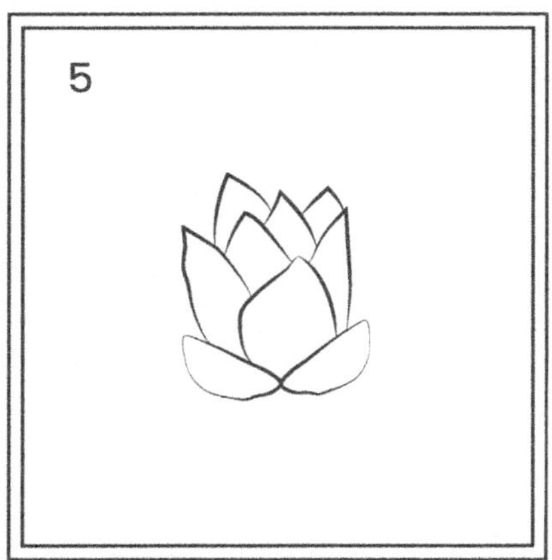

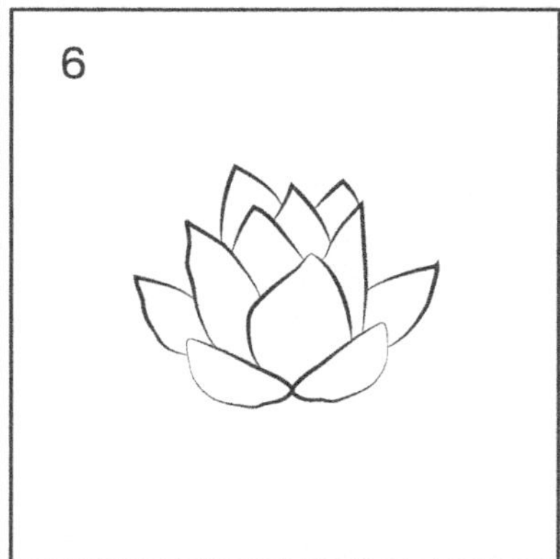

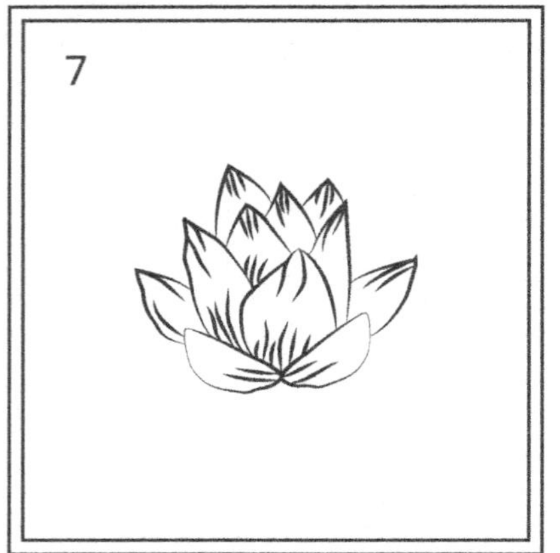

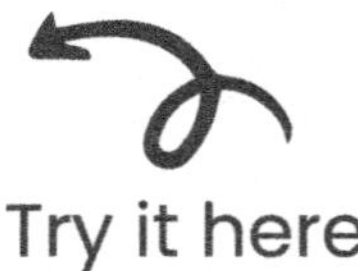

Botanical Line Drawing 1

Magnolia

31

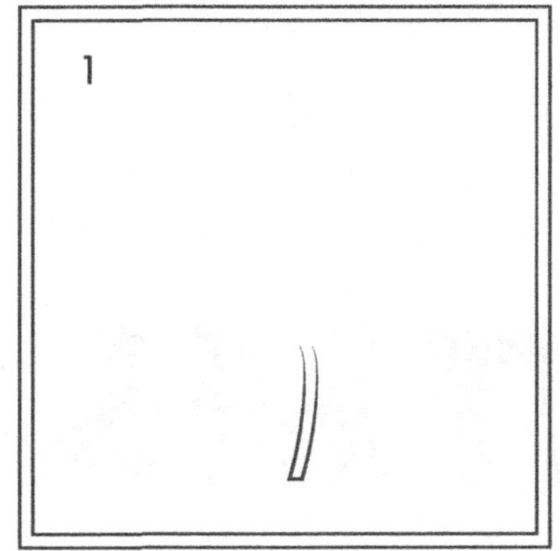

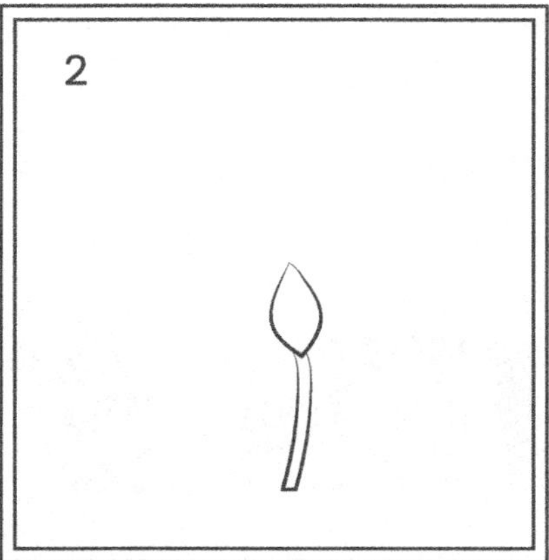

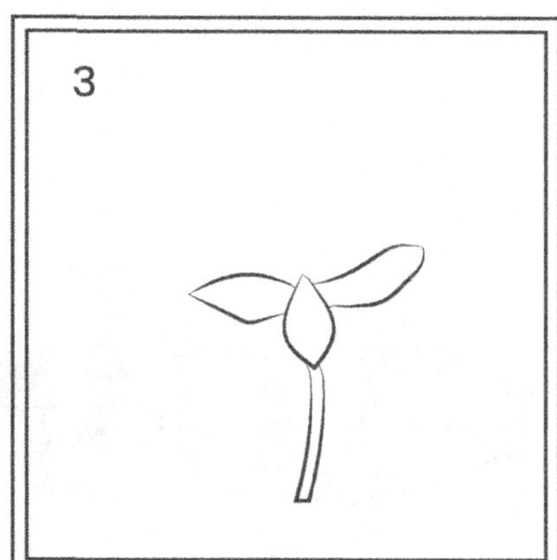

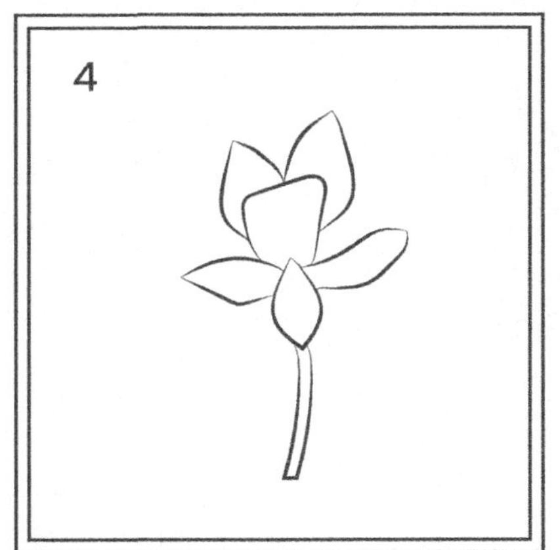

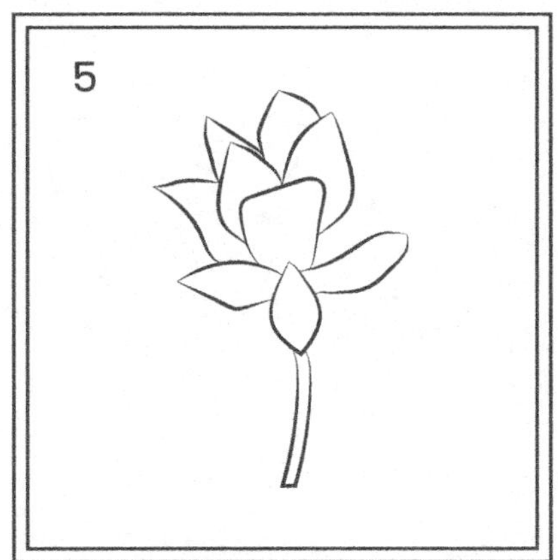

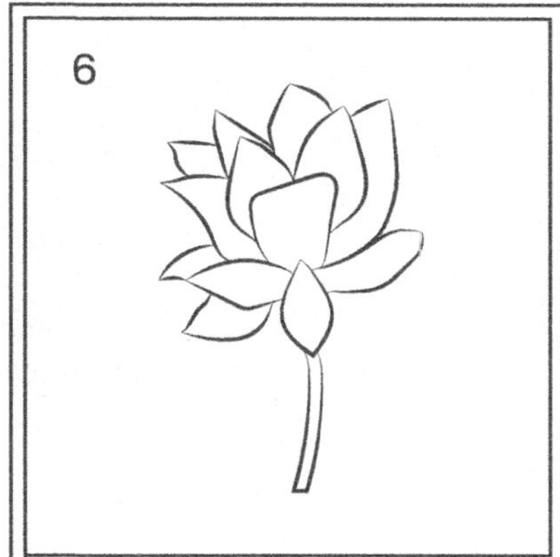

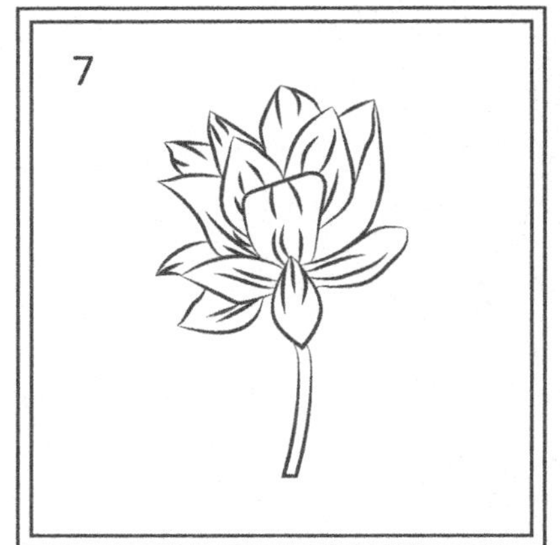

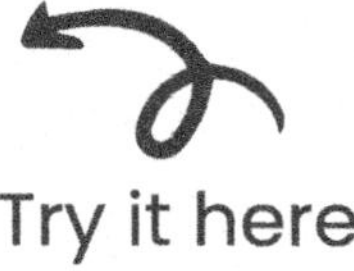

Try it here

FLOWER STEMS

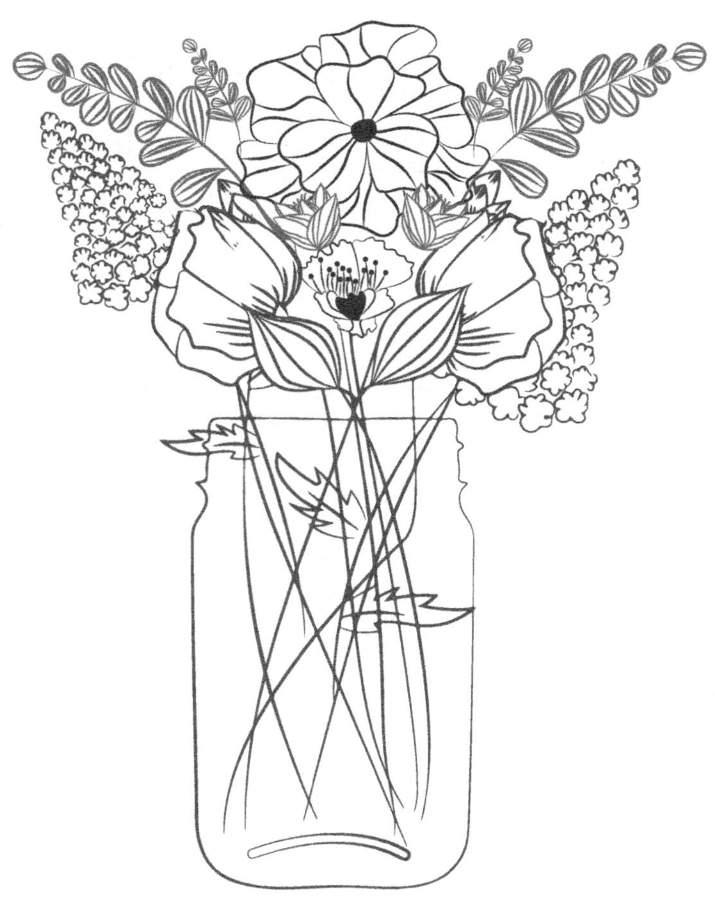

Botanical Line Drawing 1

Water Flower

32

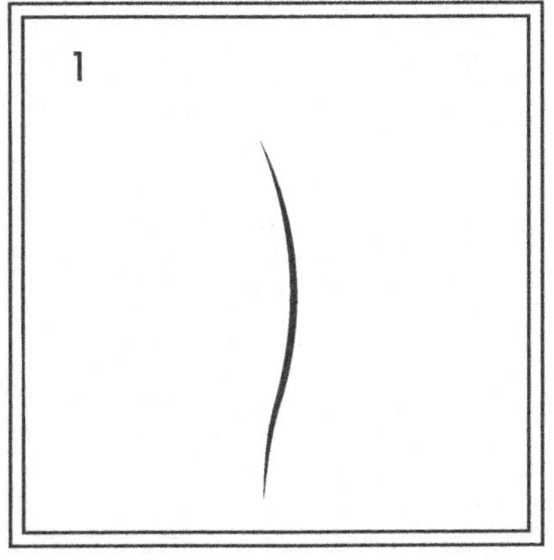

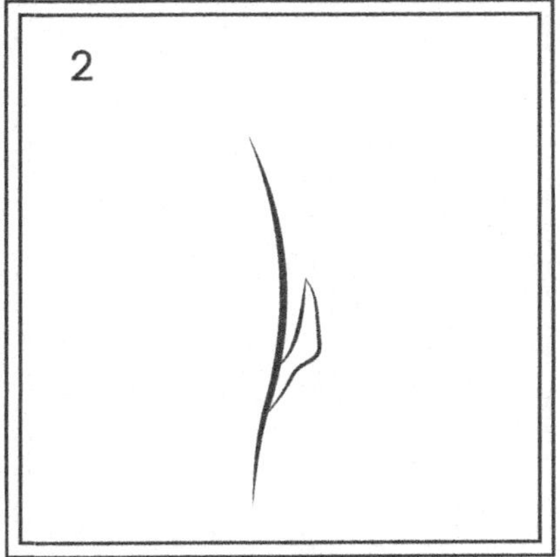

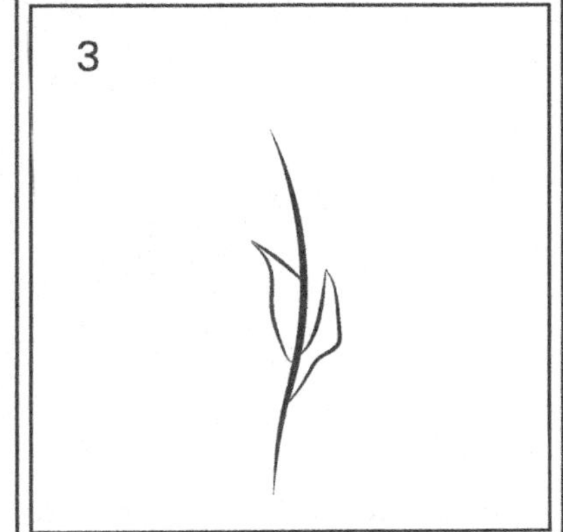

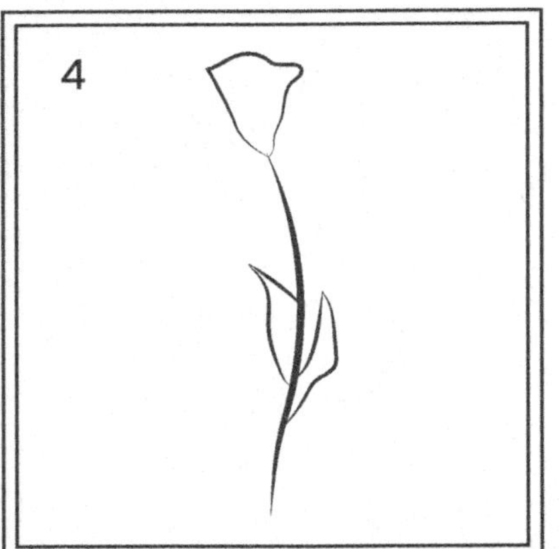

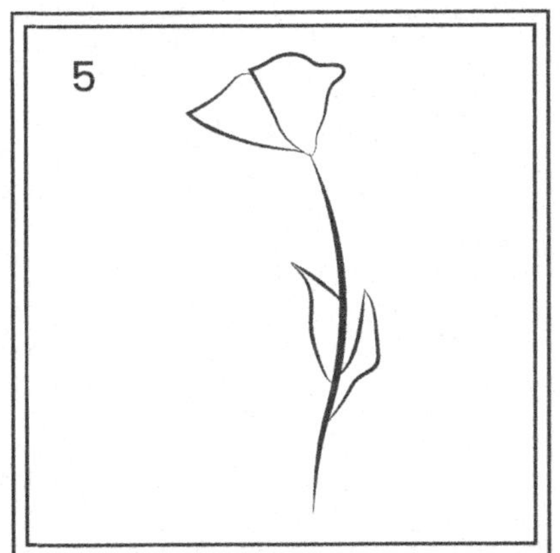

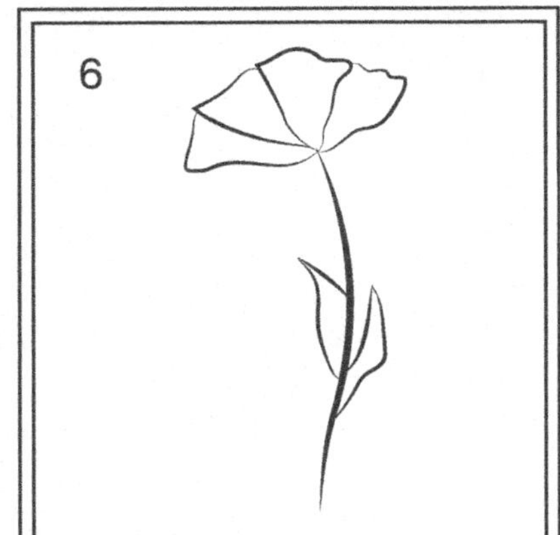

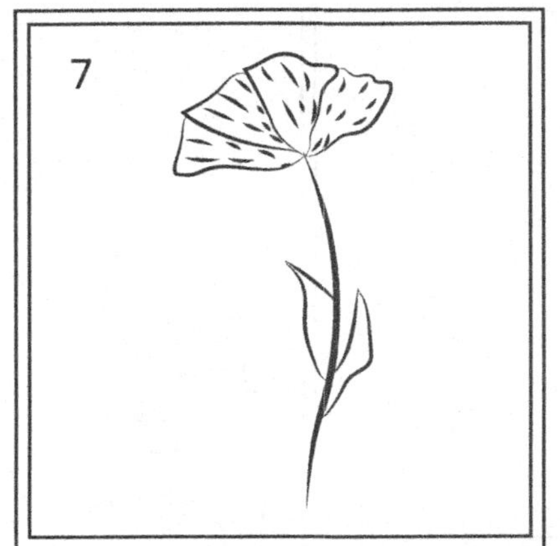

Botanical Line Drawing 1

Sunflower

33

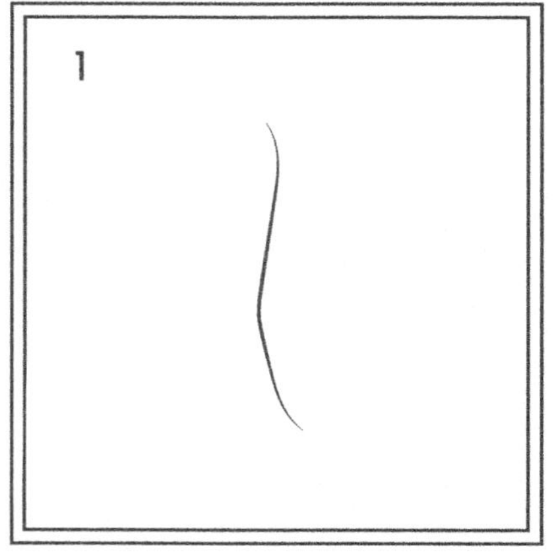

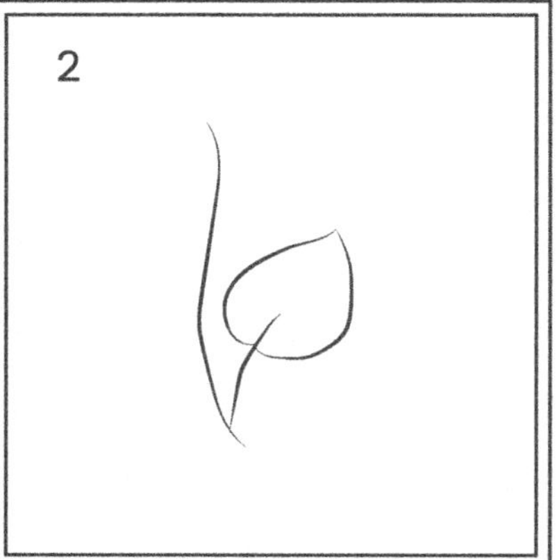

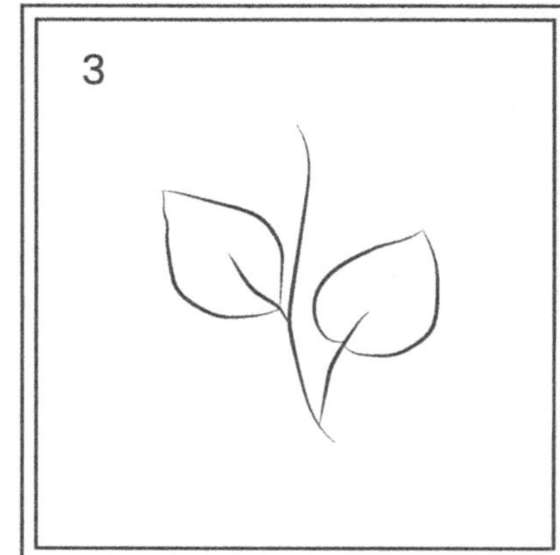

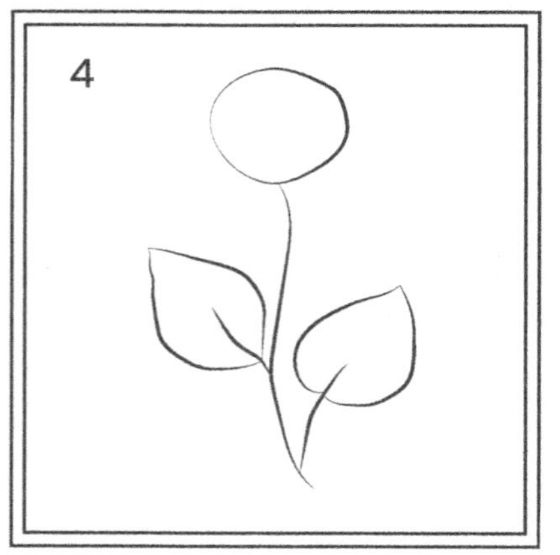

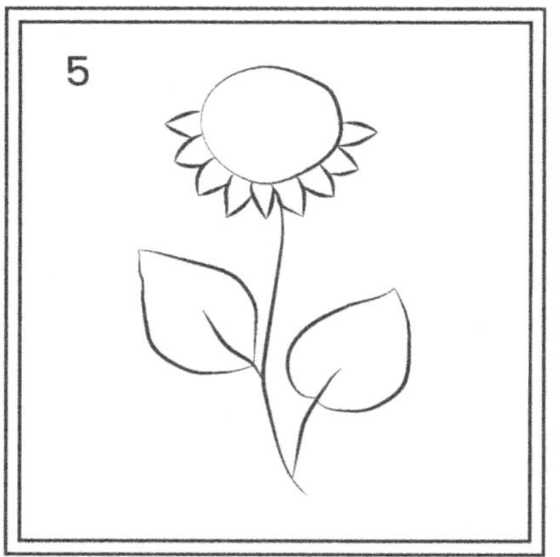

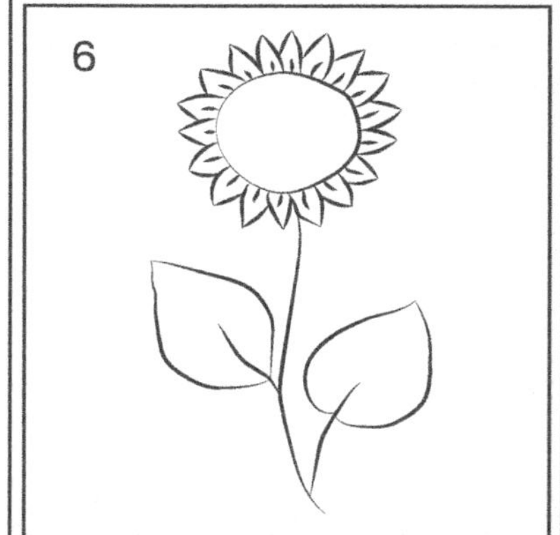

Try it here

Botanical Line Drawing 1

Bluegrass

34

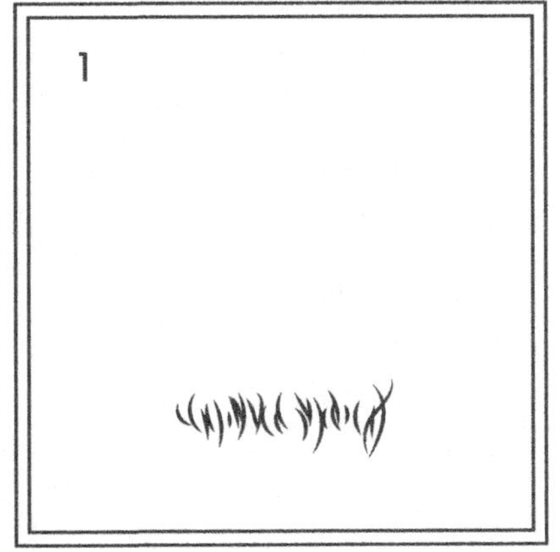

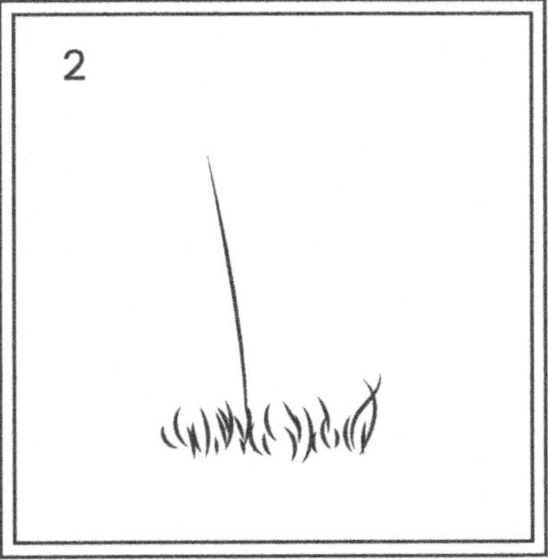

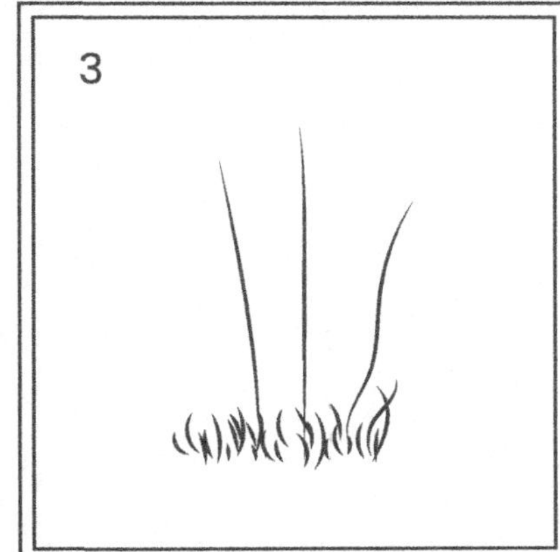

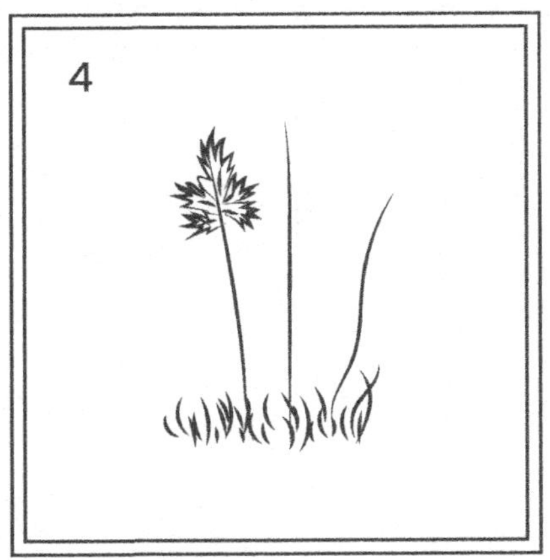

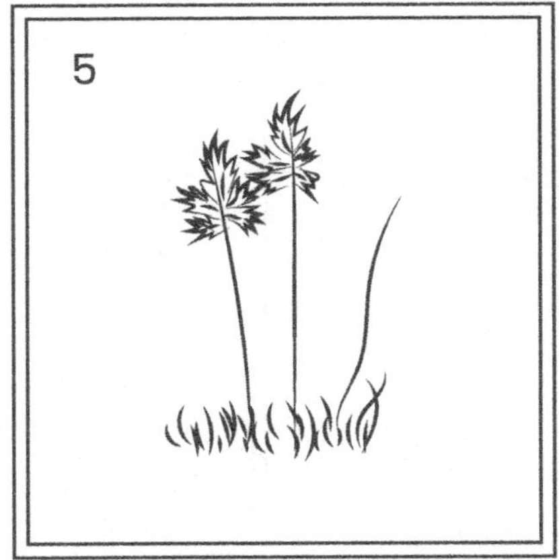

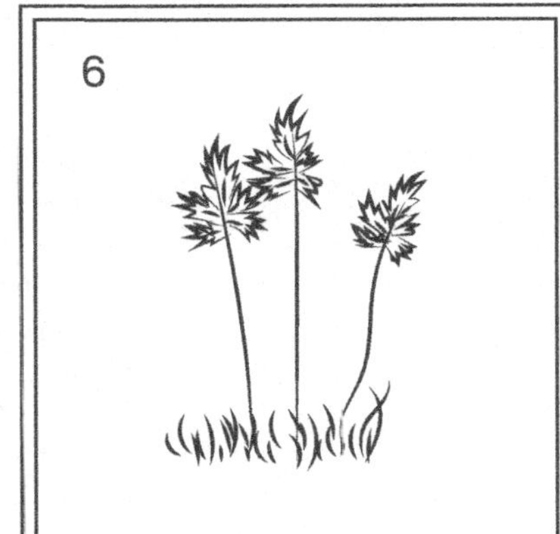

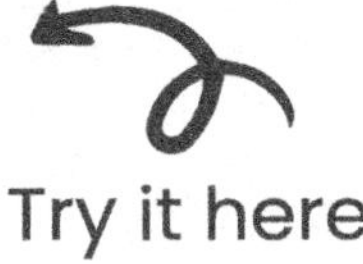

Try it here

Botanical Line Drawing 1

Lily of the Valley 35

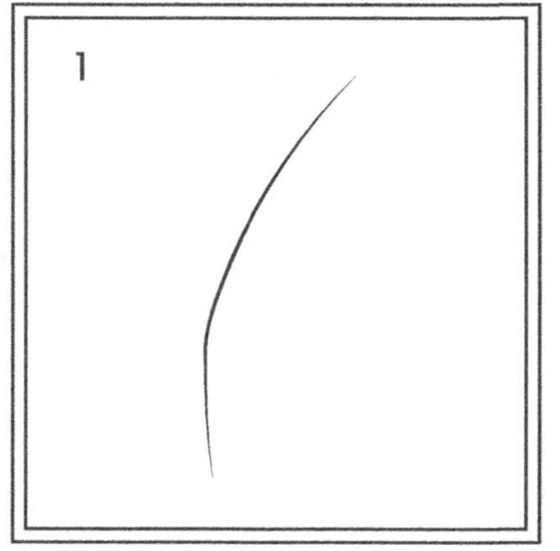

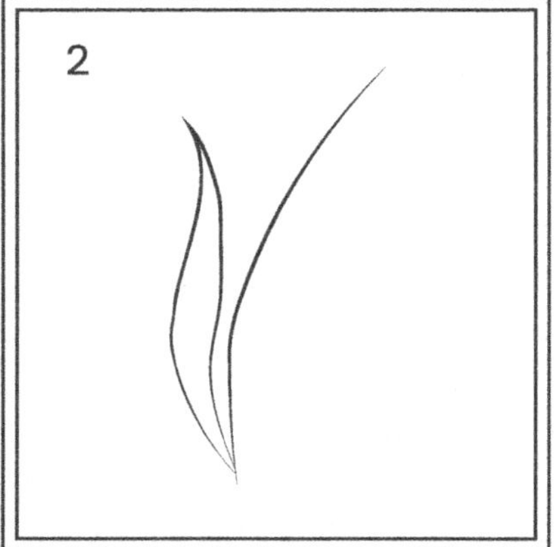

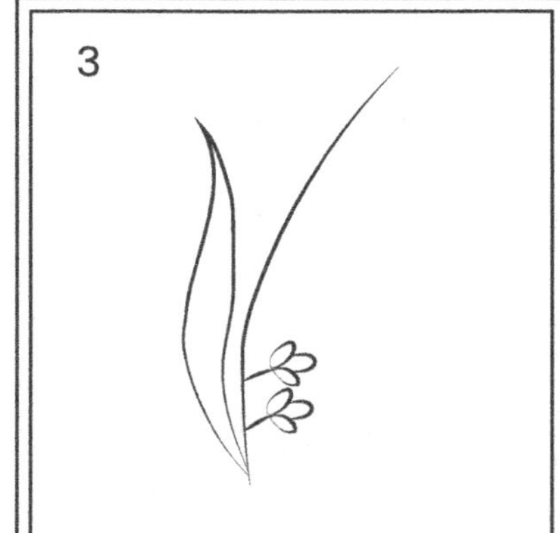

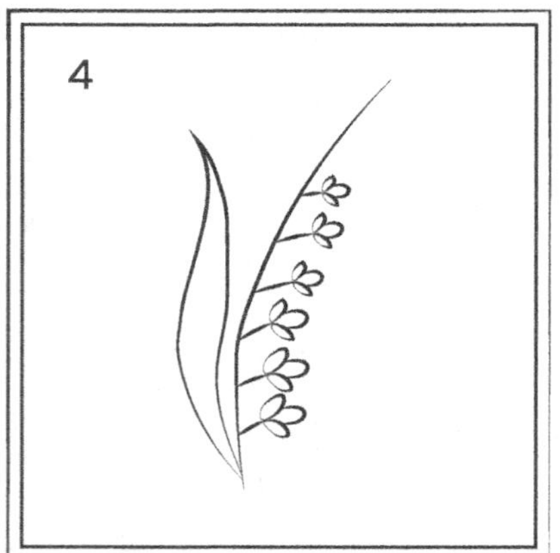

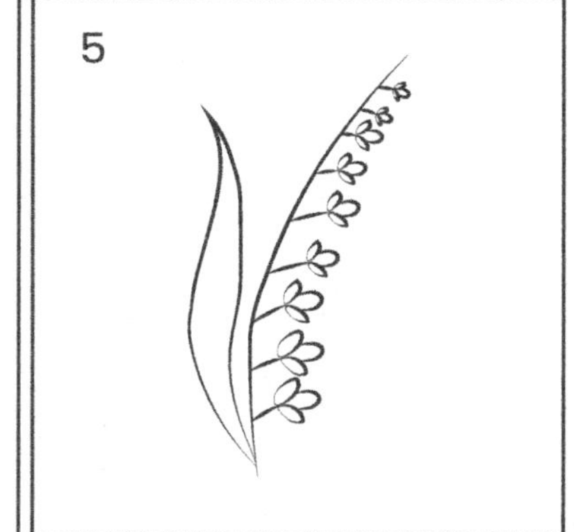

Try it here

Botanical Line Drawing 1

Camas

36

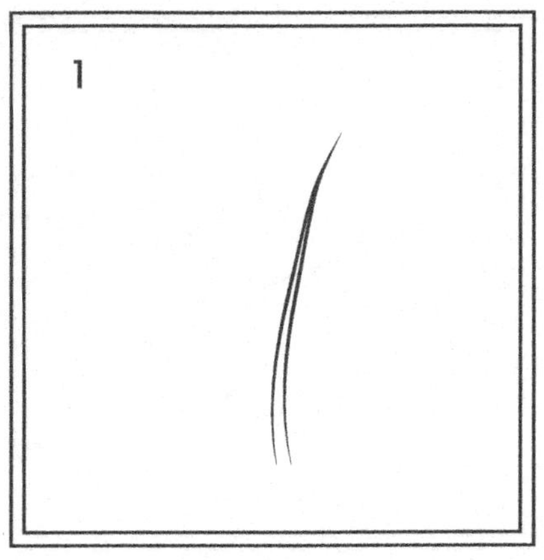

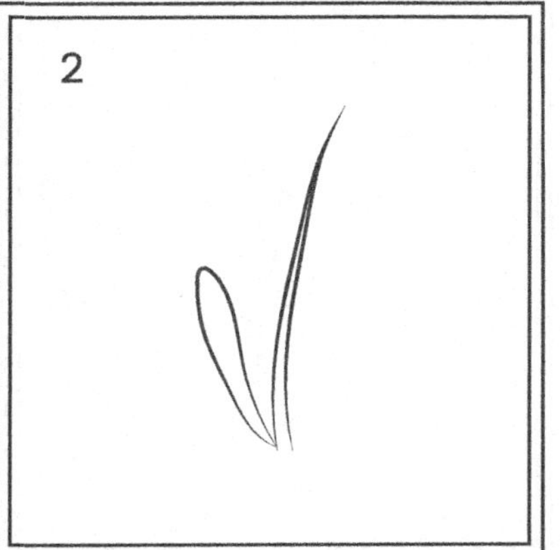

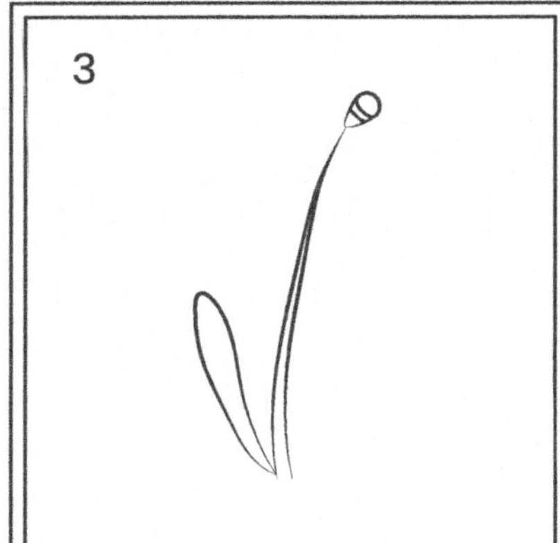

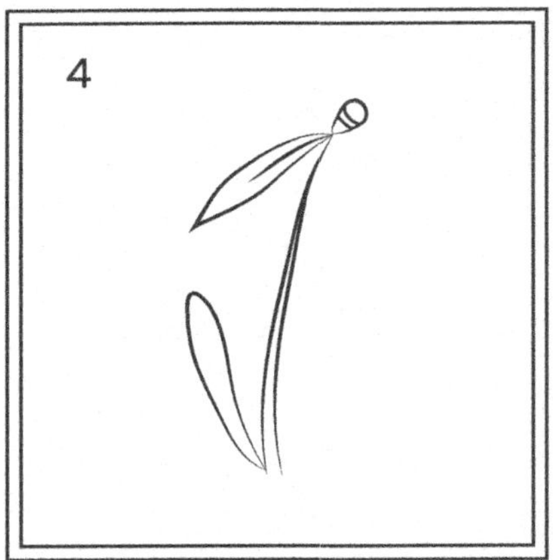

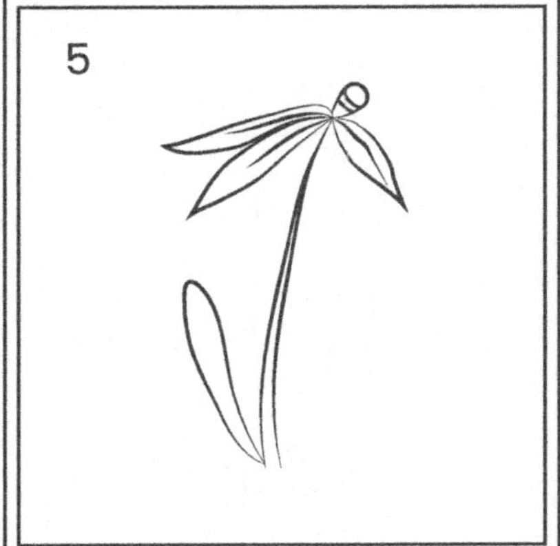

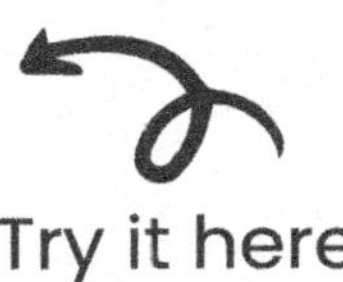

Botanical Line Drawing 1

Foxtail Millet

37

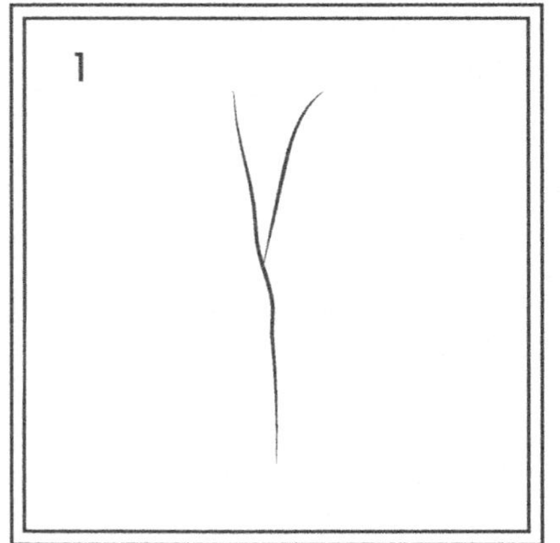

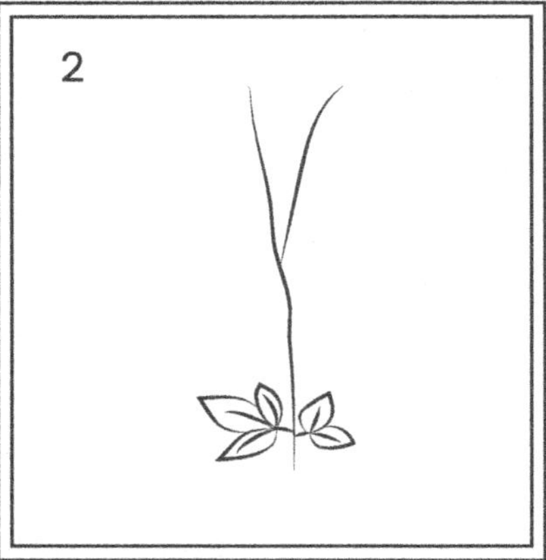

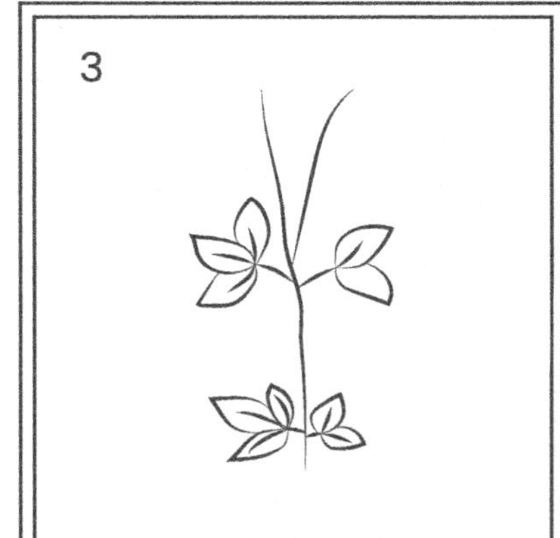

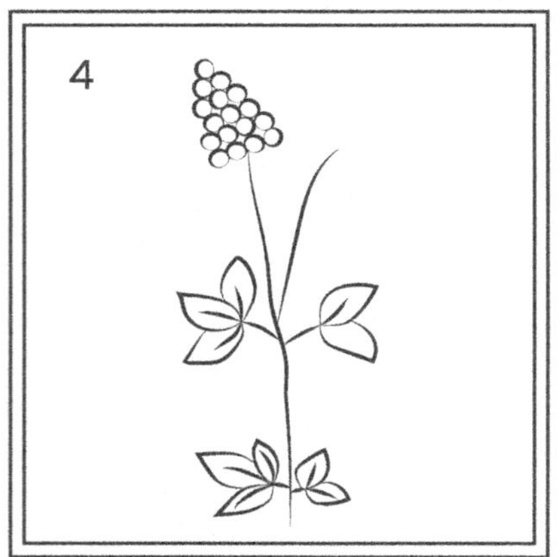

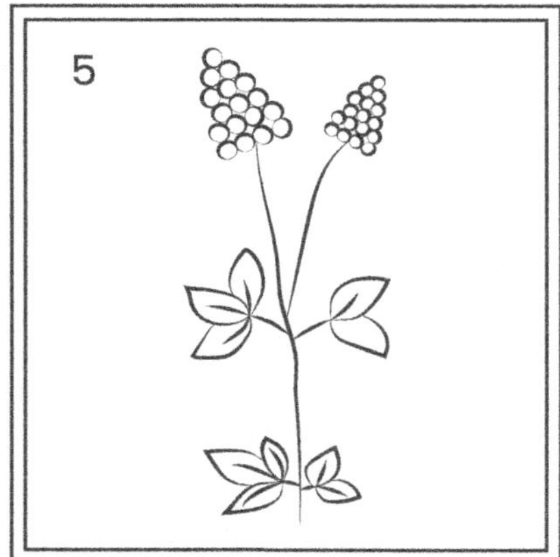

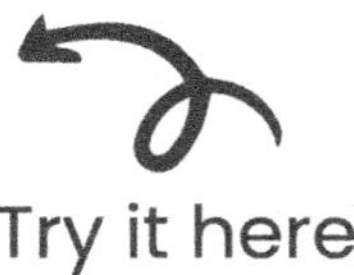

Try it here

Botanical Line Drawing 1

Poppy

38

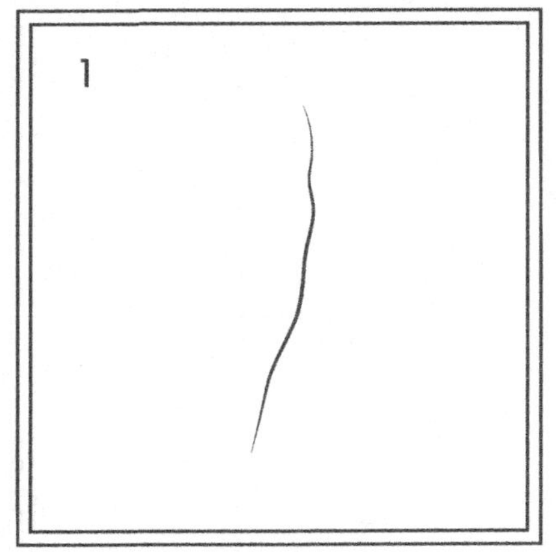

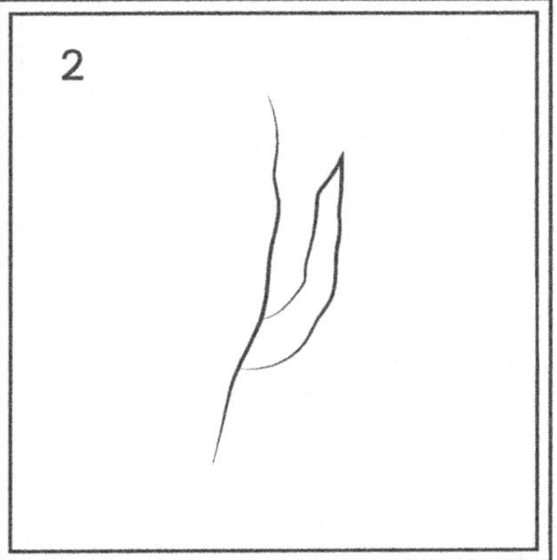

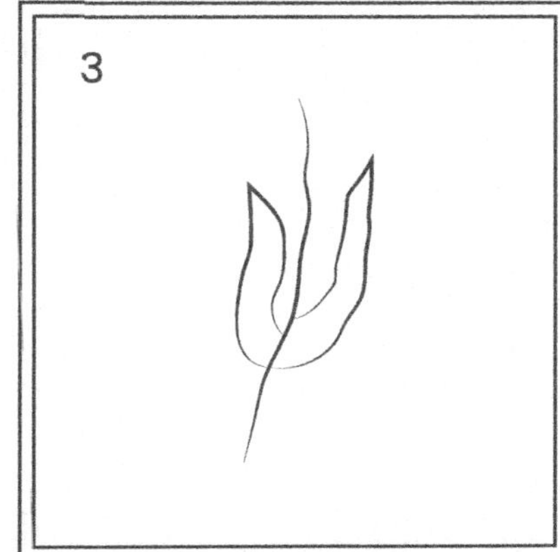

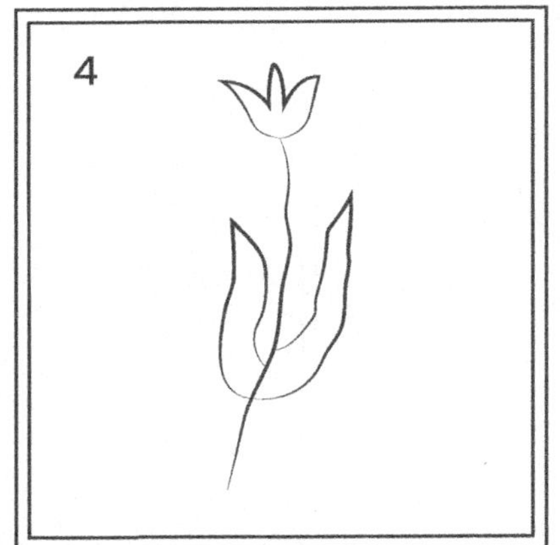

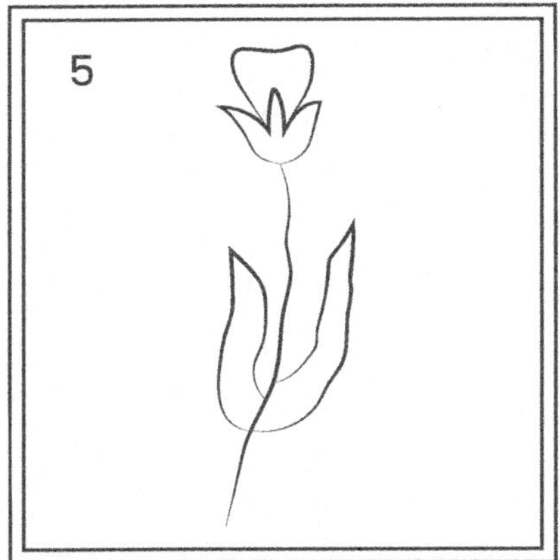

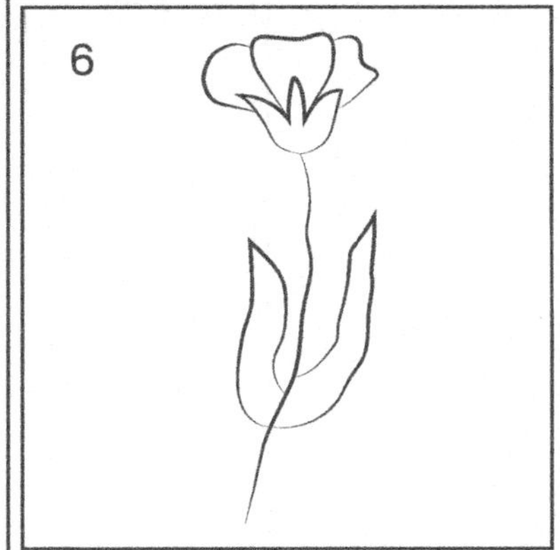

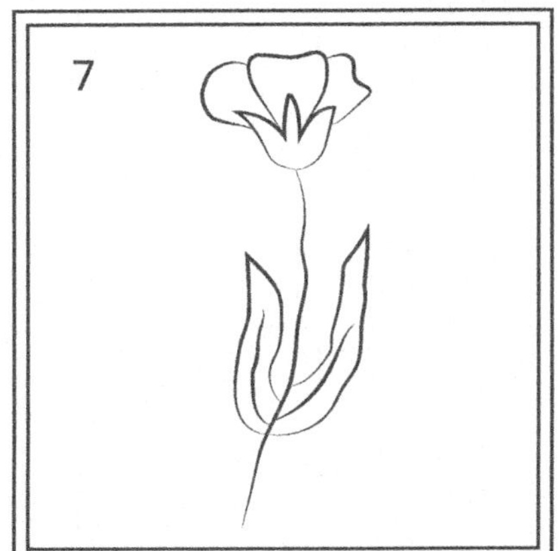

Try it here

Botanical Line Drawing 1

Linden Flower

39

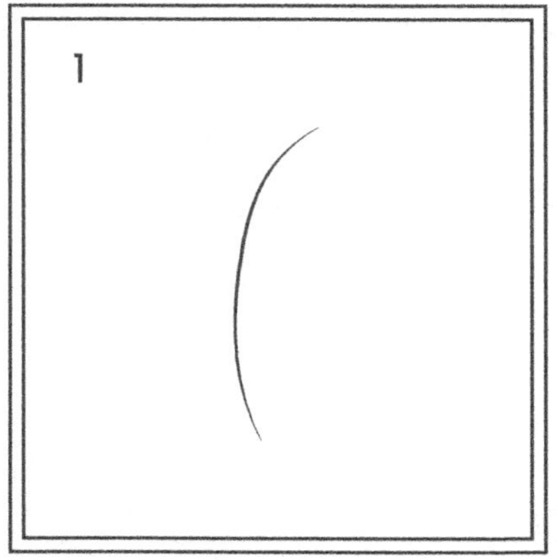

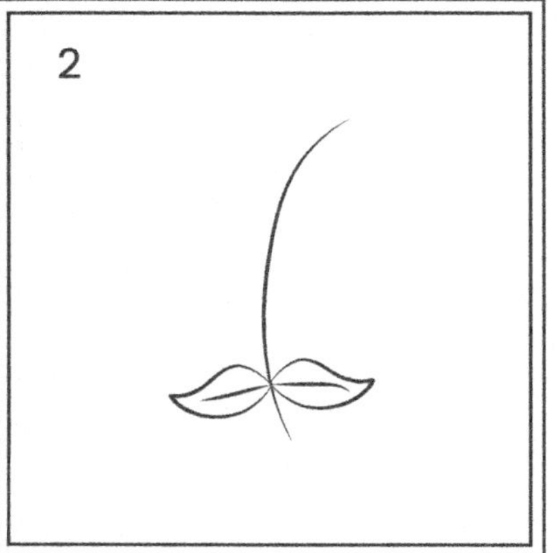

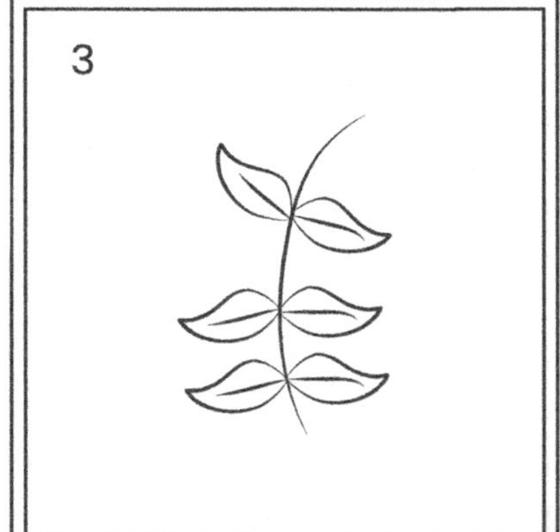

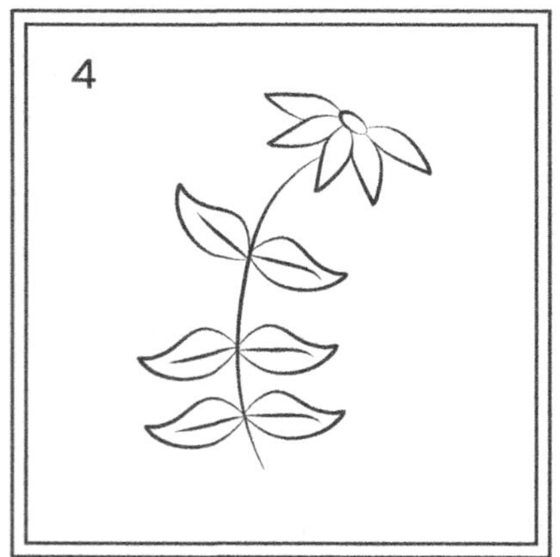

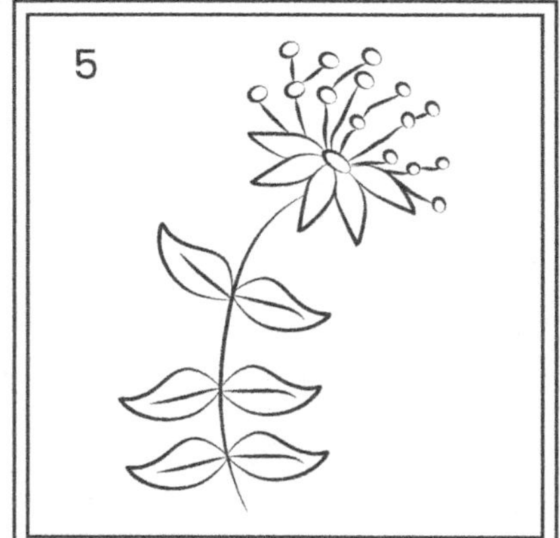

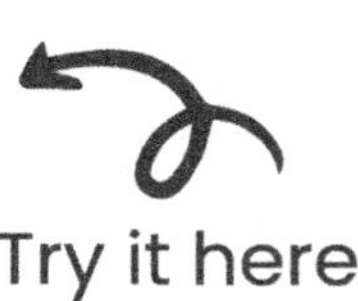

Try it here

Botanical Line Drawing 1

Ox Eye Daisy

40

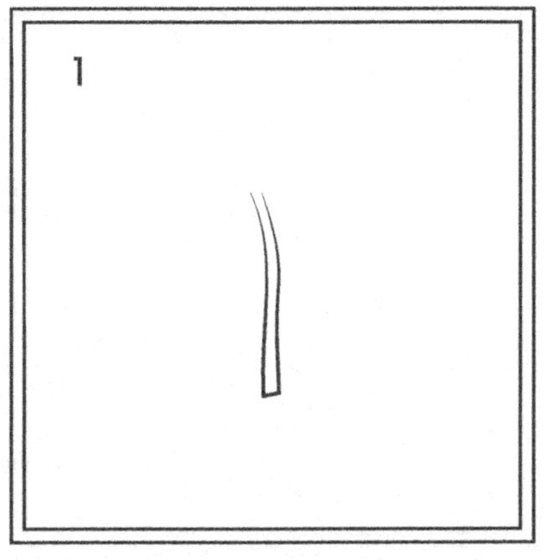

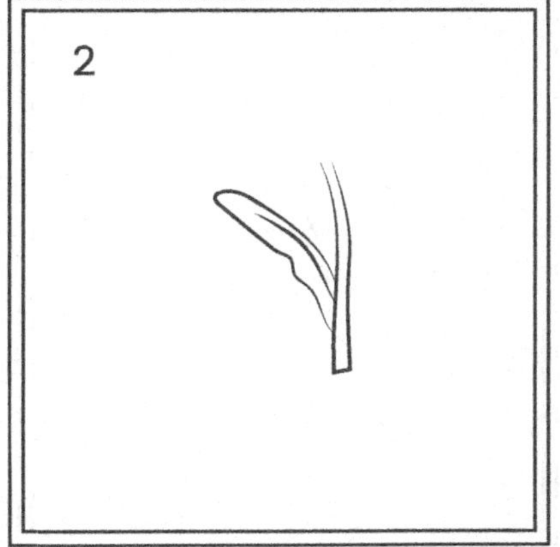

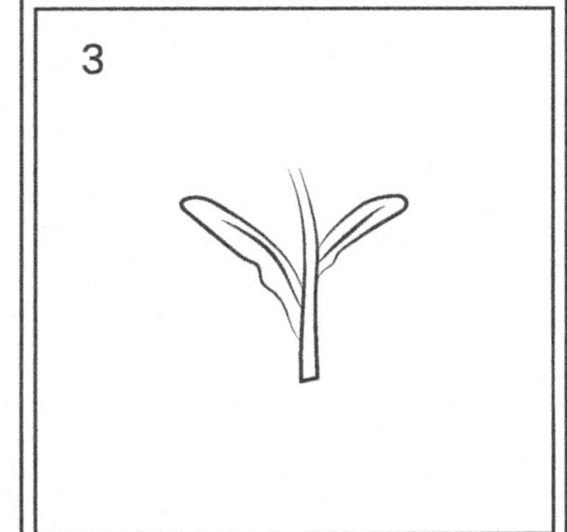

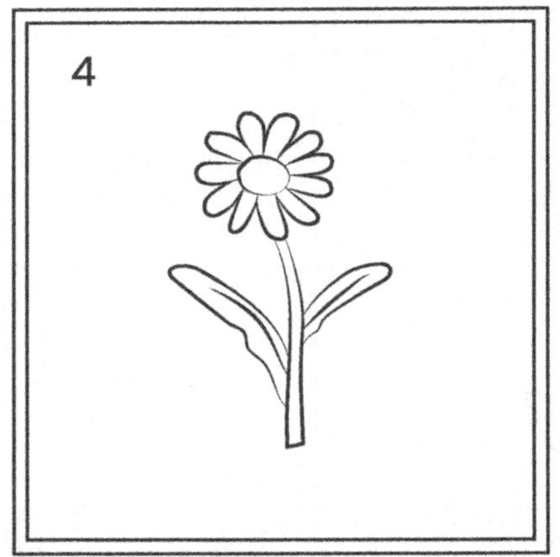

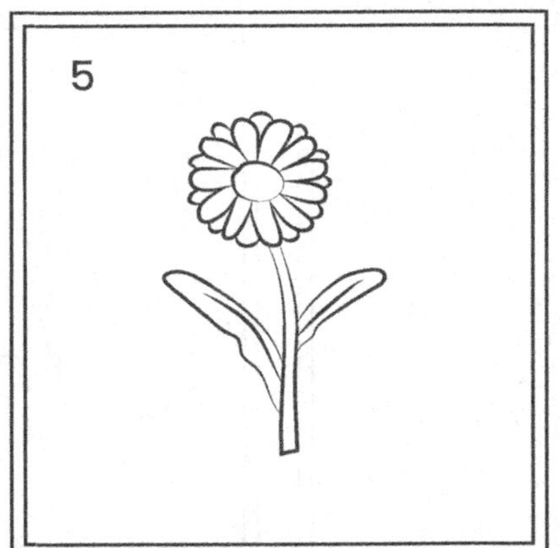

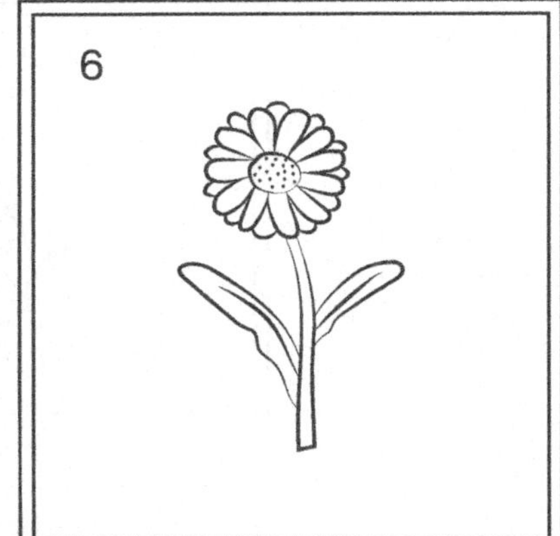

Botanical Line Drawing 1

Alfalfa

41

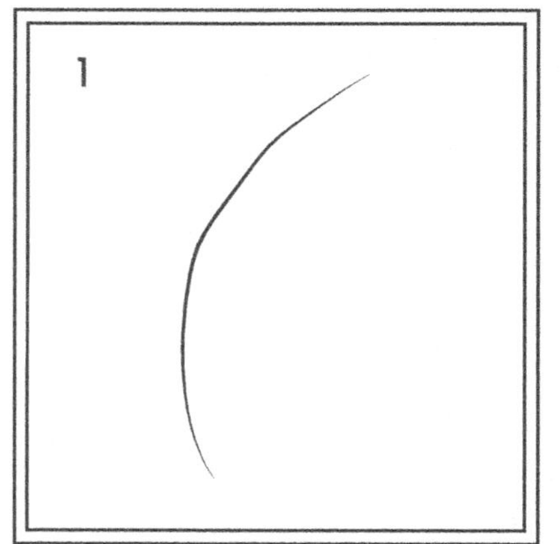

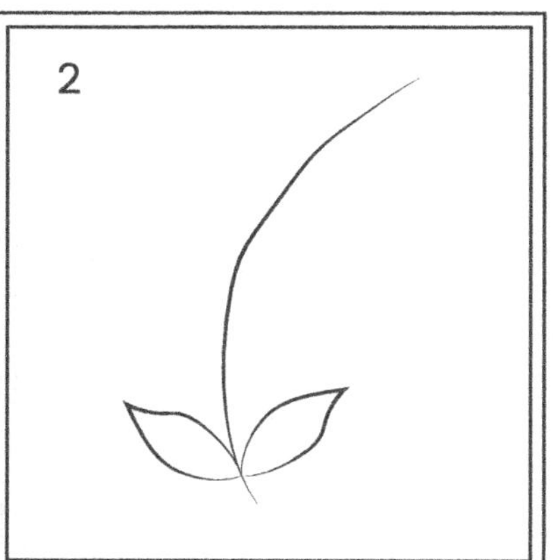

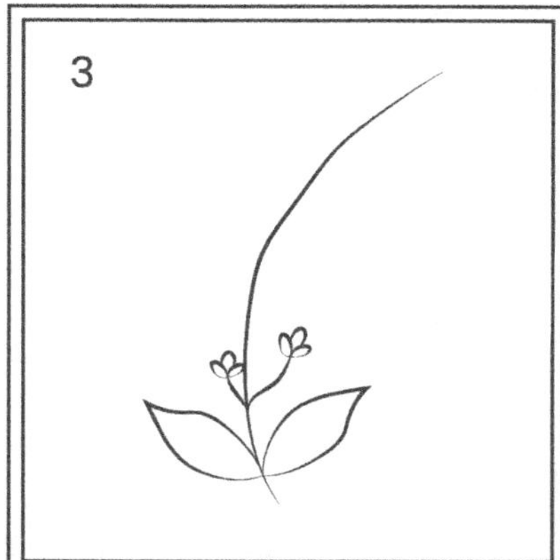

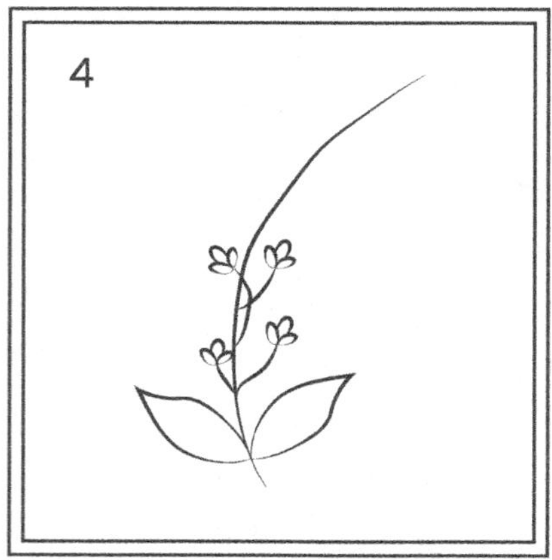

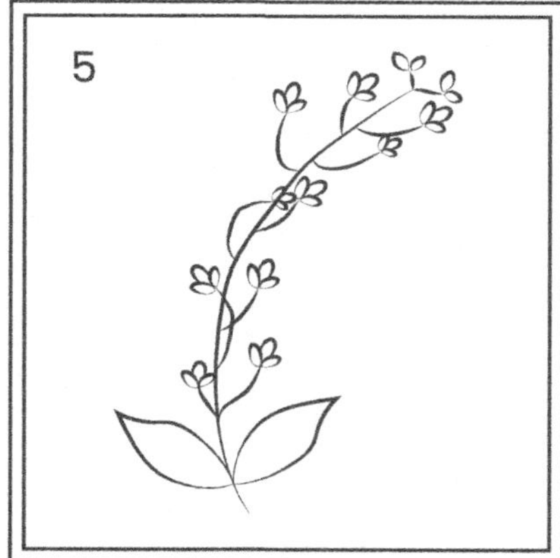

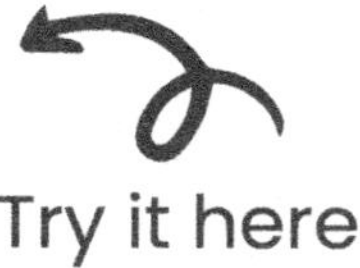

Try it here

Botanical Line Drawing 1

Bay Laurel

42

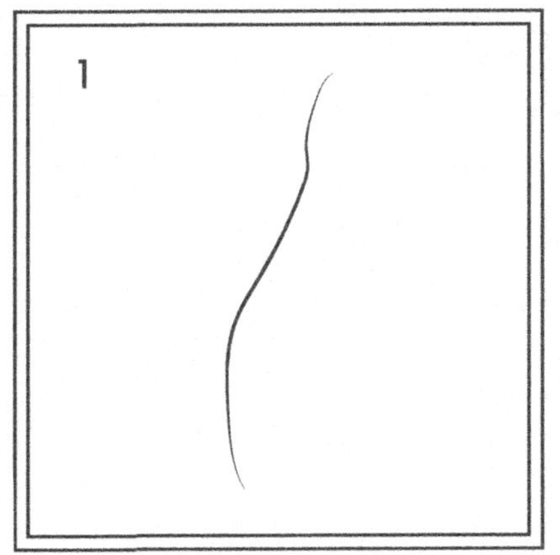

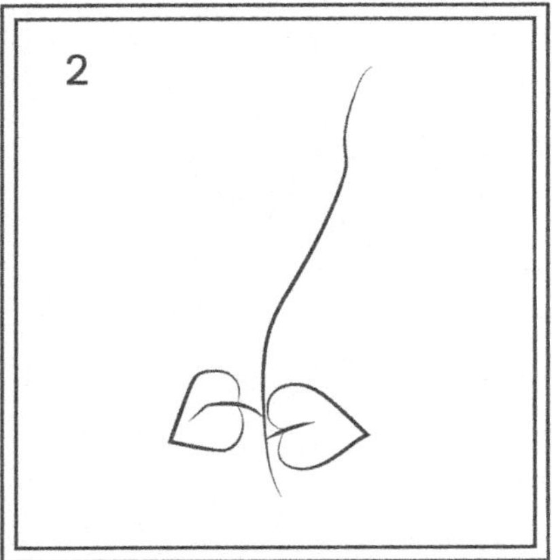

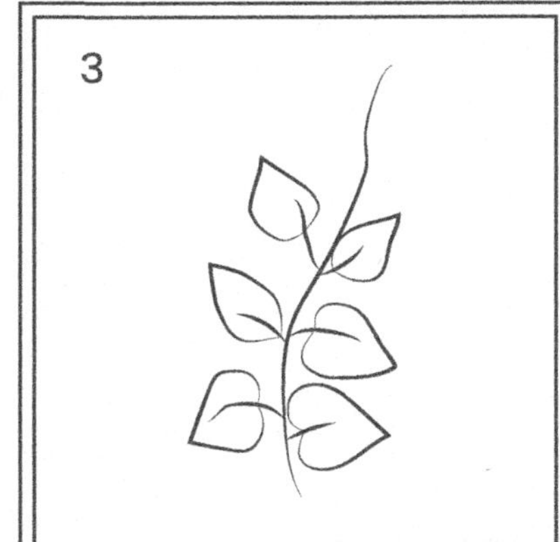

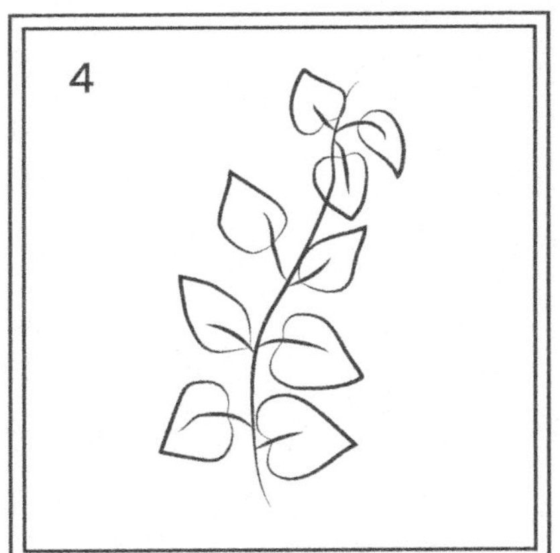

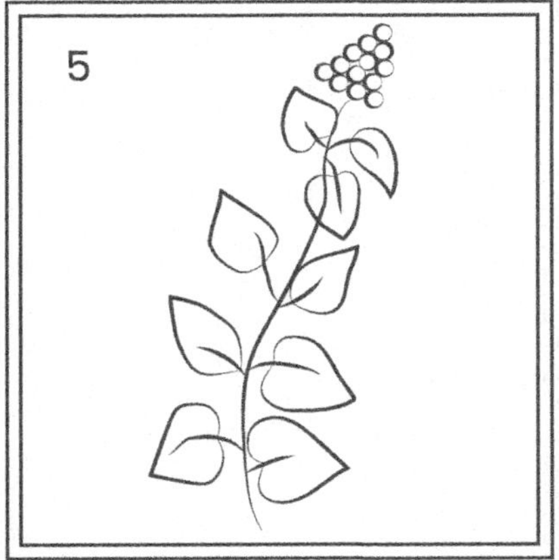

Try it here

Botanical Line Drawing 1

Freesia

43

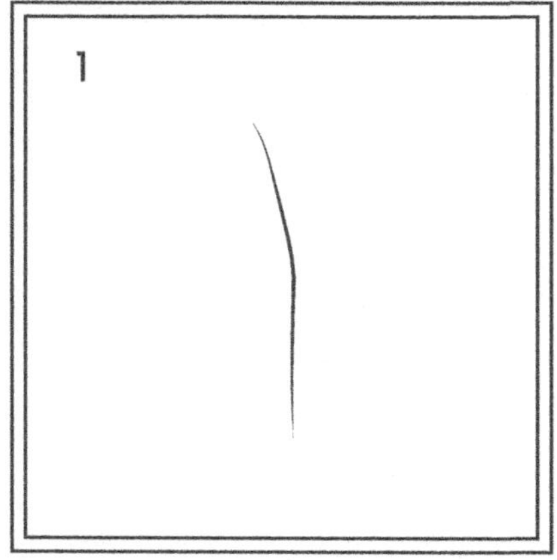

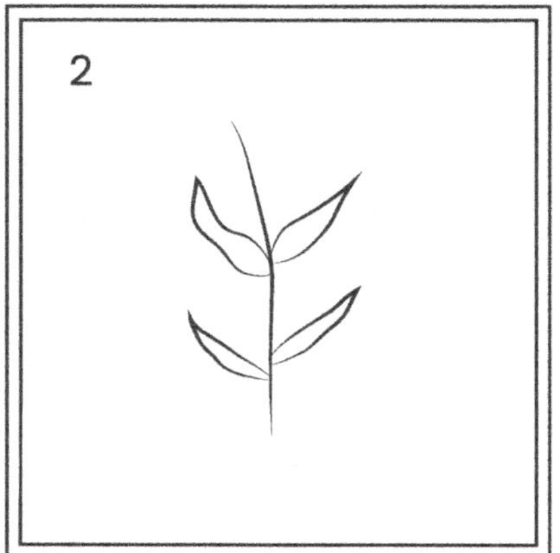

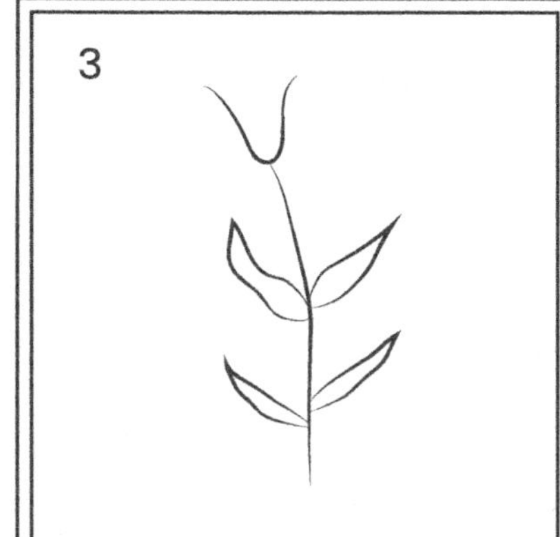

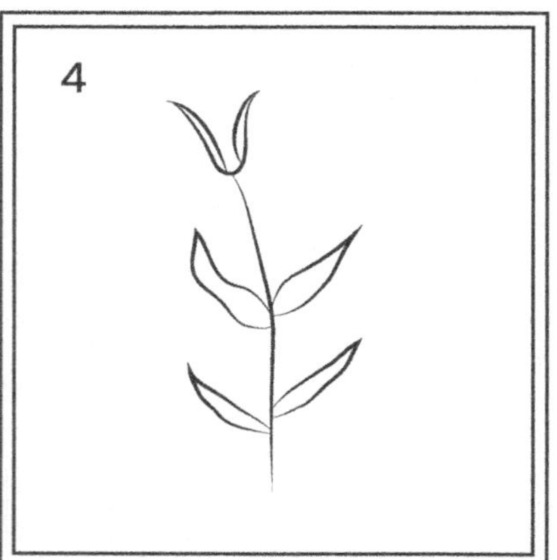

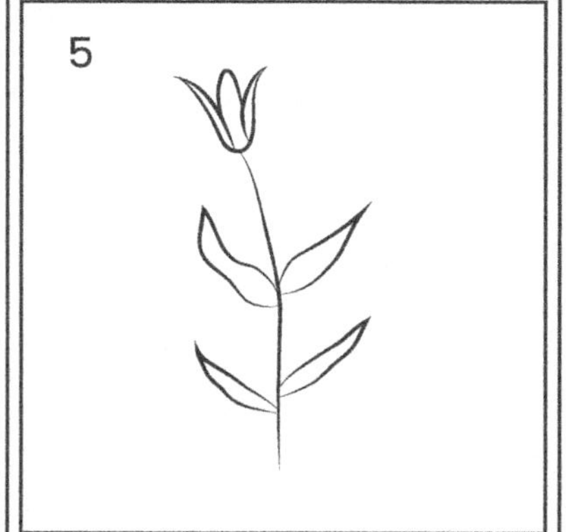

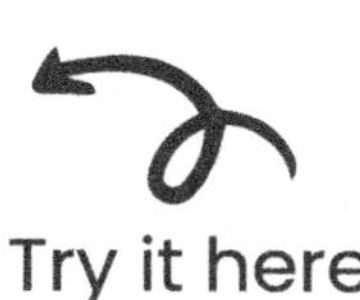

Try it here

Botanical Line Drawing 1

Giant Onion

44

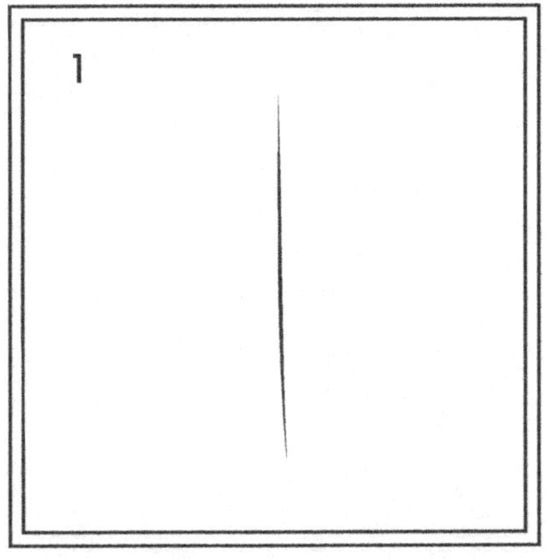

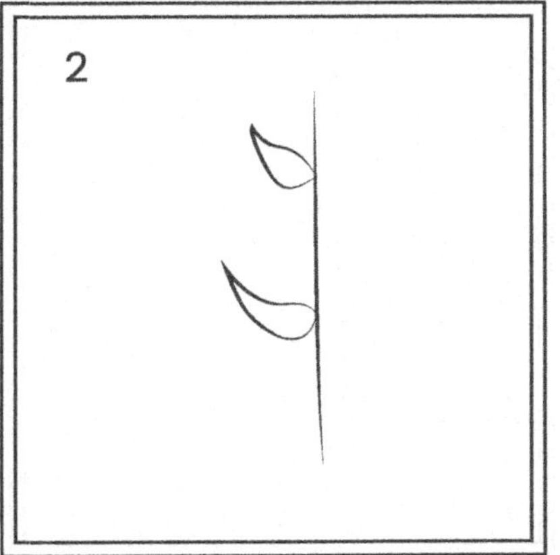

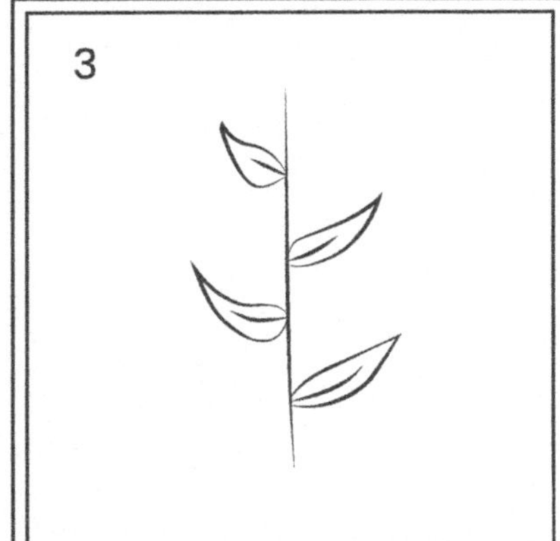

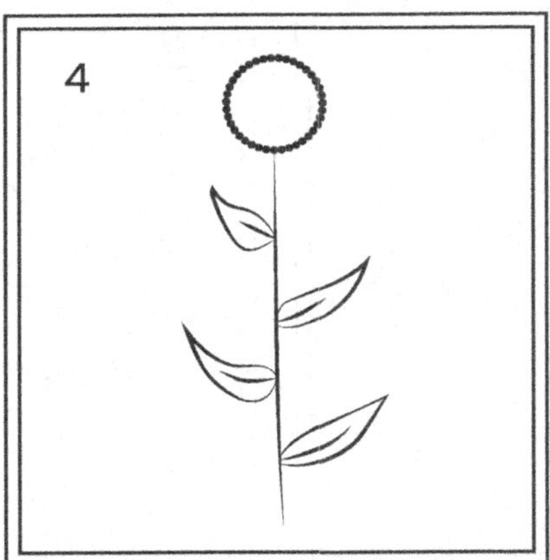

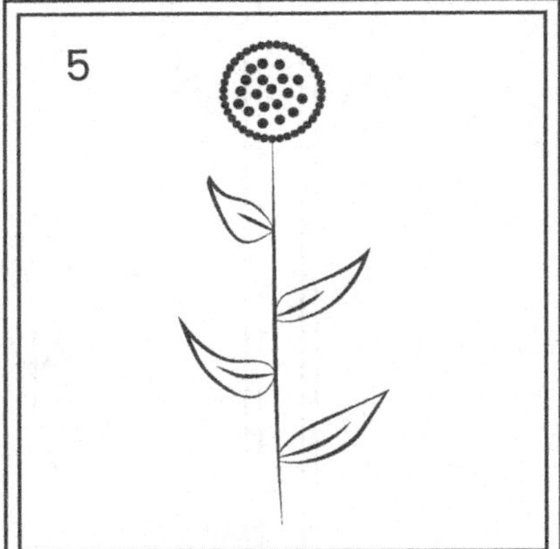

Try it here

Botanical Line Drawing 1

Lavender

45

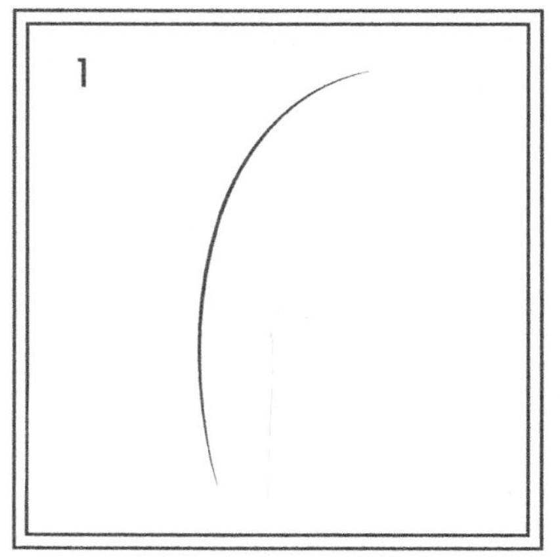

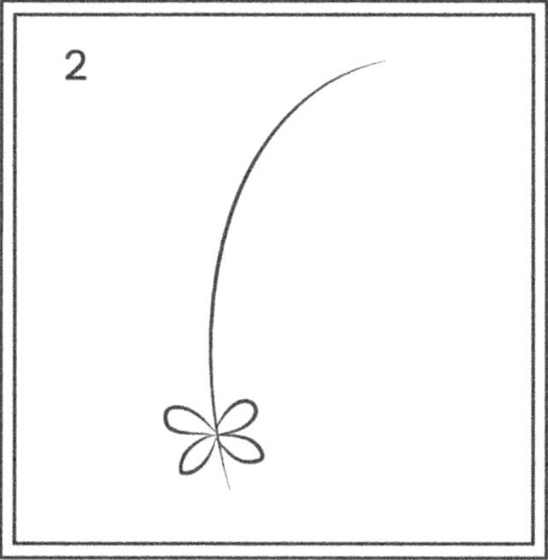

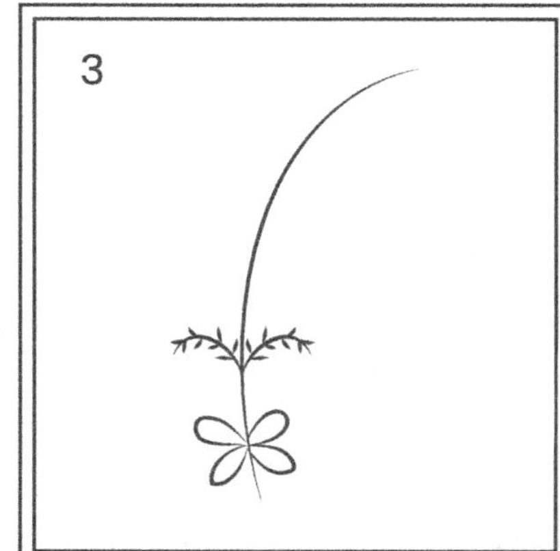

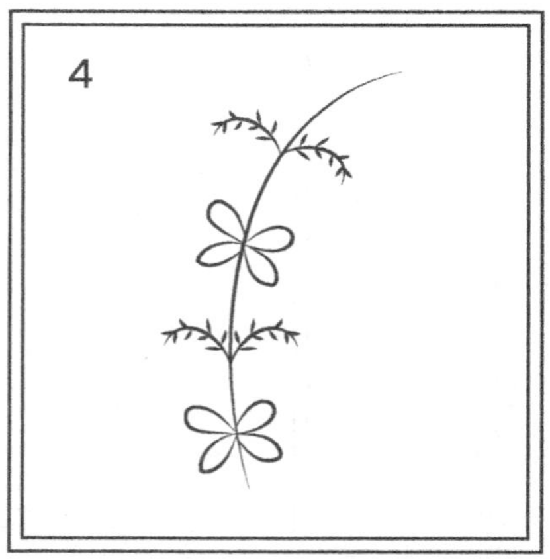

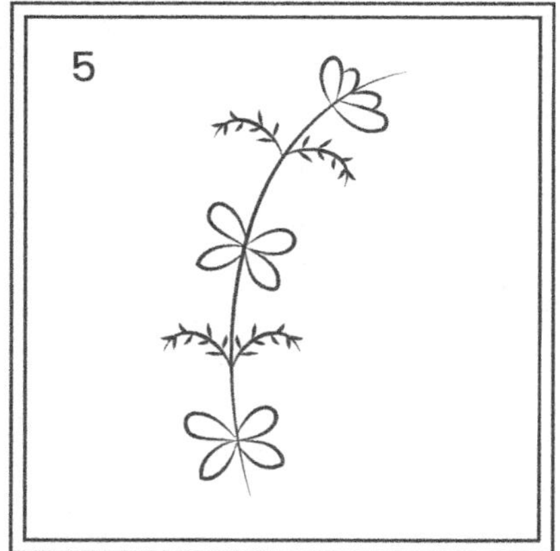

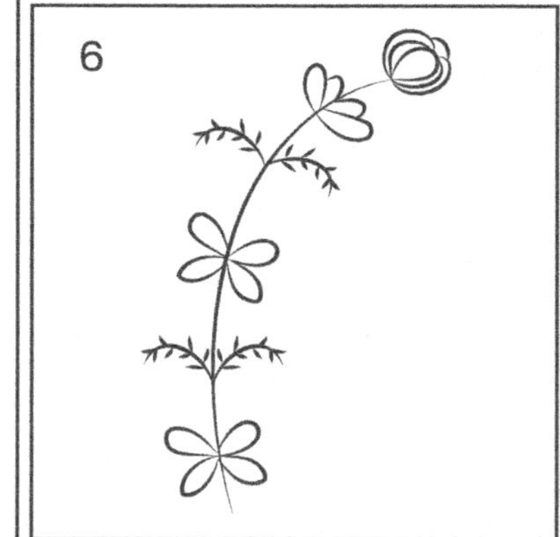

Try it here

Botanical Line Drawing 1

Periwinkle

46

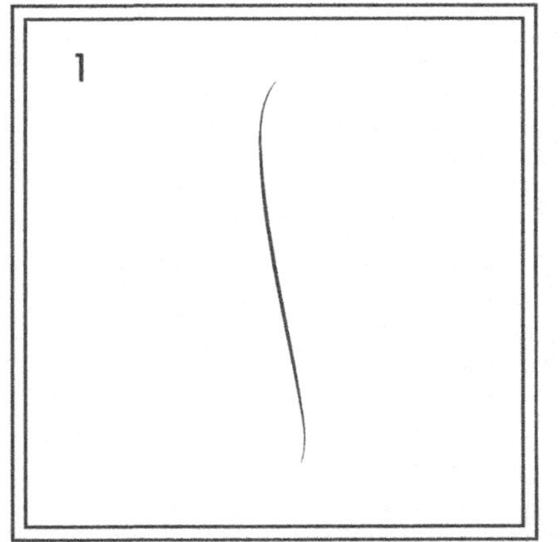

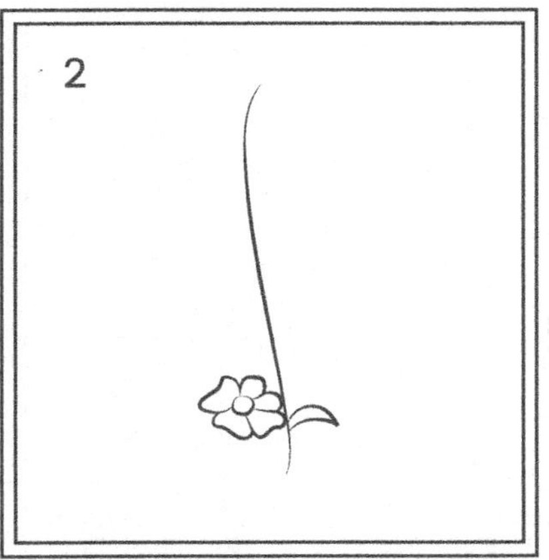

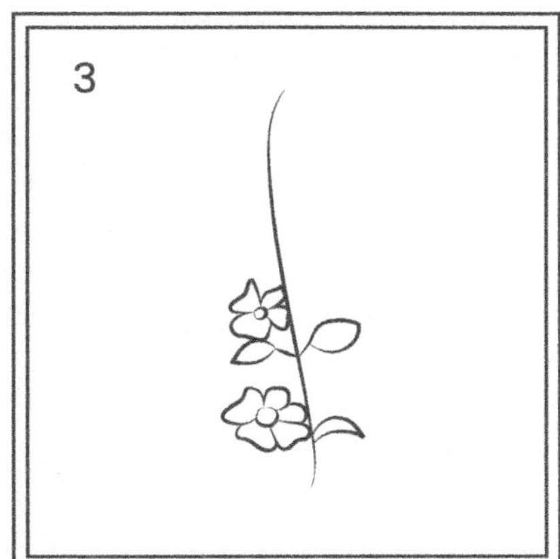

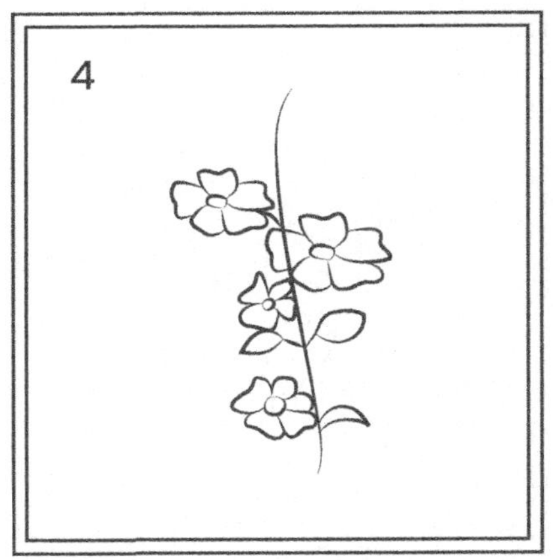

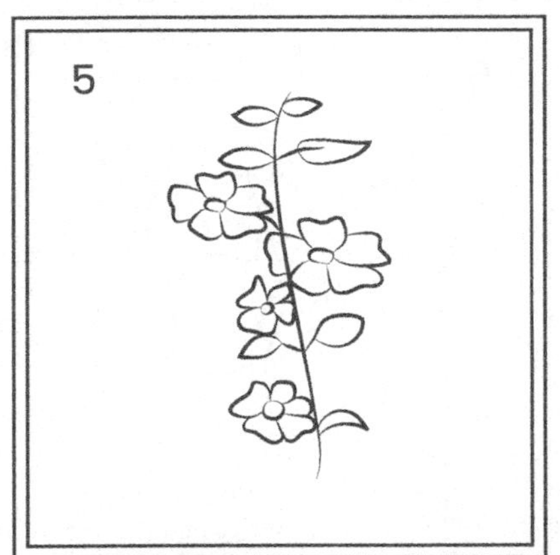

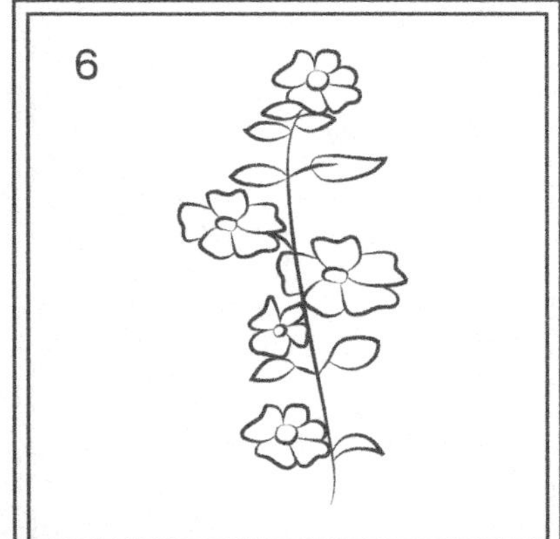

Try it here

Botanical Line Drawing 1

Morning Glory

47

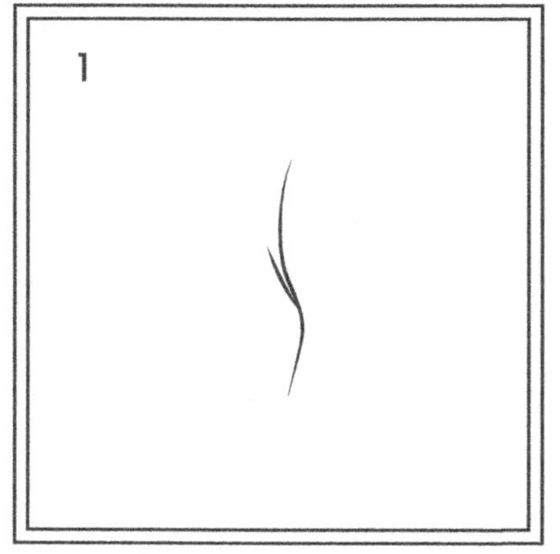

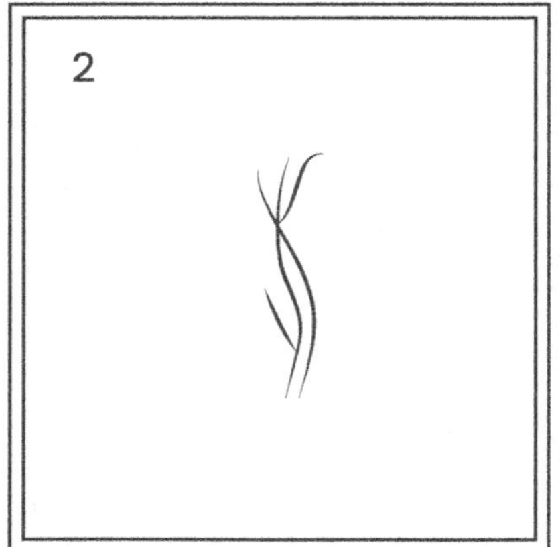

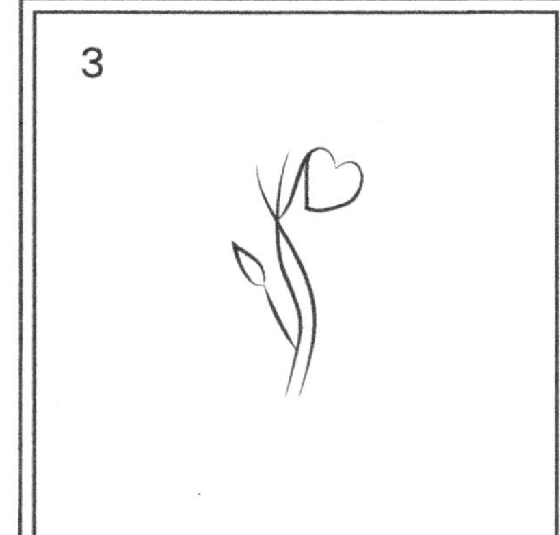

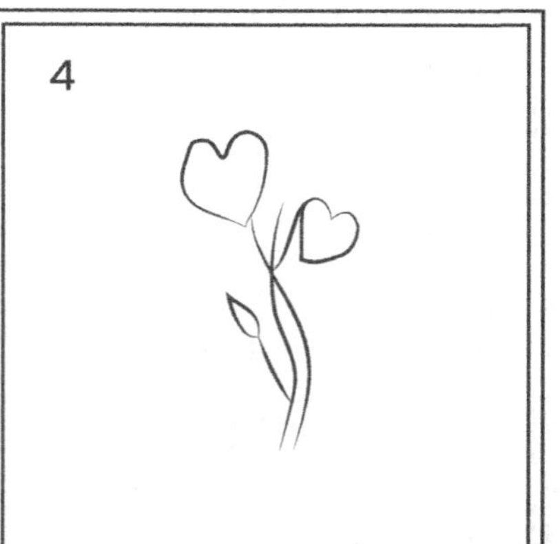

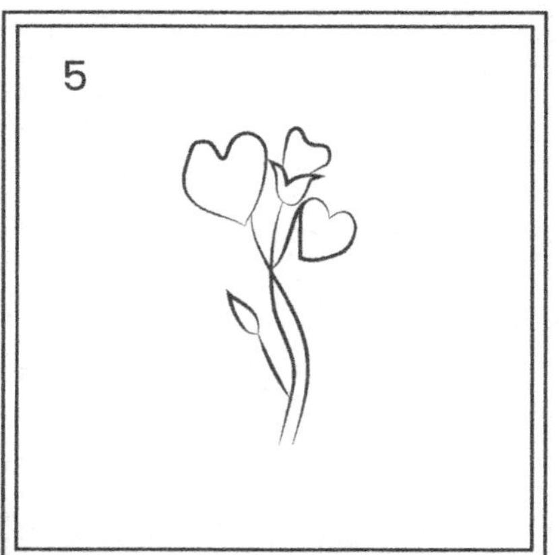

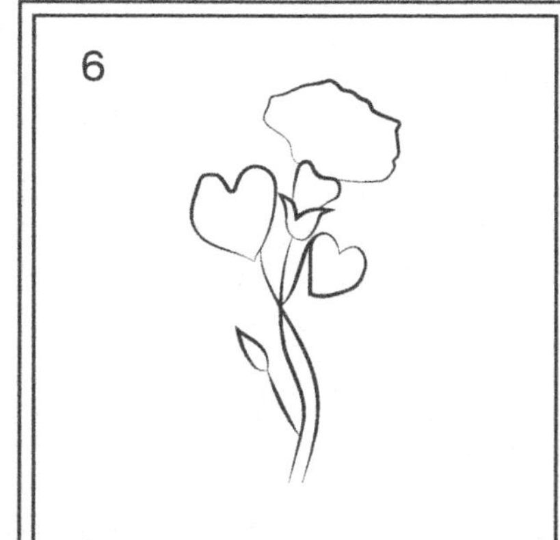

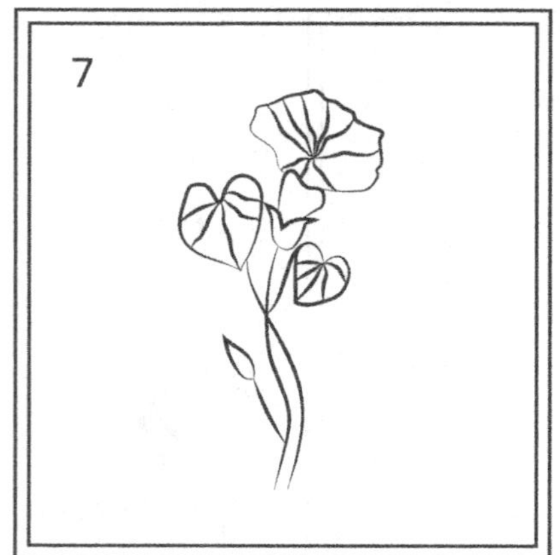

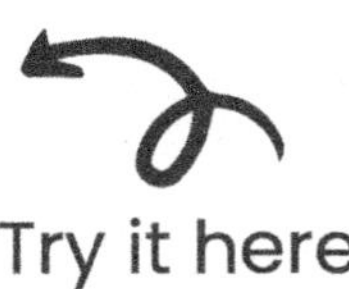

Try it here

Botanical Line Drawing 1

Lily of the Valley 48

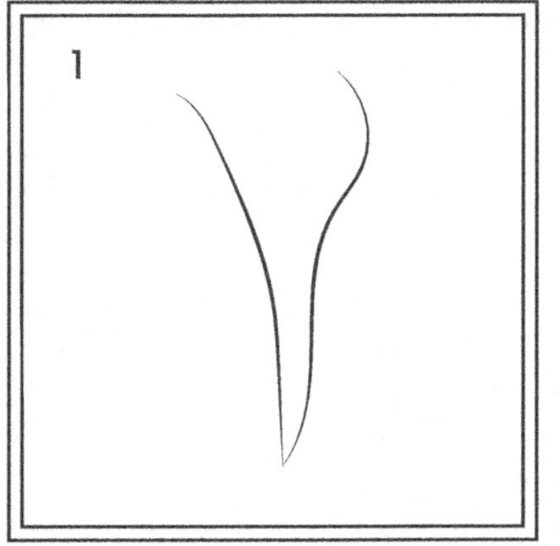

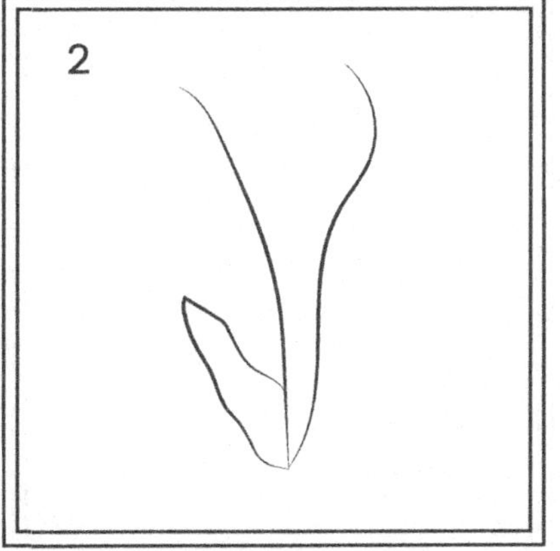

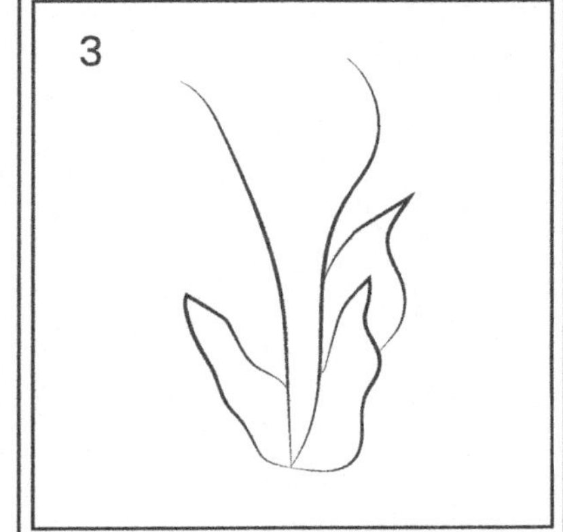

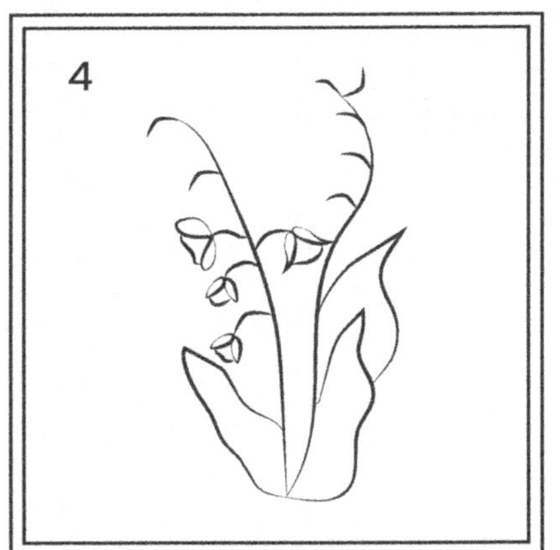

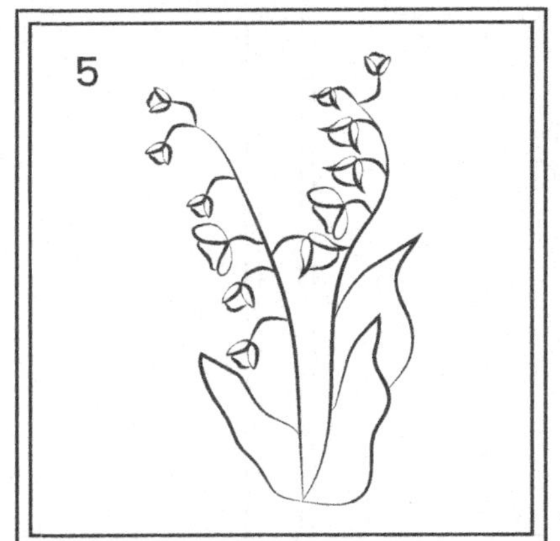

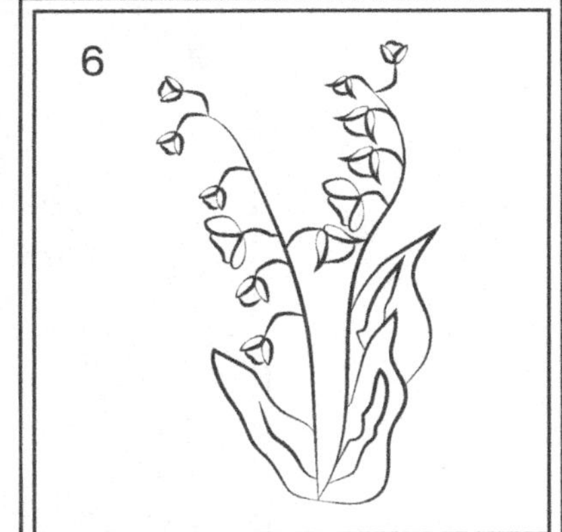

Try it here

Botanical Line Drawing 1

Daisy Vine

49

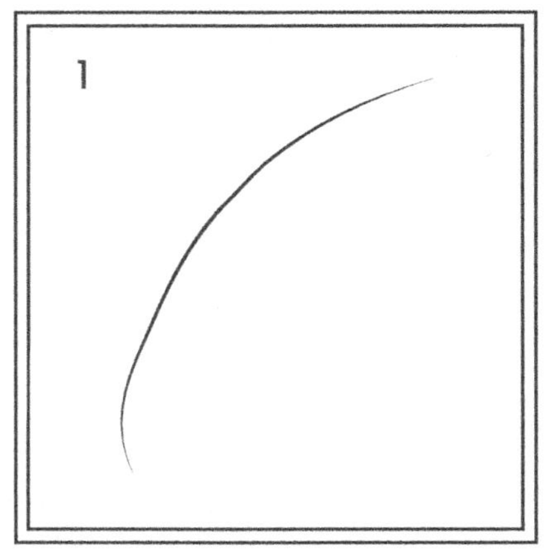

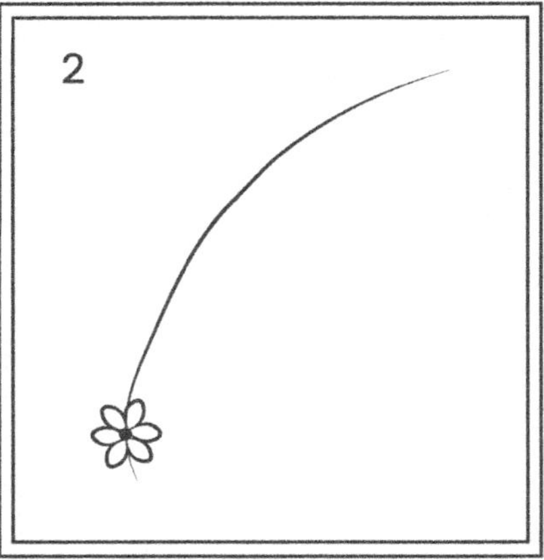

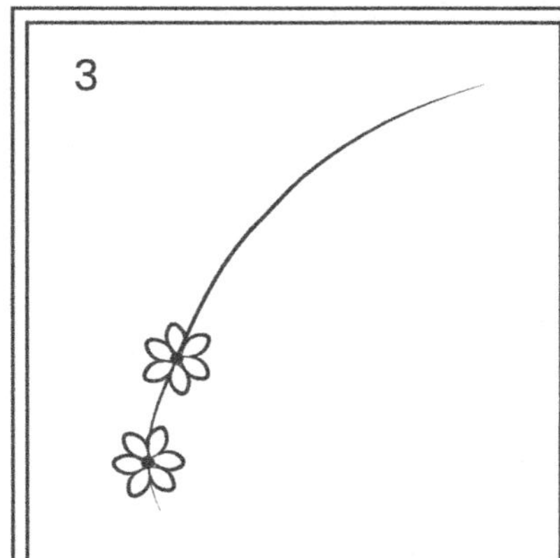

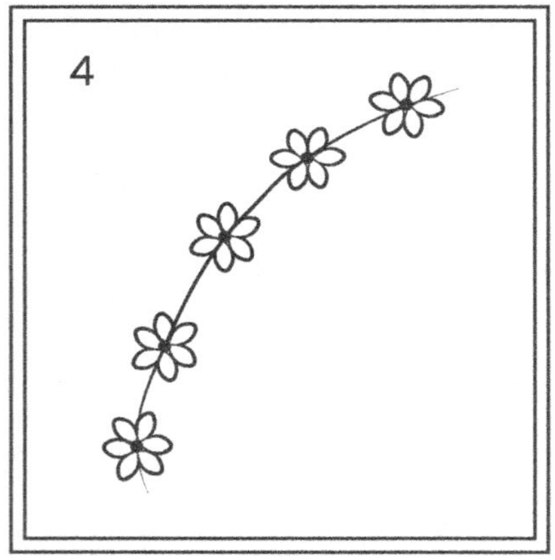

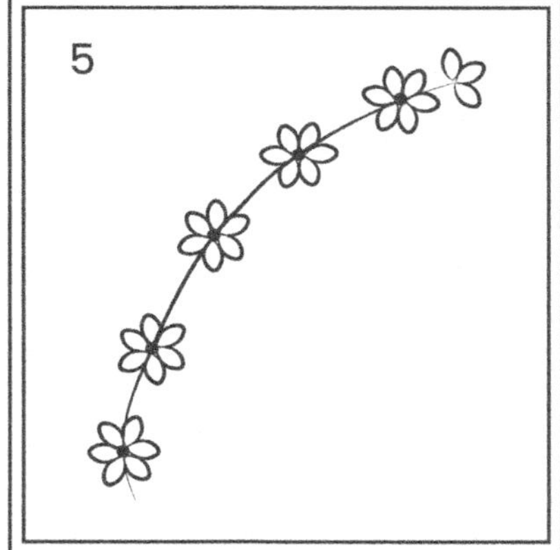

Try it here

Botanical Line Drawing 1

Daisy

50

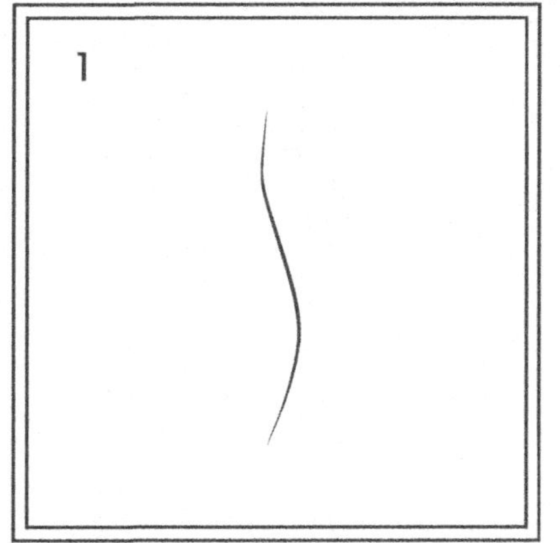

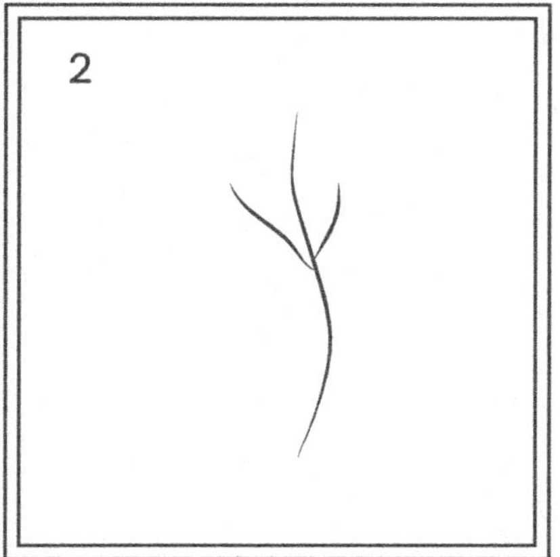

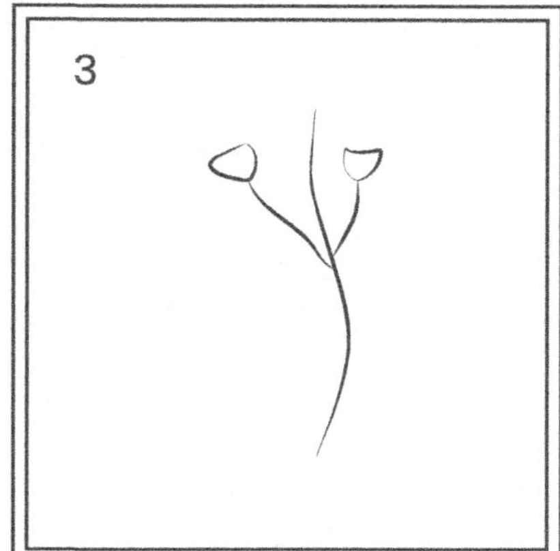

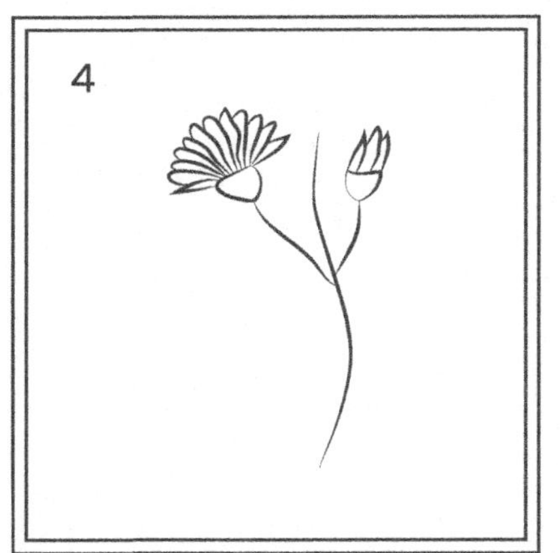

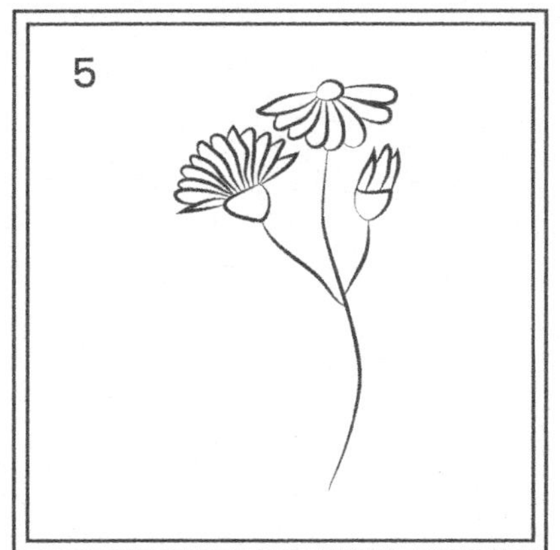

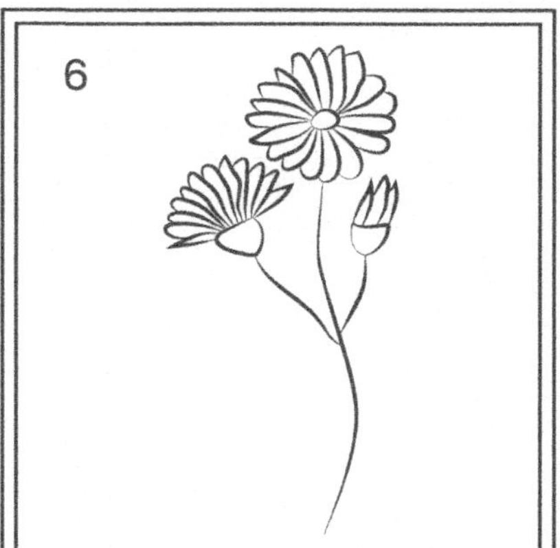

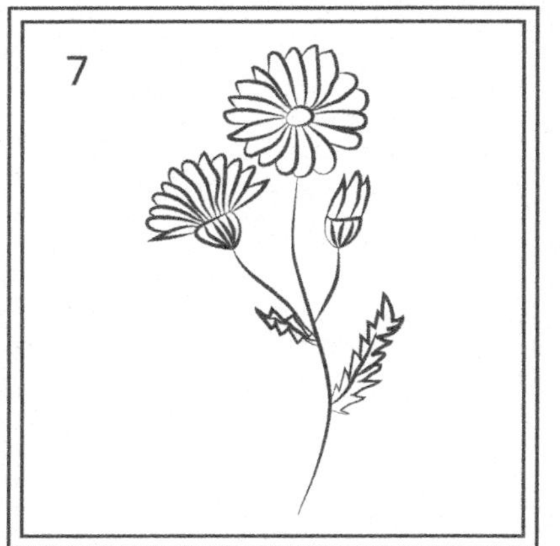

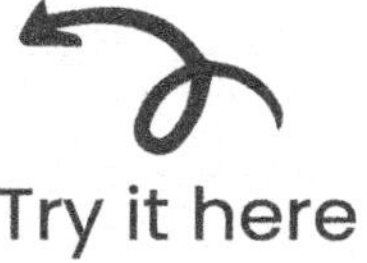

Try it here

Botanical Line Drawing 1

Sakura

51

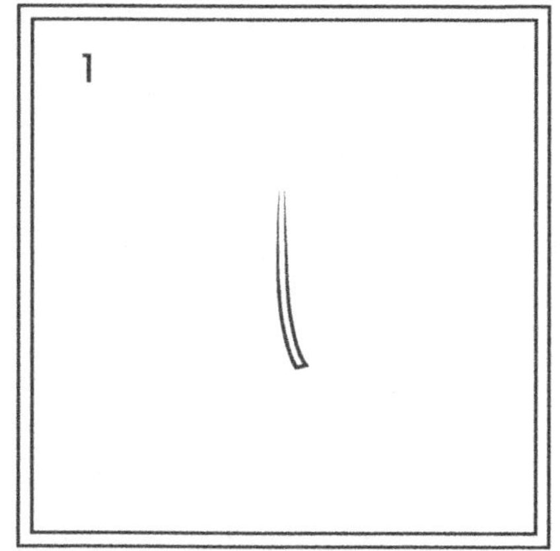

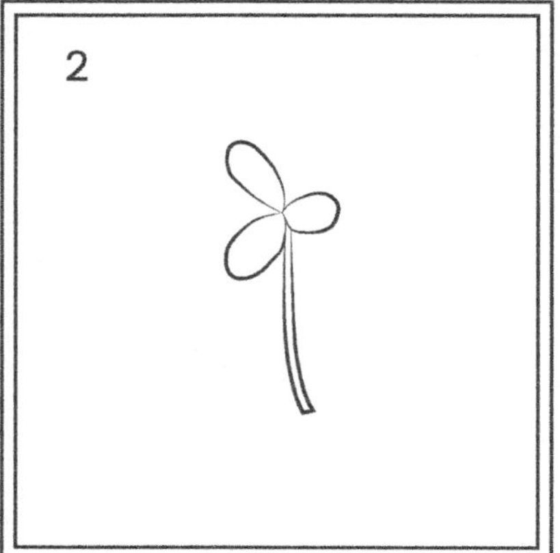

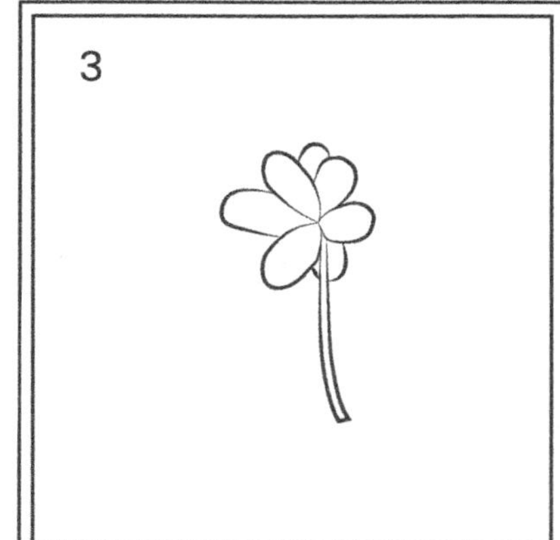

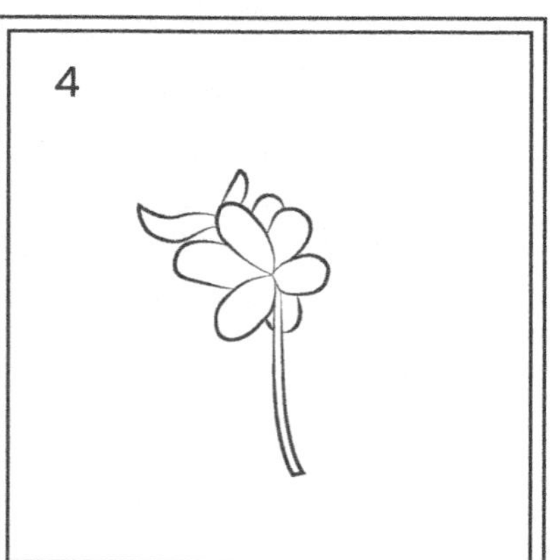

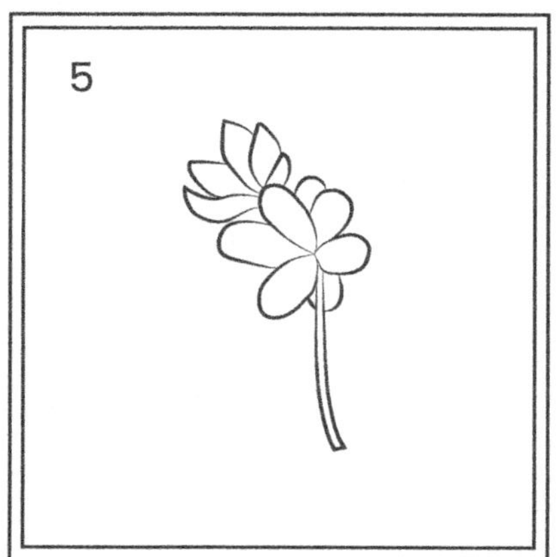

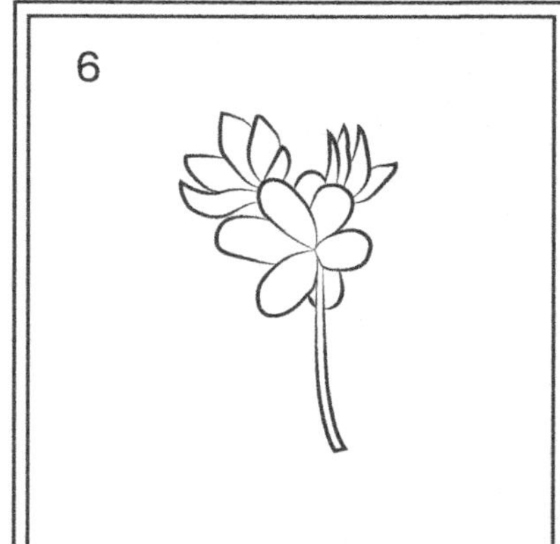

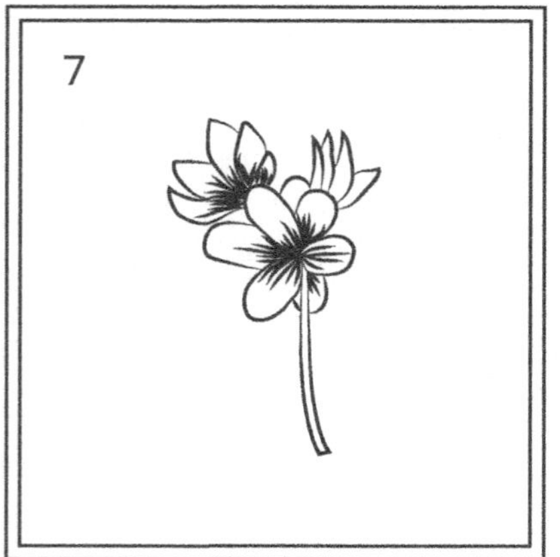

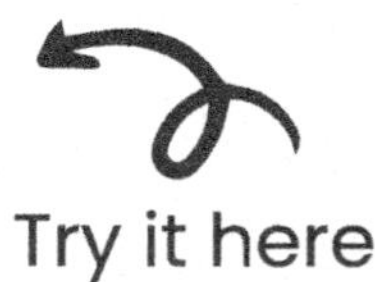

Try it here

Botanical Line Drawing 1

Lotus Water Lily 52

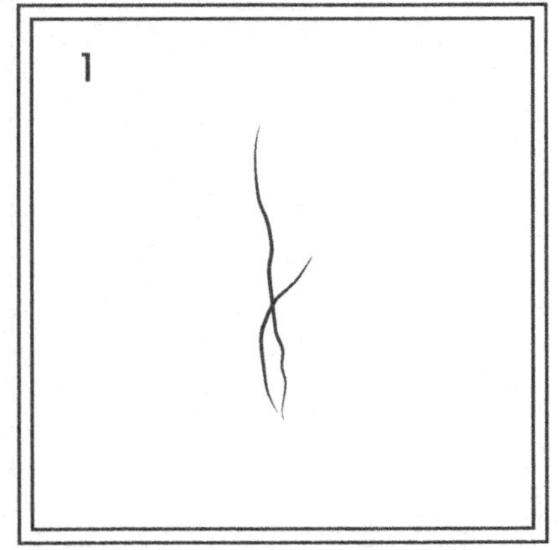

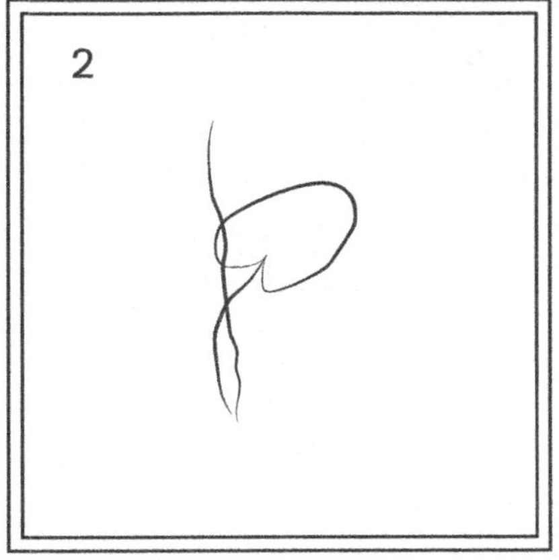

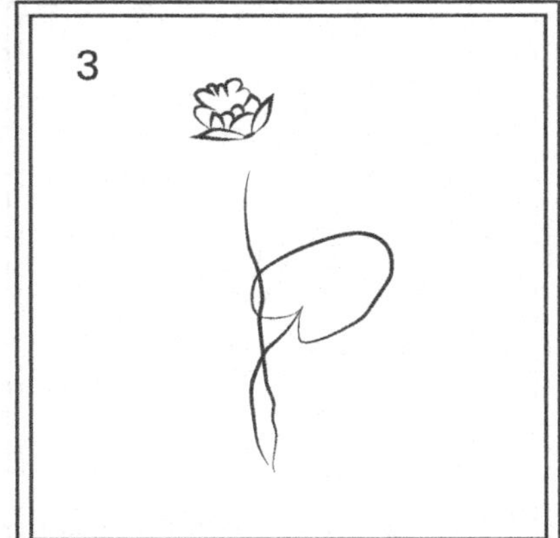

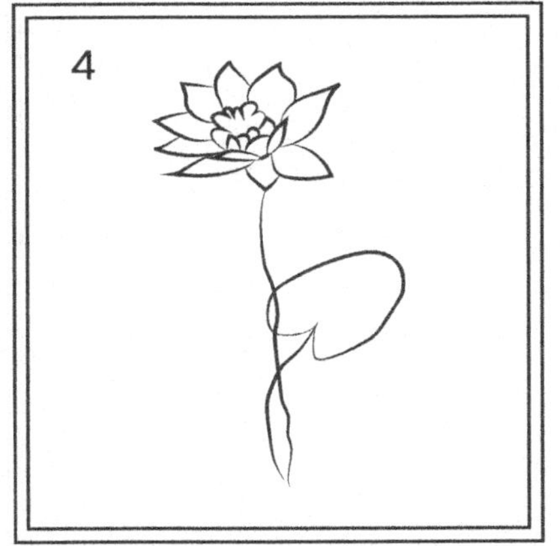

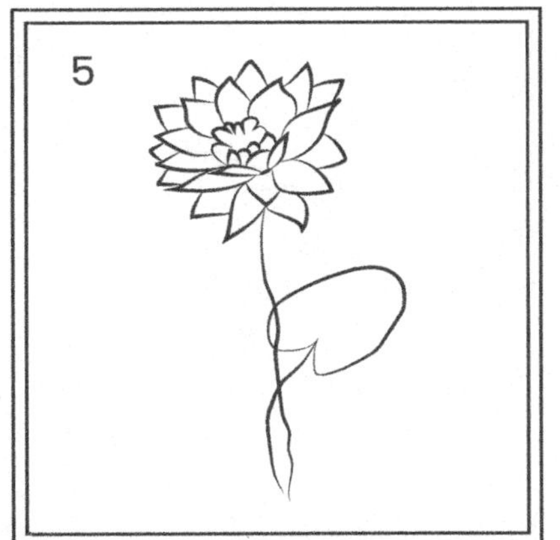

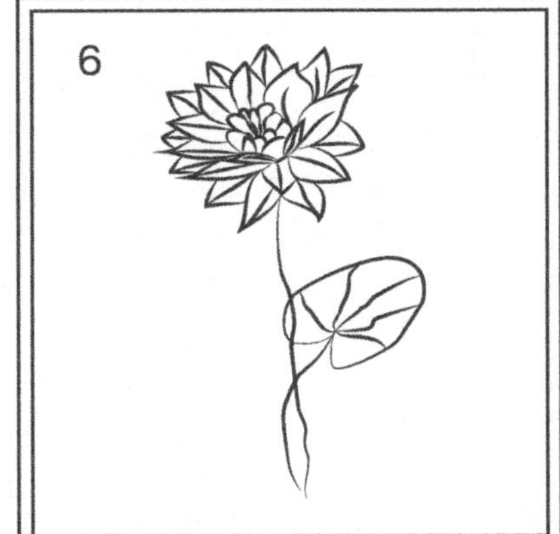

Botanical Line Drawing 1

Cosmos

53

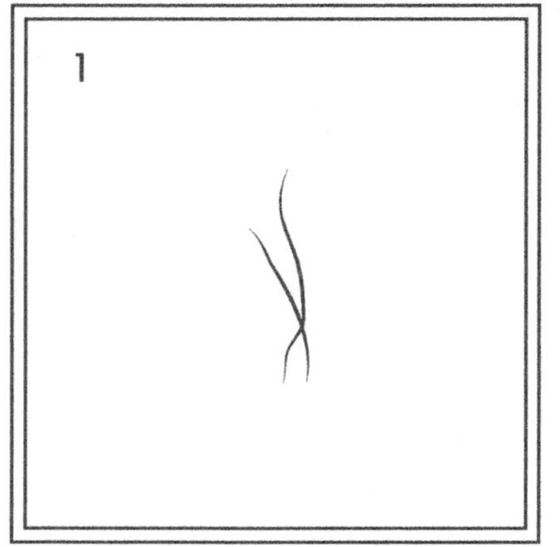

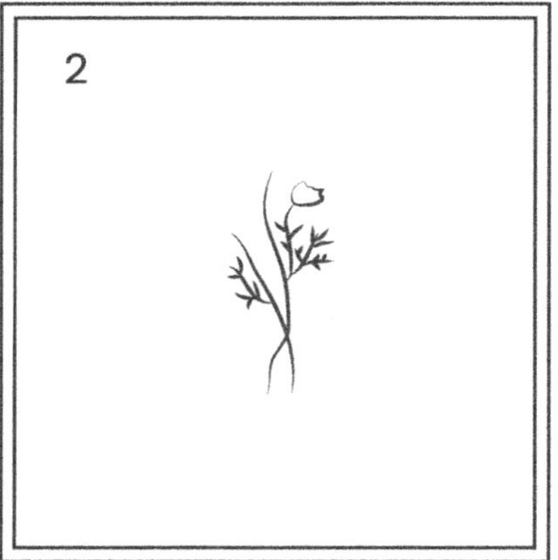

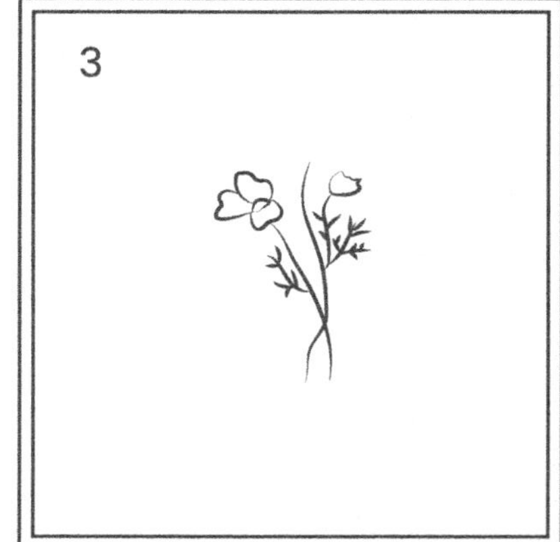

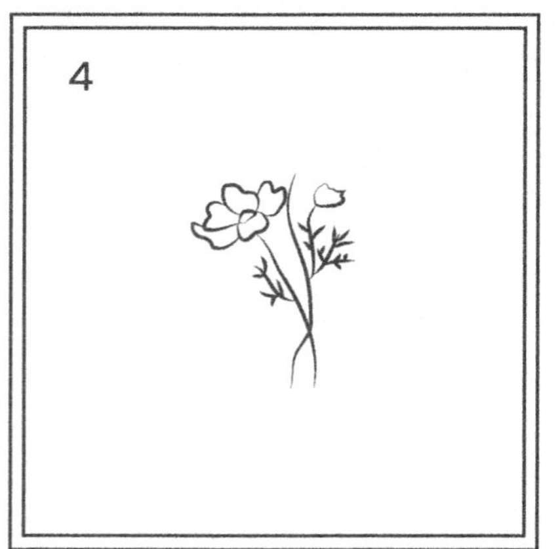

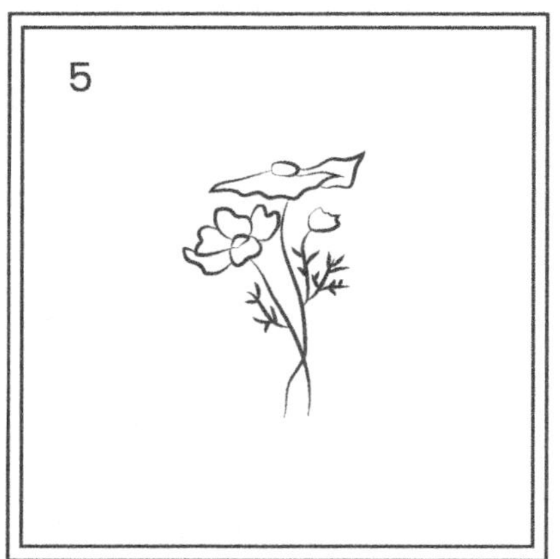

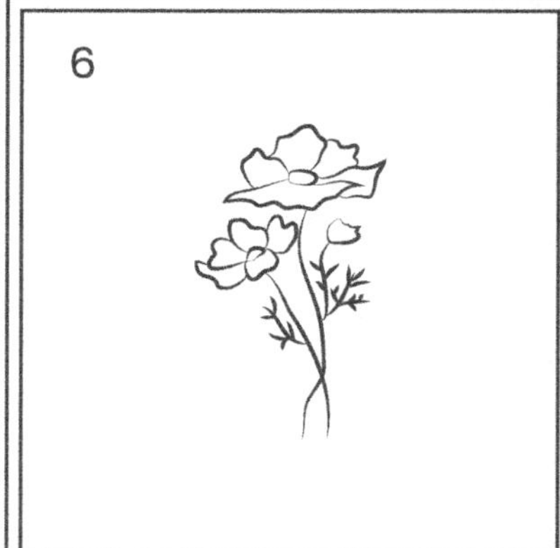

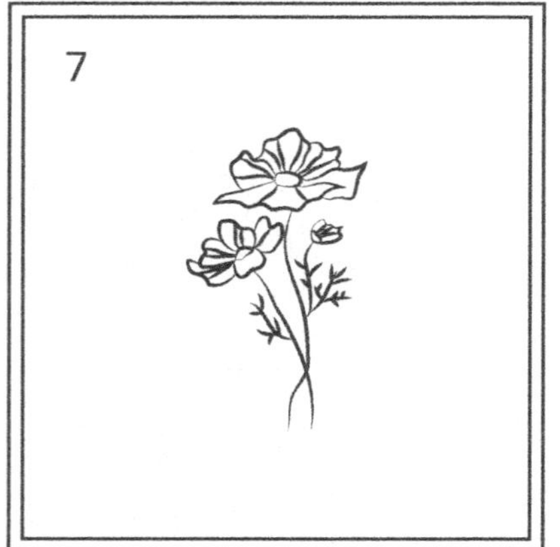

Try it here

Botanical Line Drawing 1

Poppy 2

54

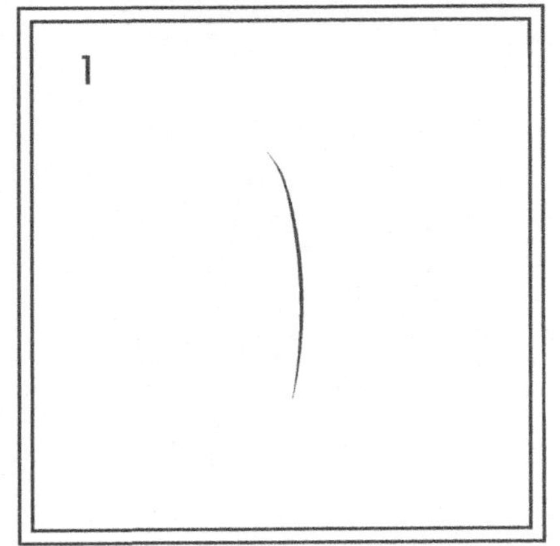

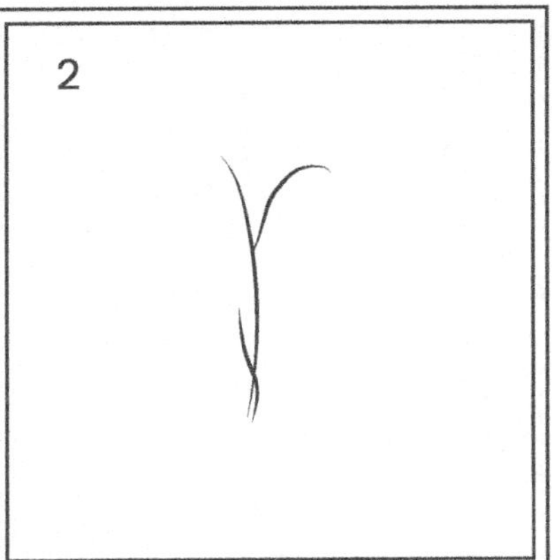

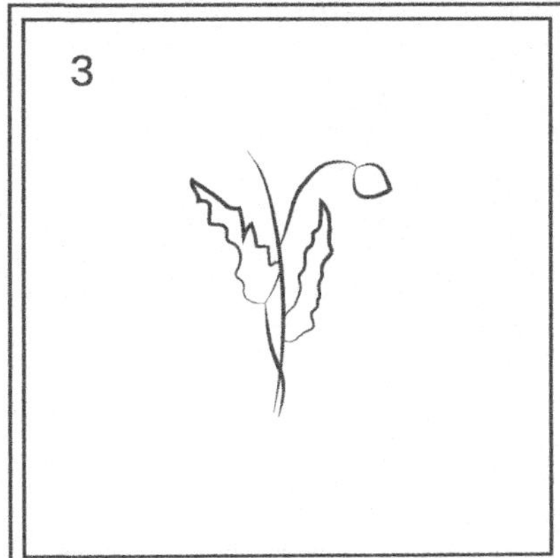

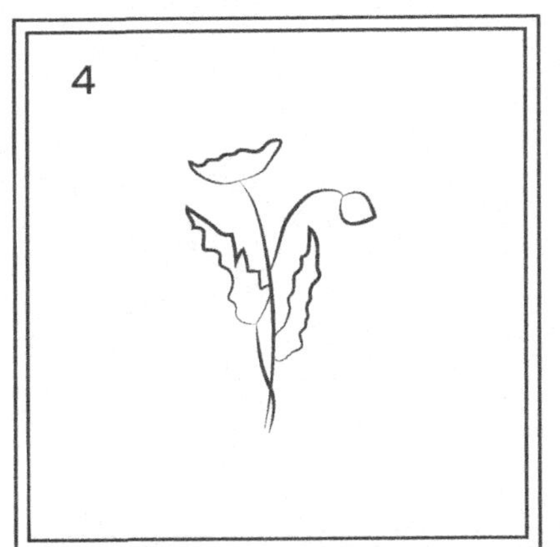

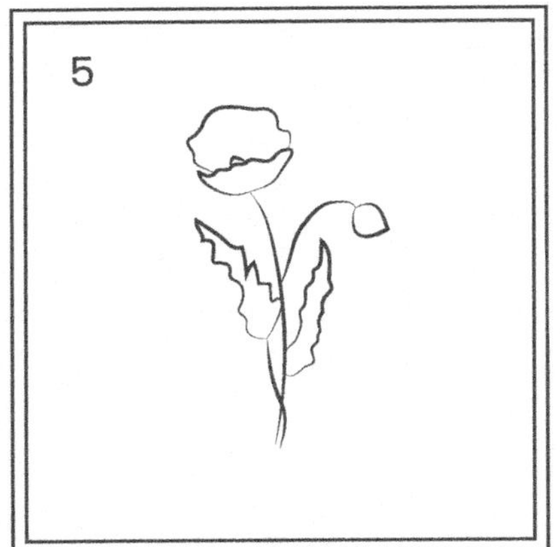

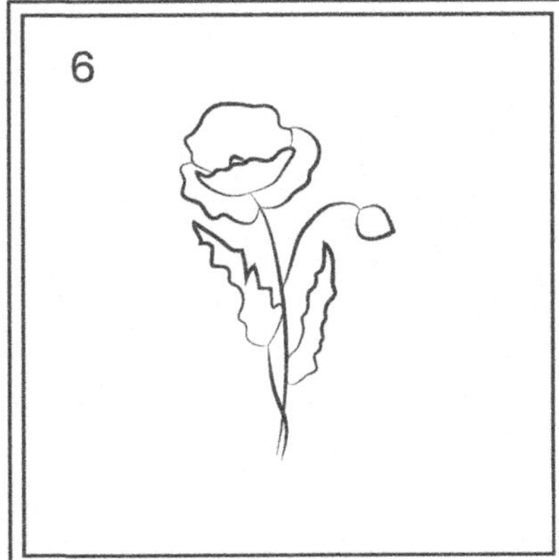

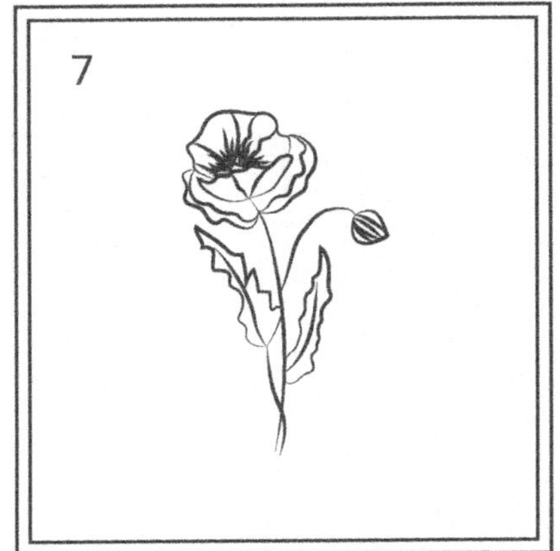

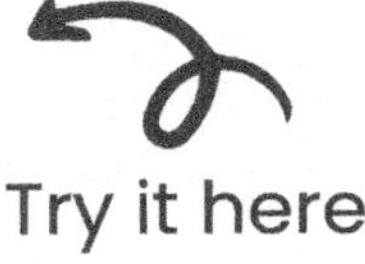

Try it here

Botanical Line Drawing 1

Crocus

55

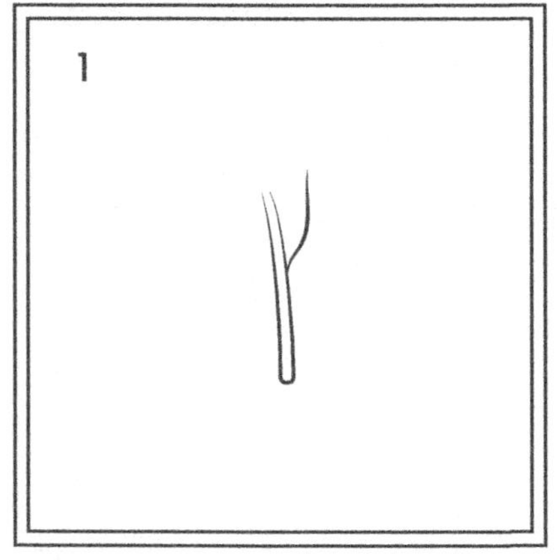

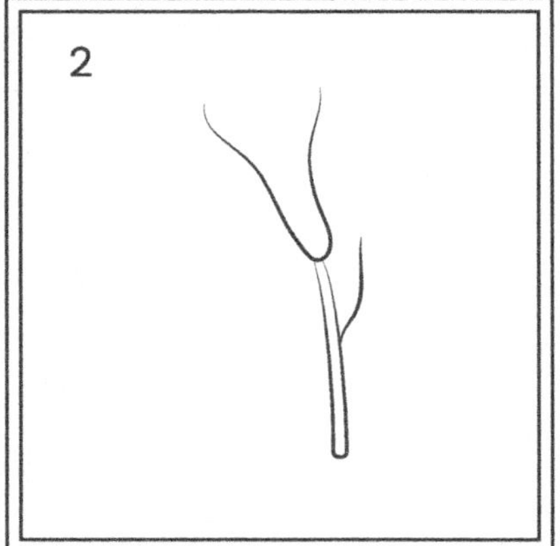

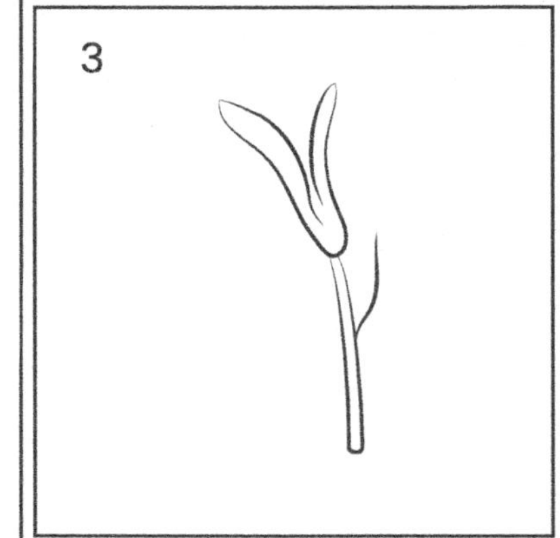

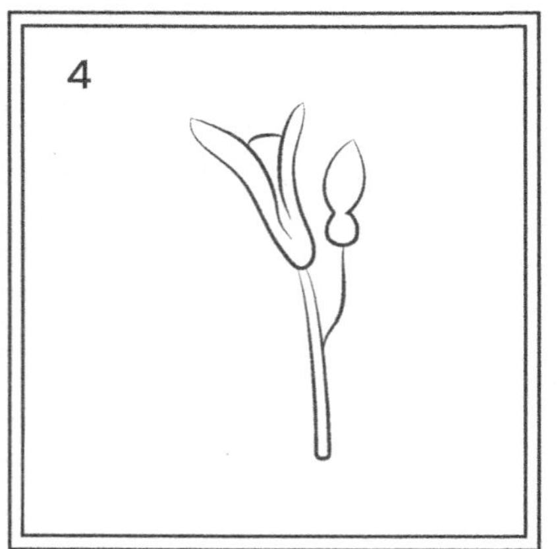

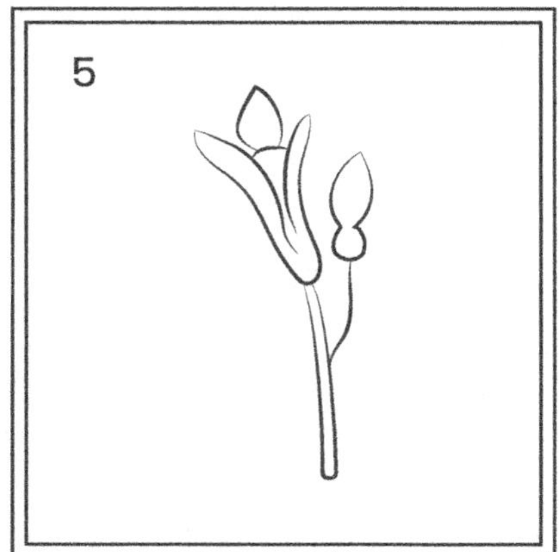

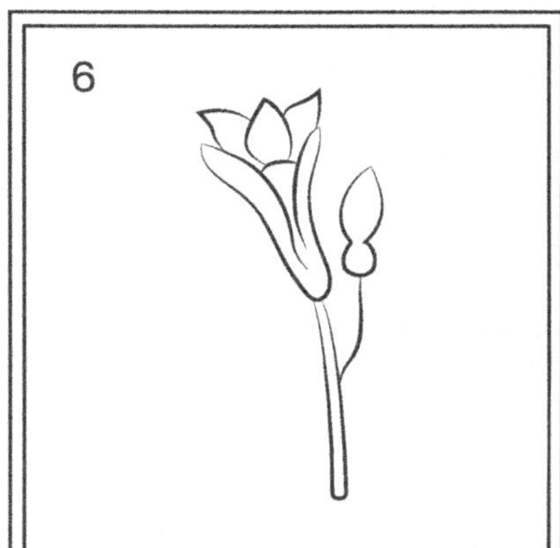

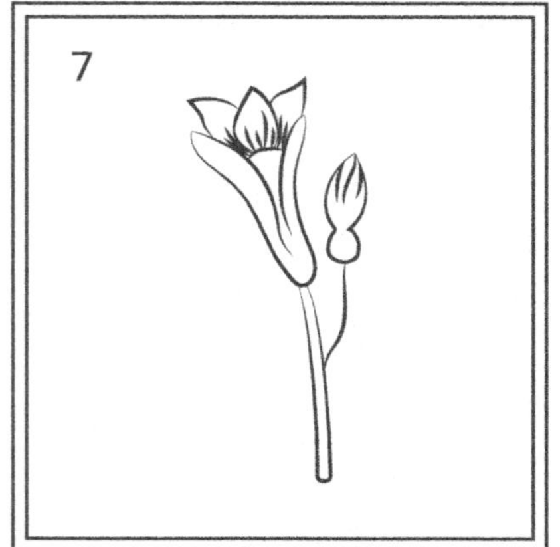

Try it here

Botanical Line Drawing 1

Chrysanthemum 56

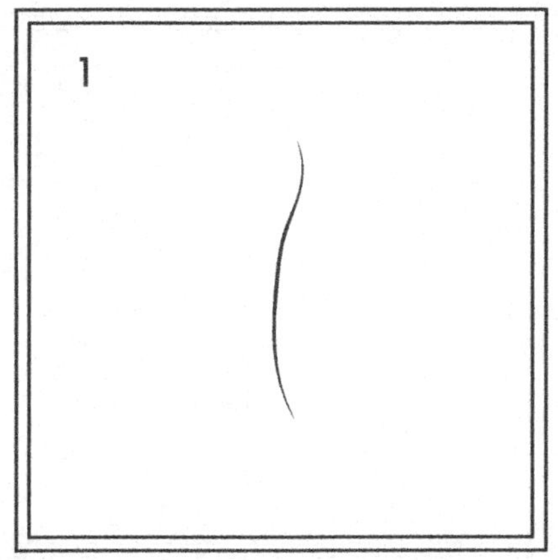

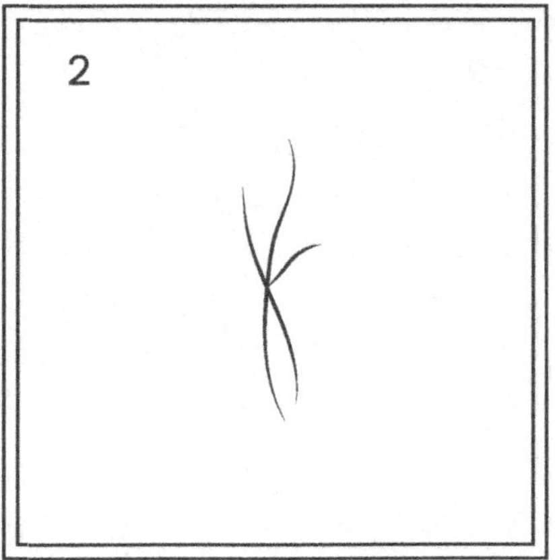

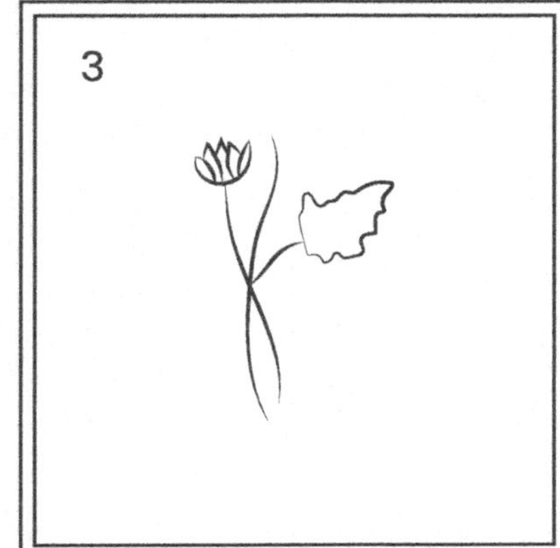

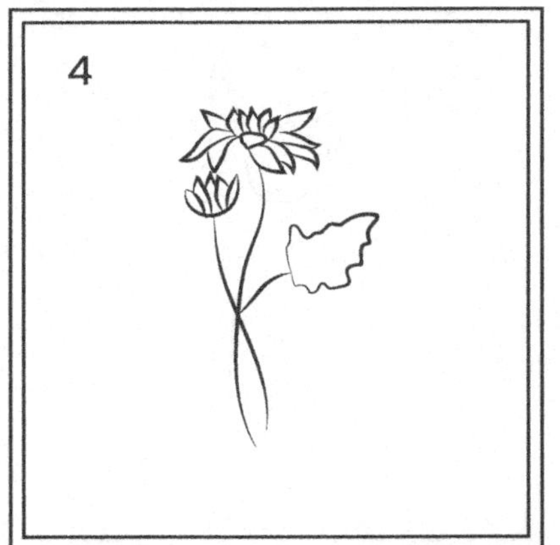

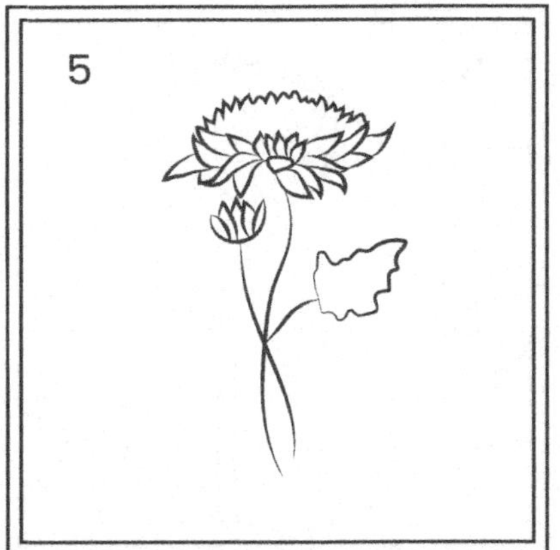

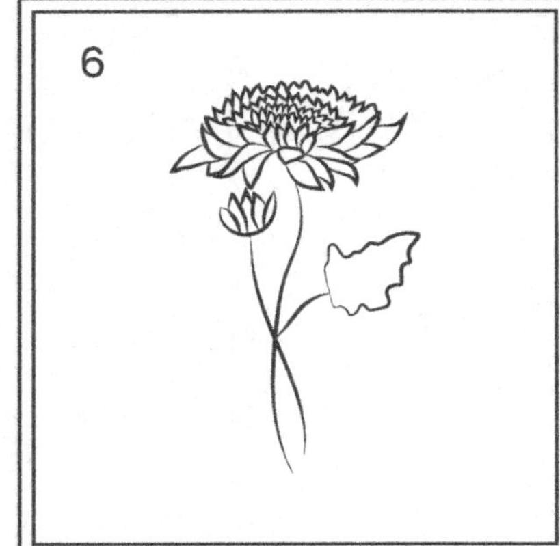

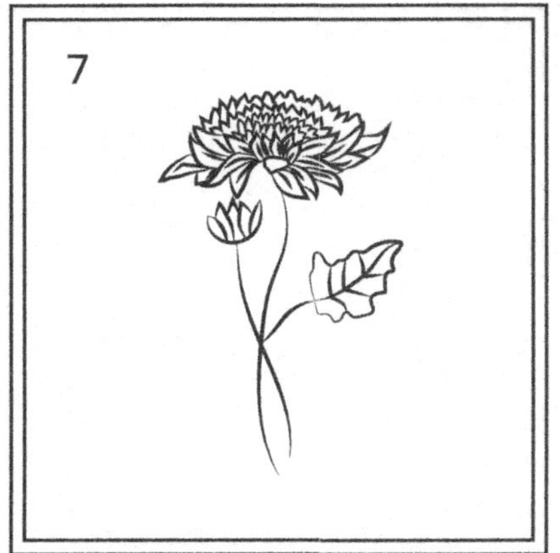

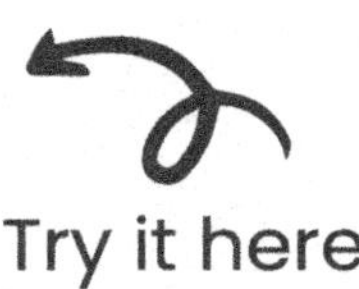

Try it here

Botanical Line Drawing 1

Rose

57

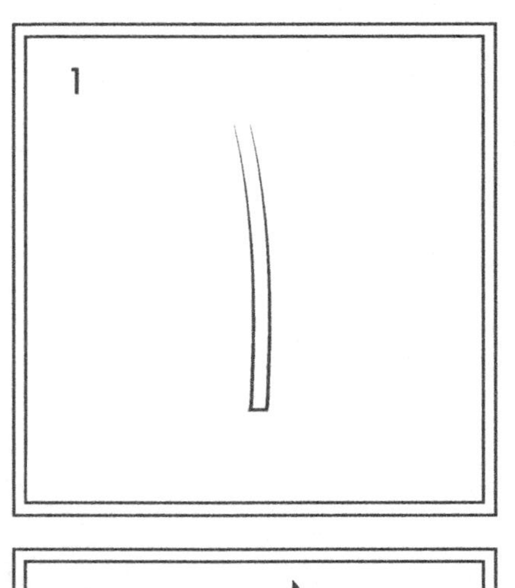

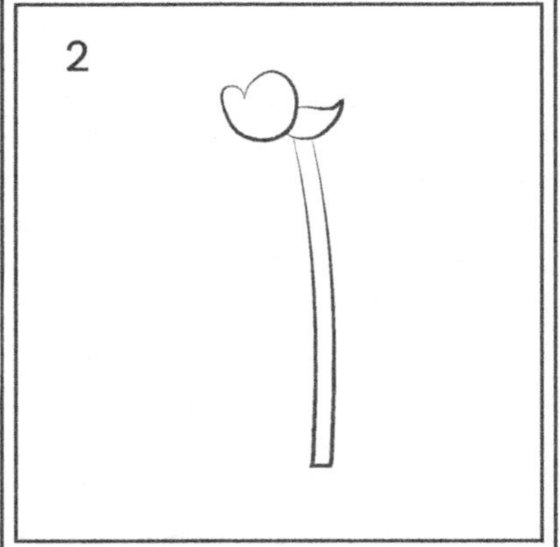

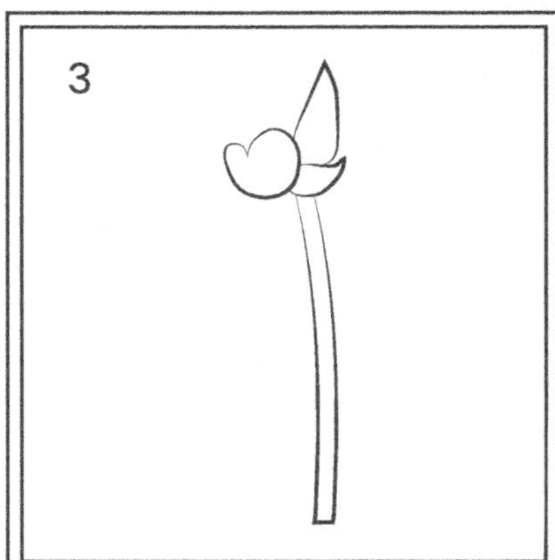

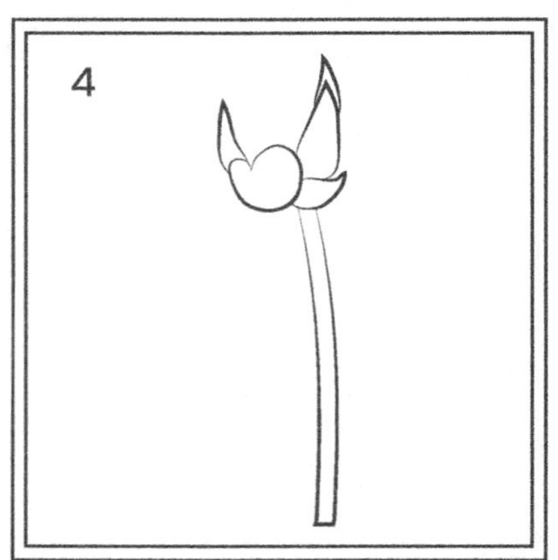

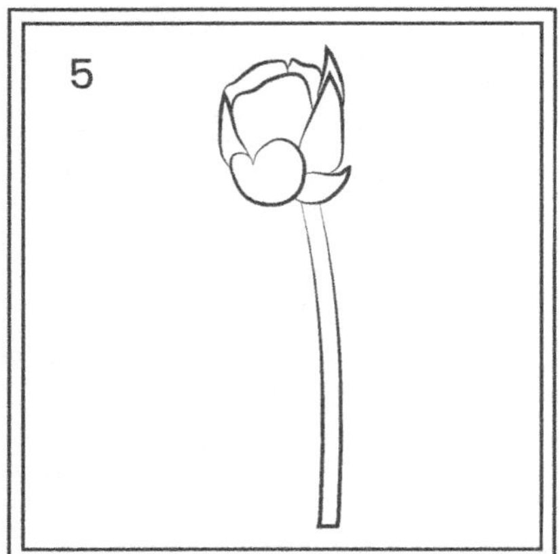

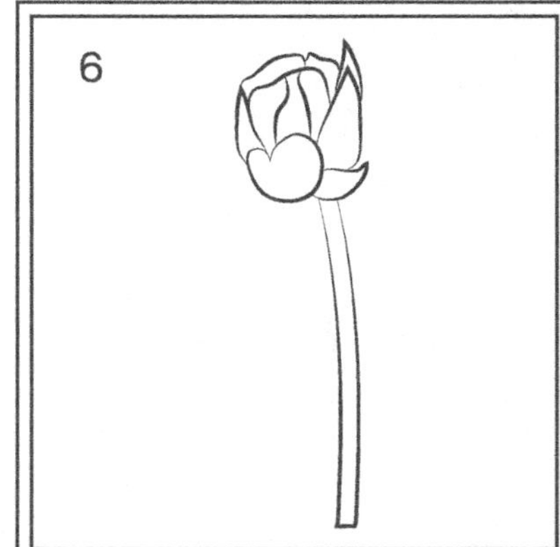

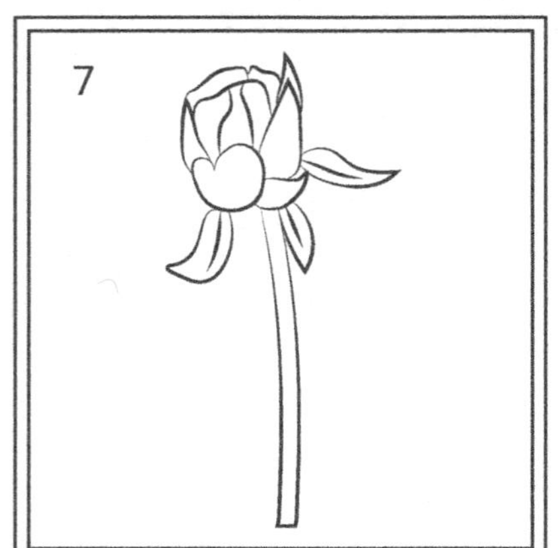

Try it here

Botanical Line Drawing 1

Tulip

58

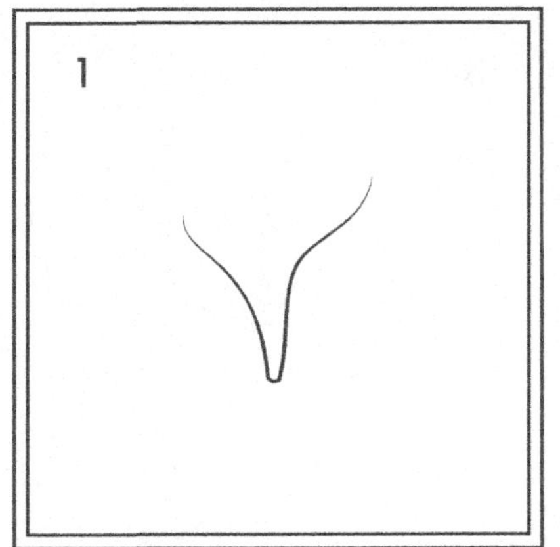

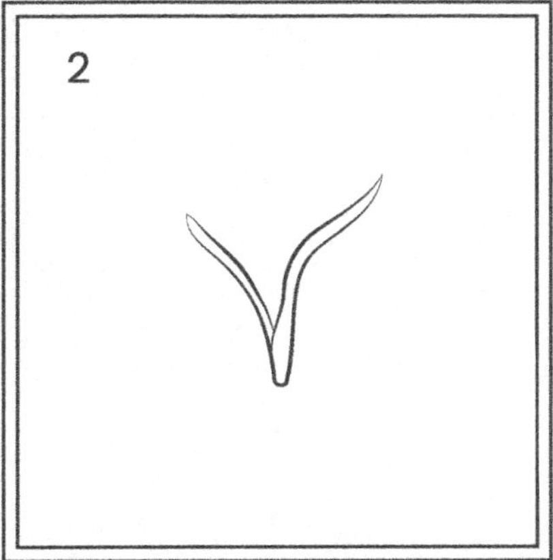

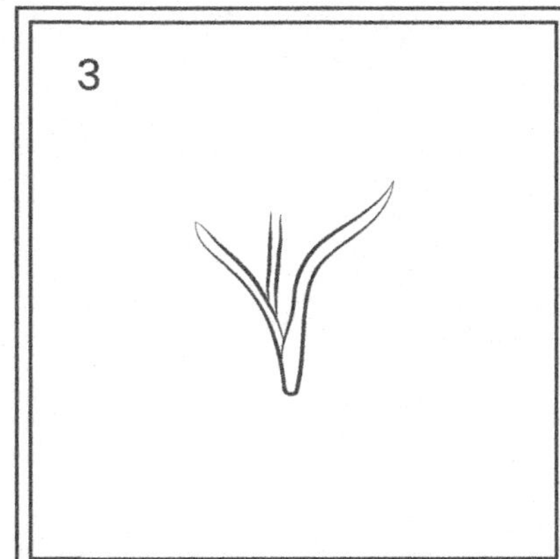

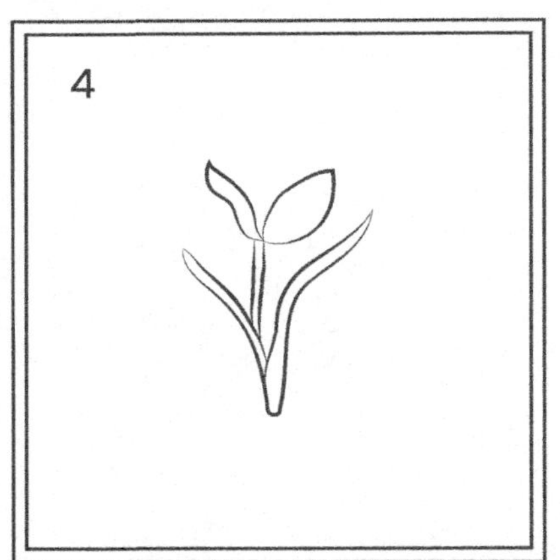

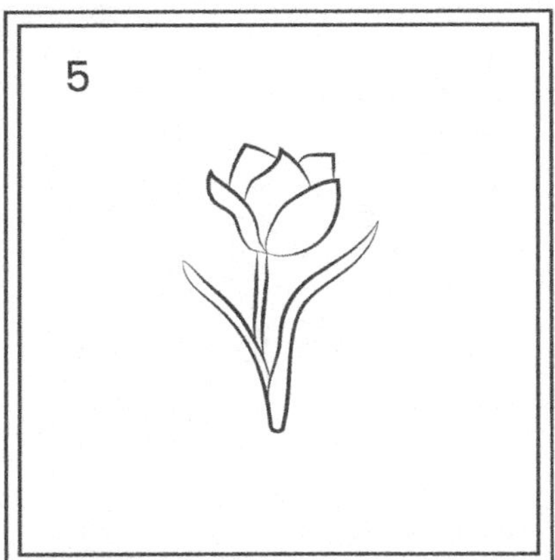

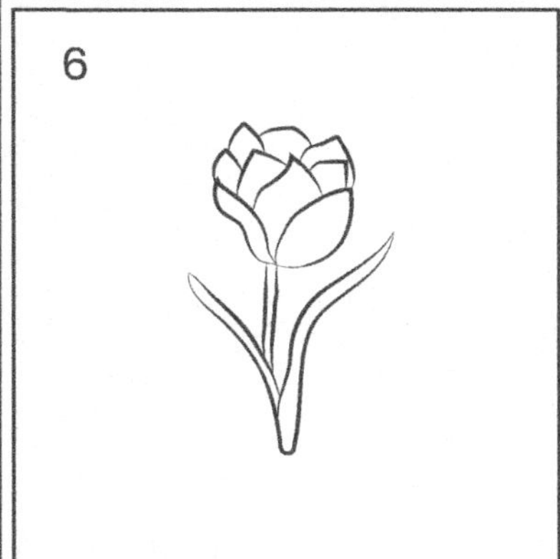

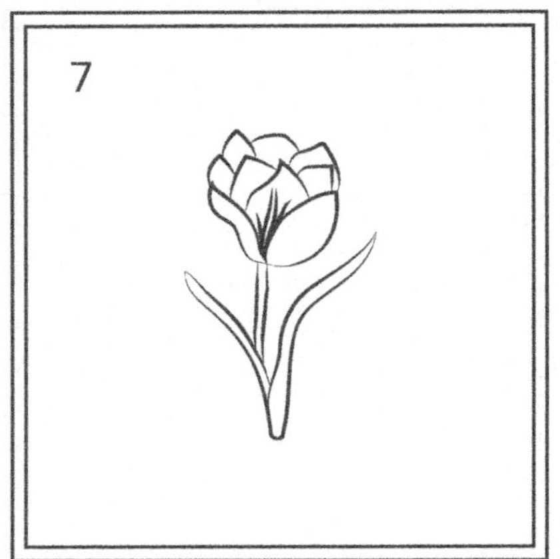

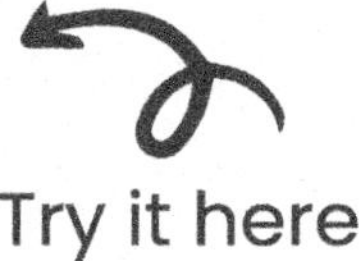

Try it here

Botanical Line Drawing 1

Magnolia

59

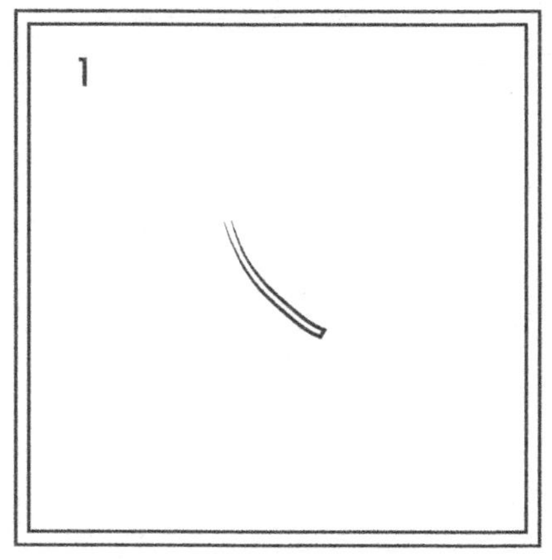

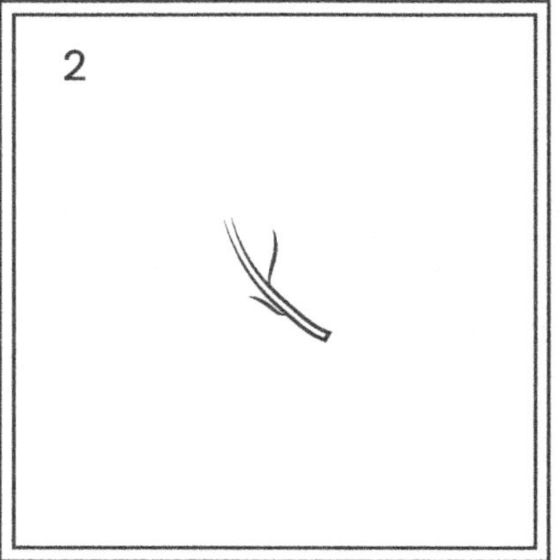

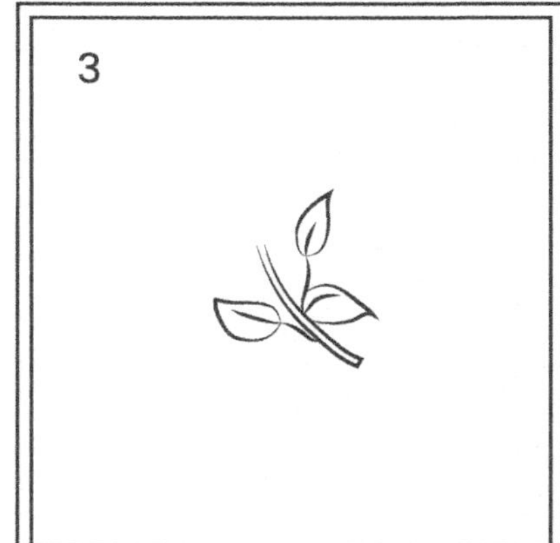

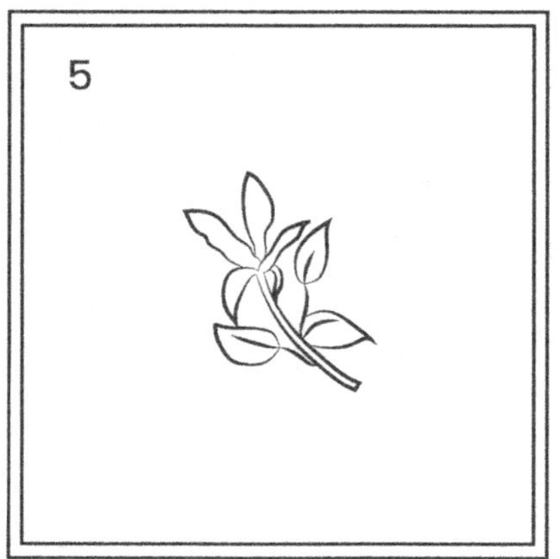

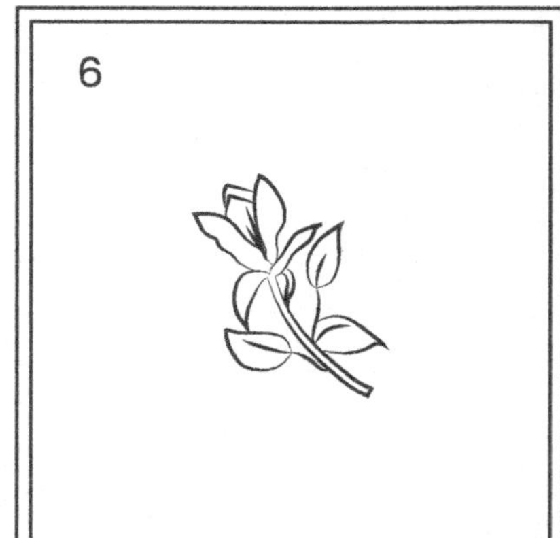

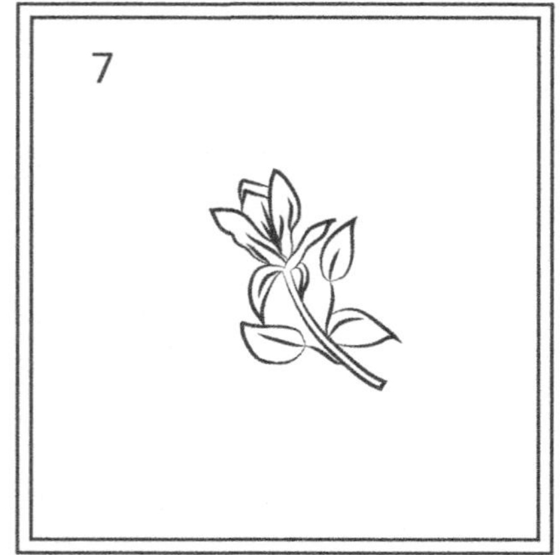

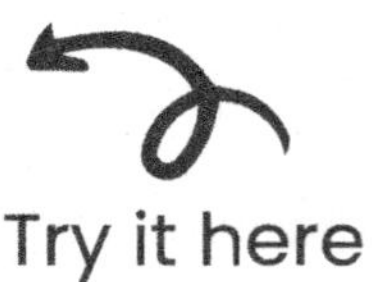

Try it here

Botanical Line Drawing 1

Protea

60

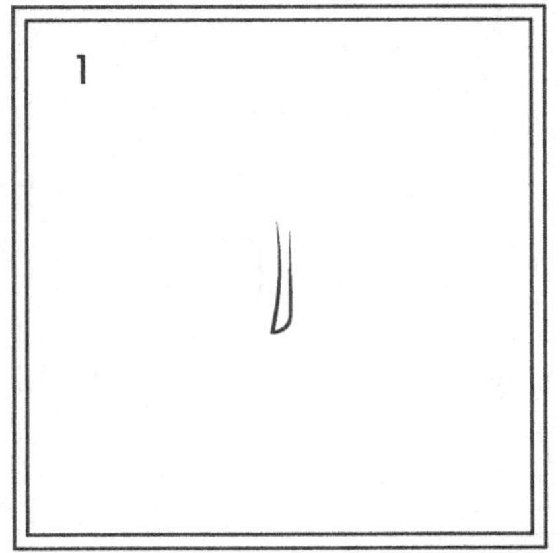

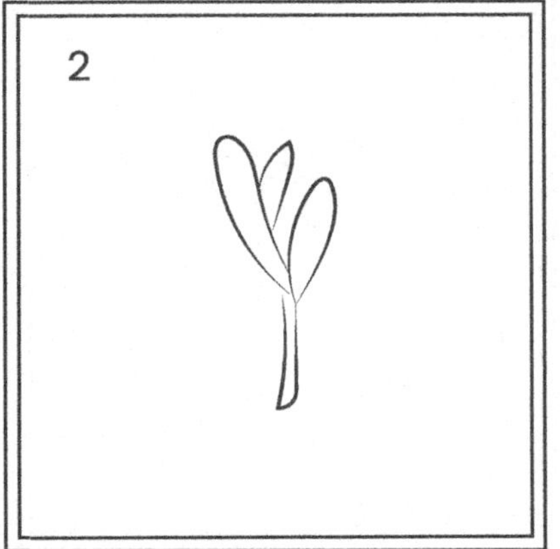

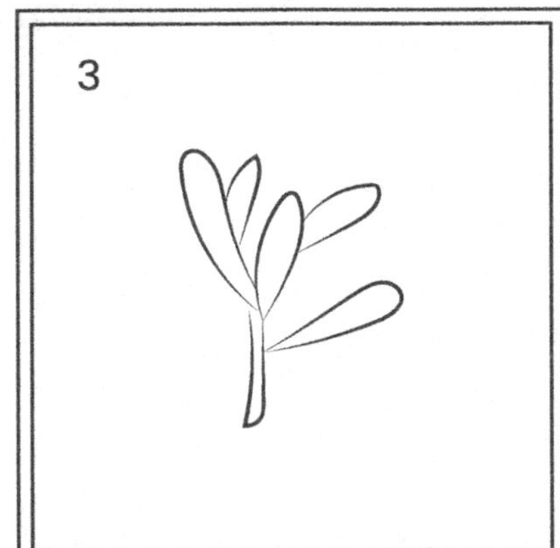

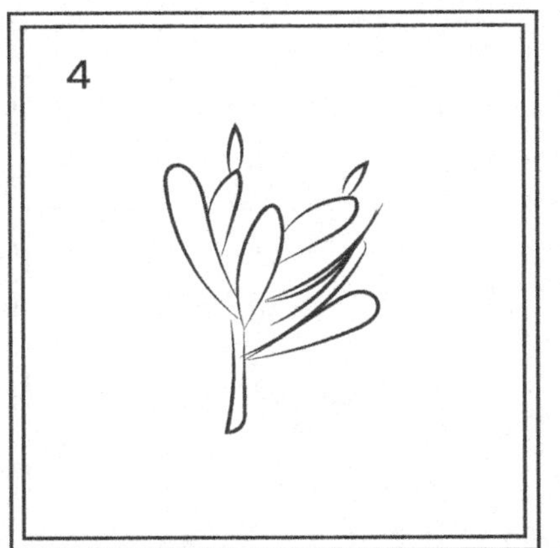

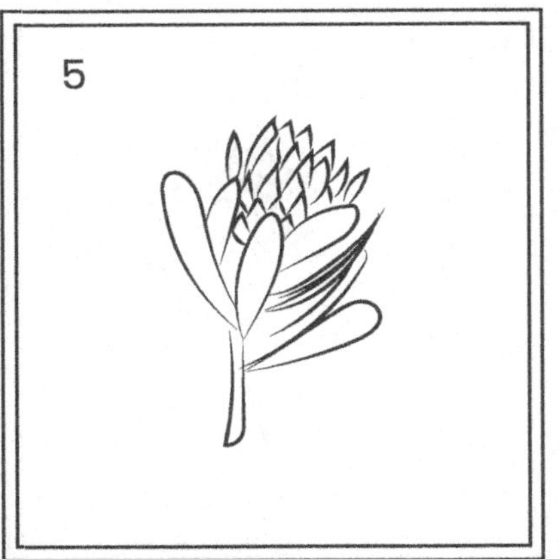

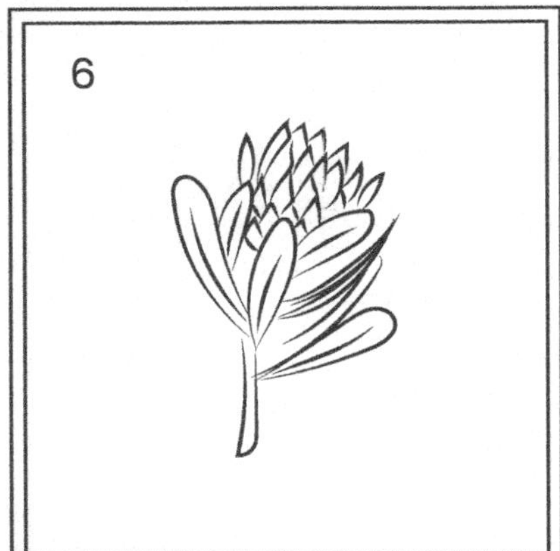

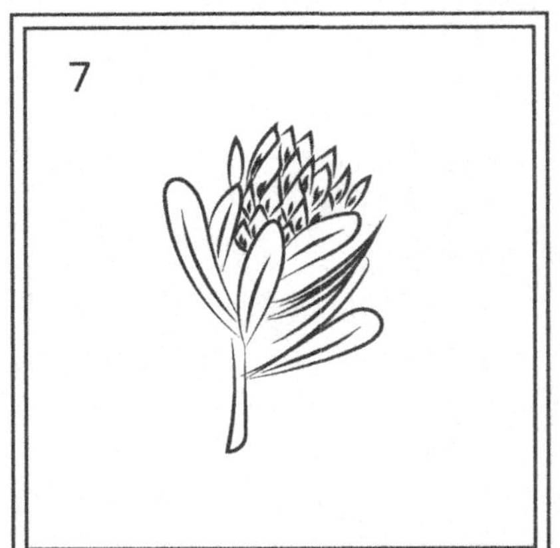

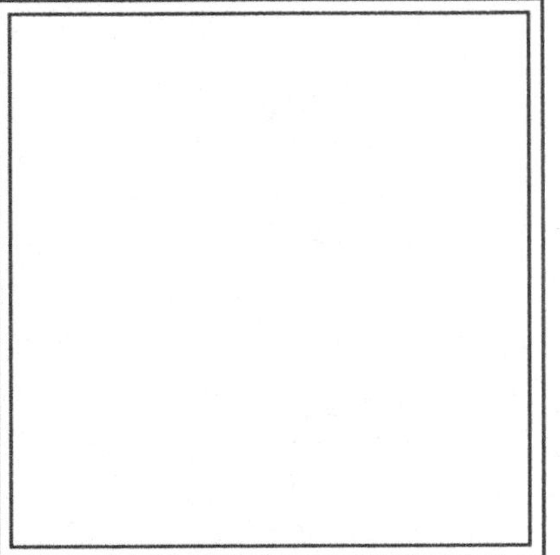

Try it here

Botanical Line Drawing 1

Chia

61

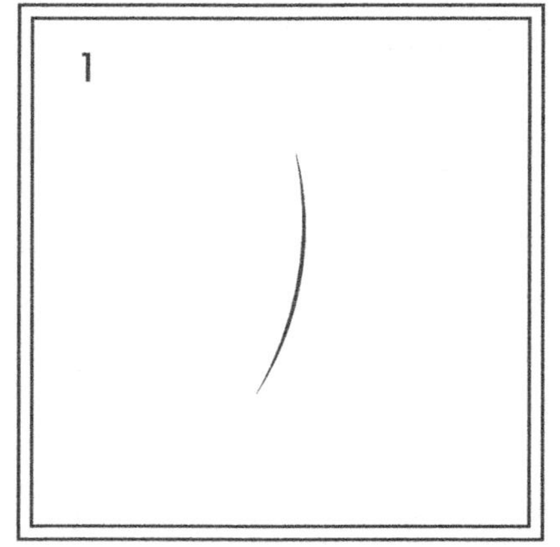

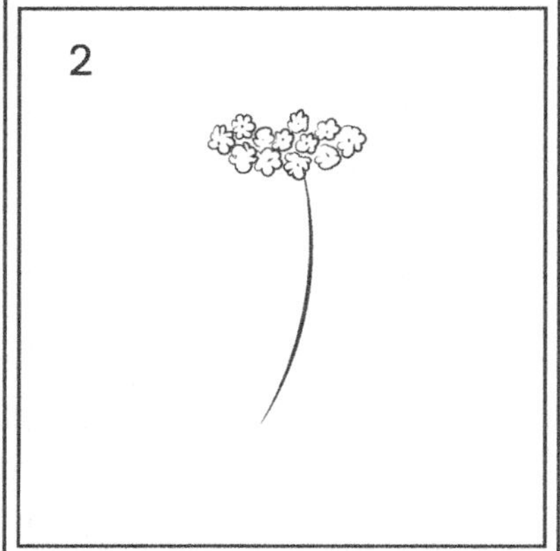

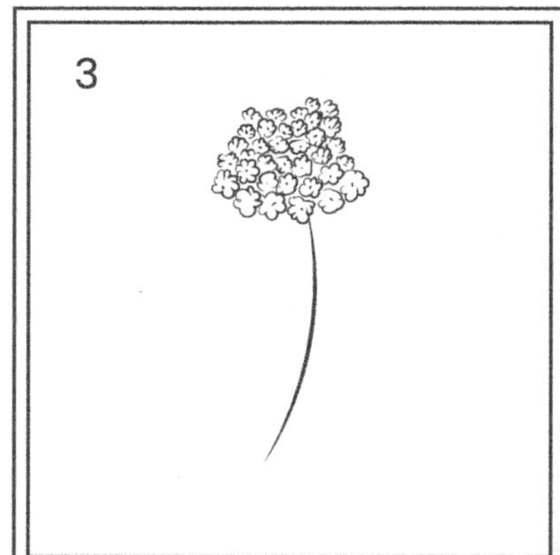

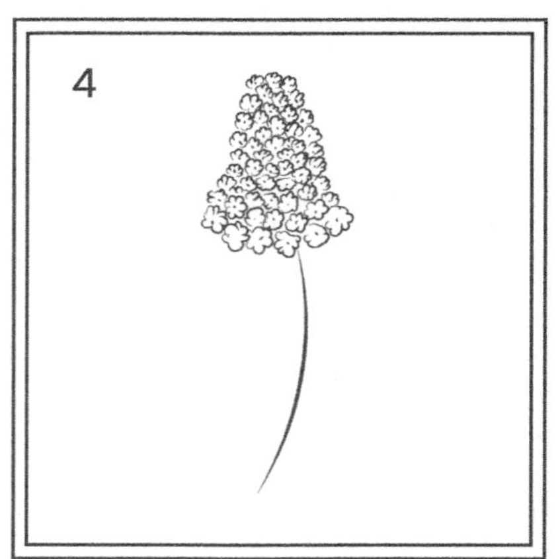

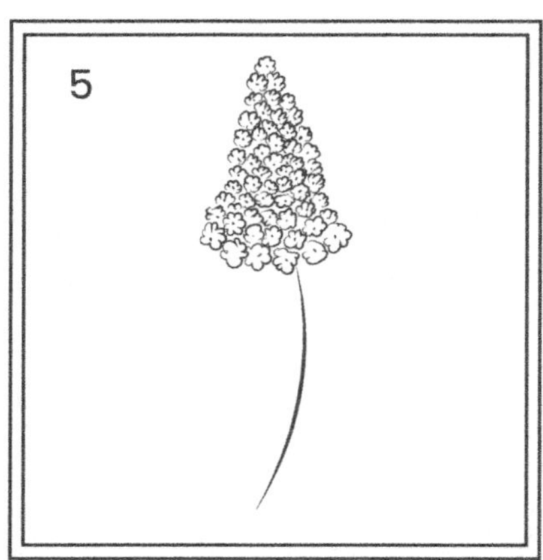

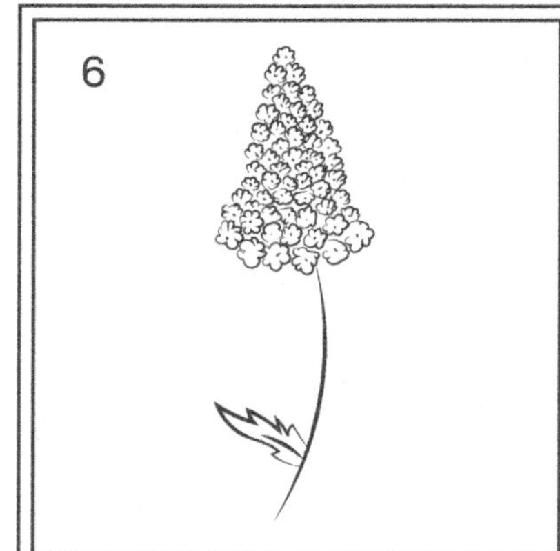

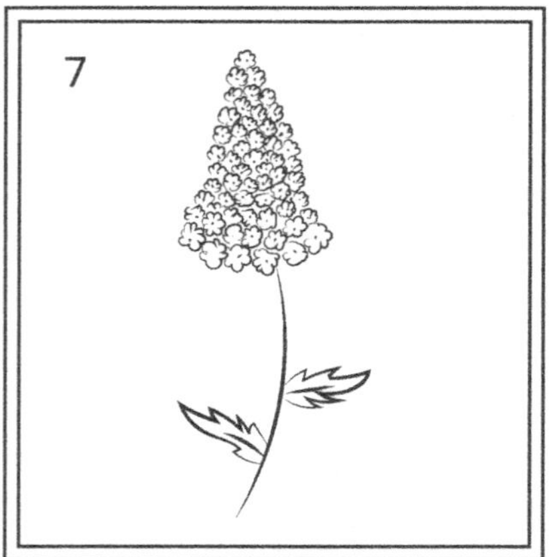

Try it here

Botanical Line Drawing 1

Eucalyptus 2

62

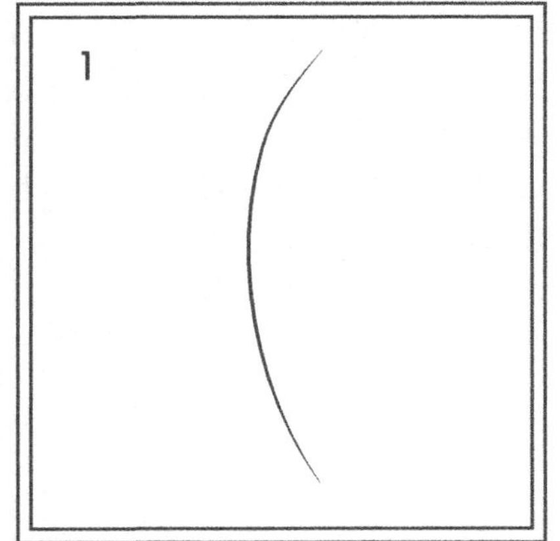

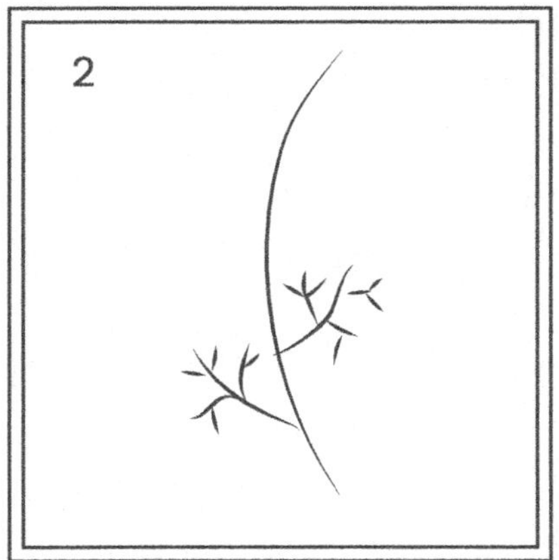

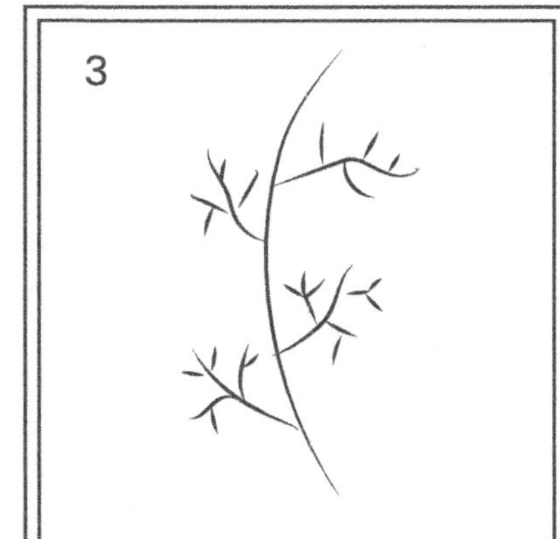

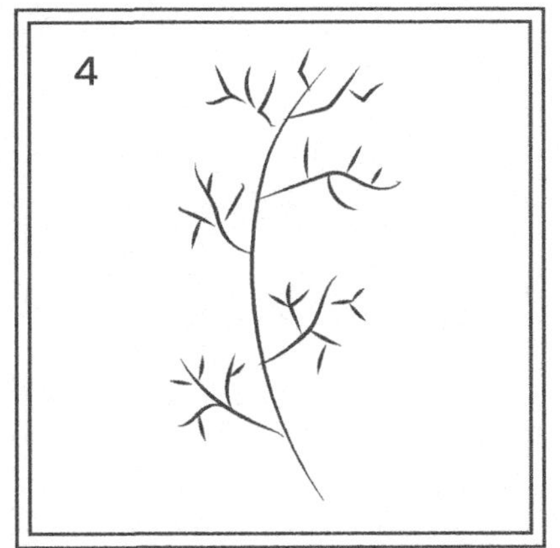

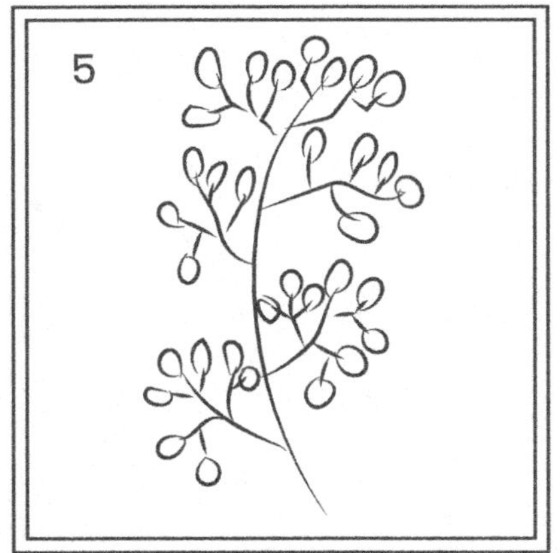

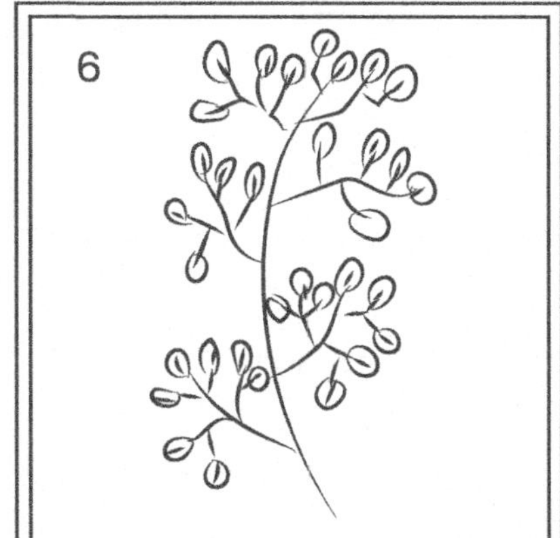

Try it here

Botanical Line Drawing 1

Jewels of Opar 63

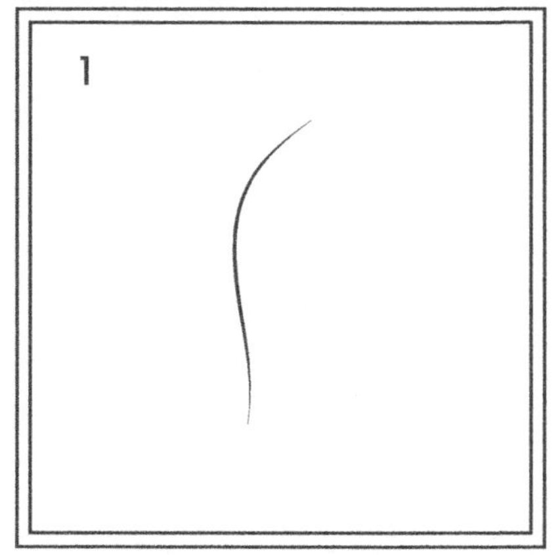

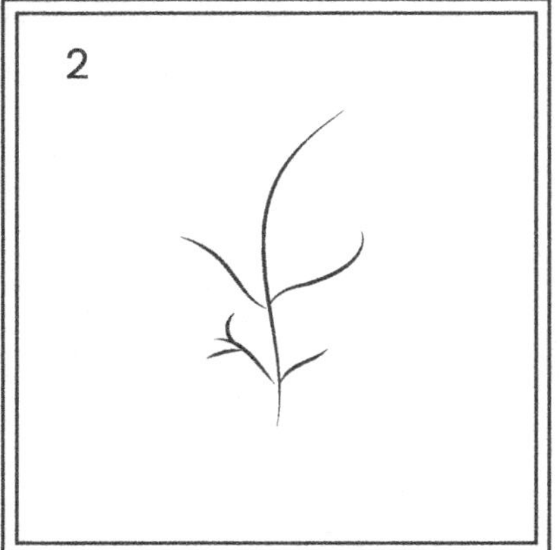

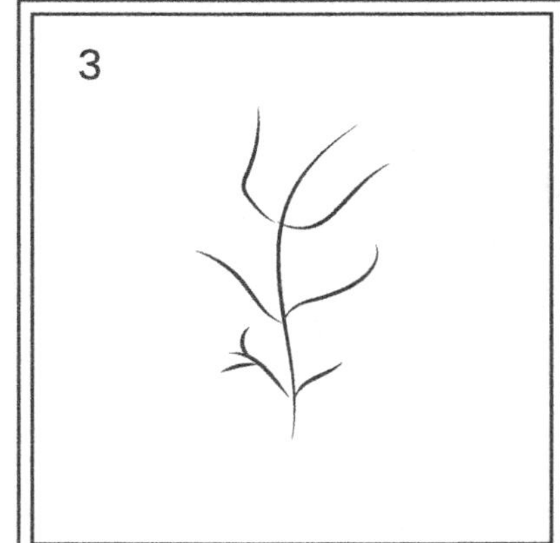

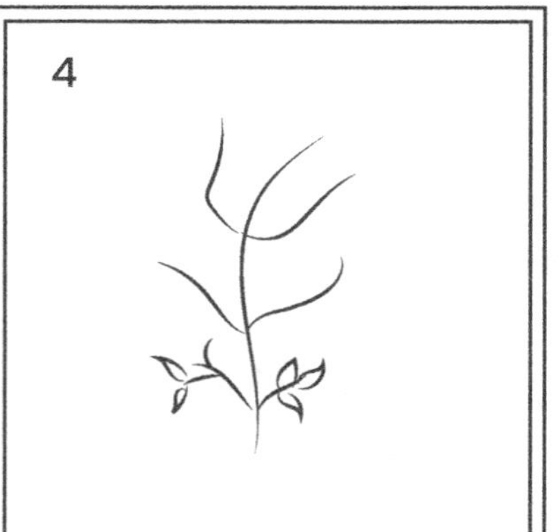

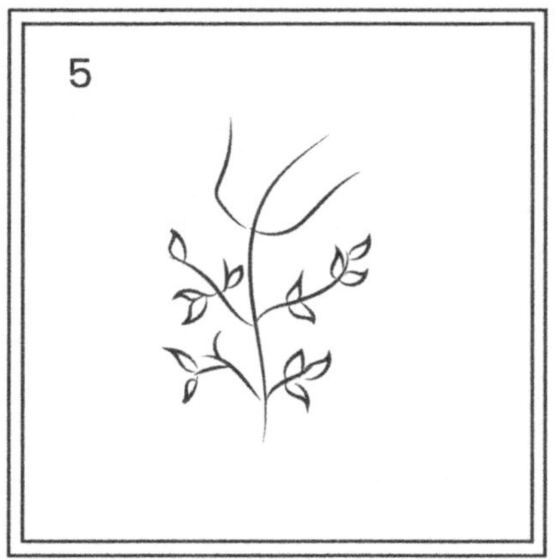

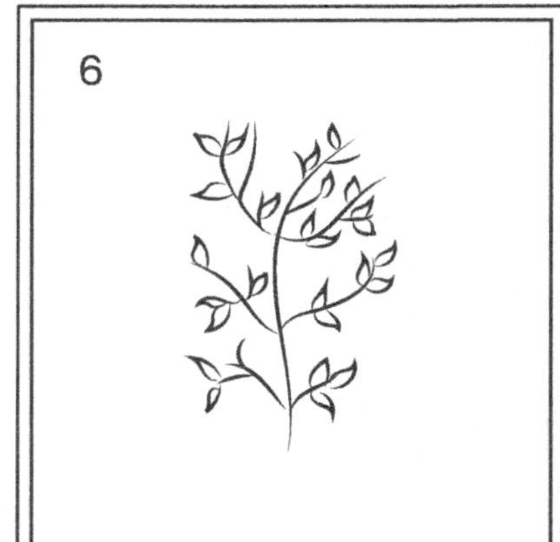

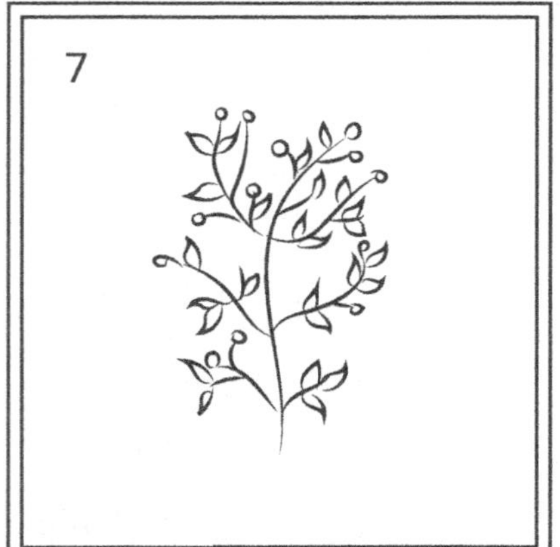

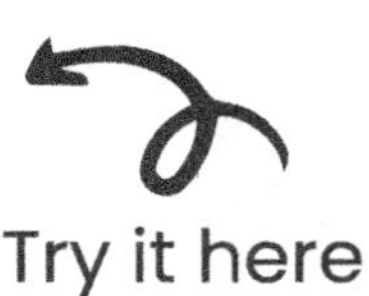

Botanical Line Drawing 1

Wild Tulip

64

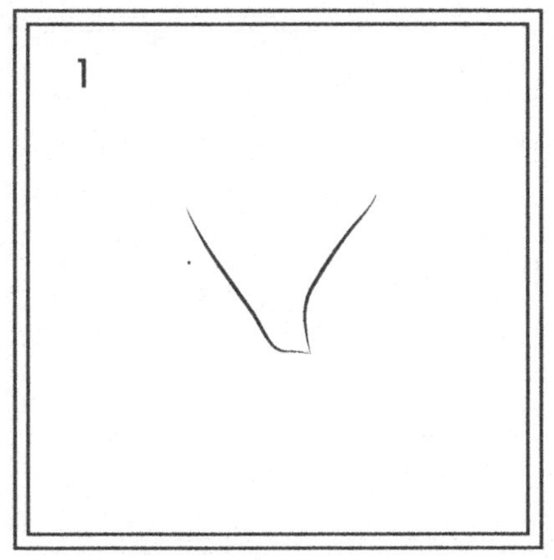

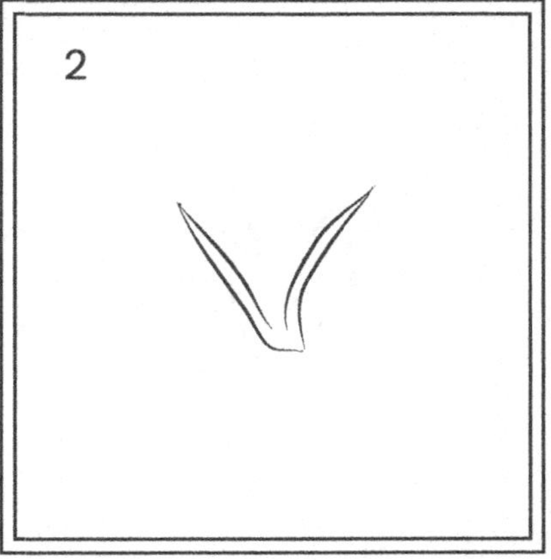

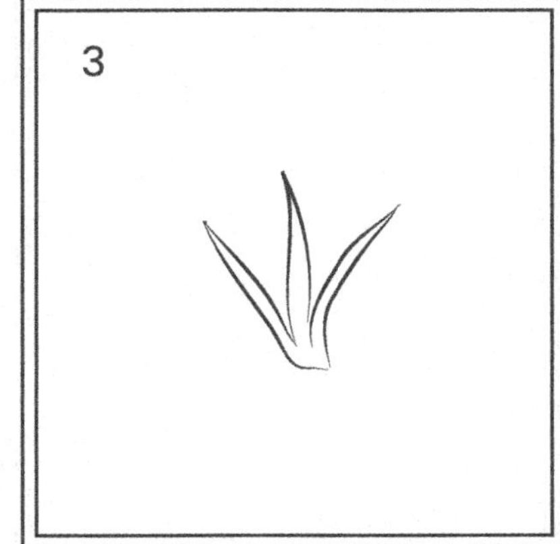

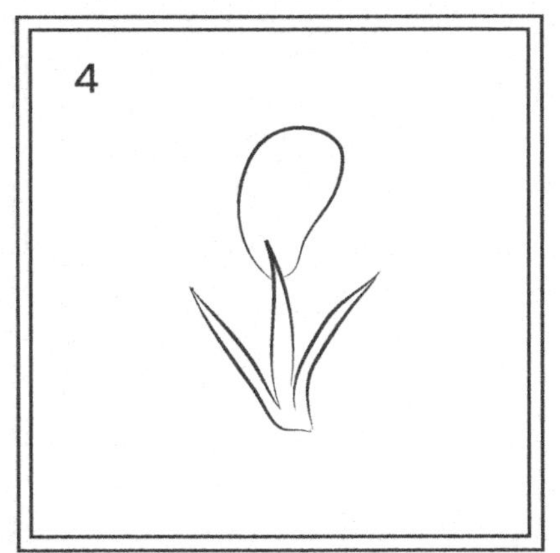

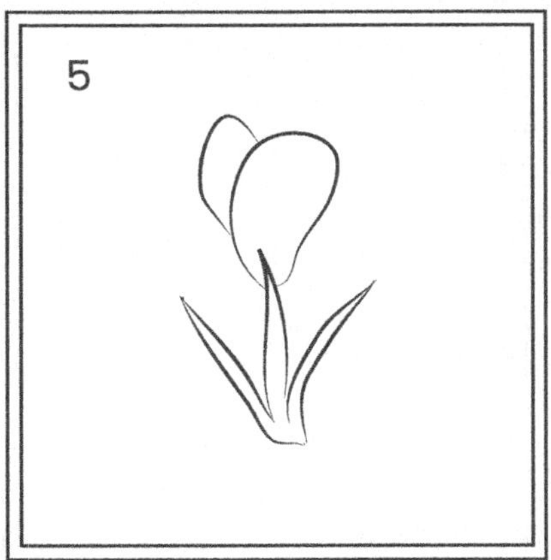

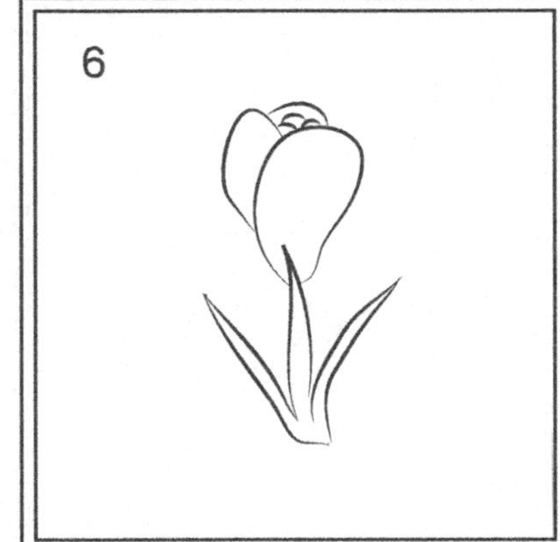

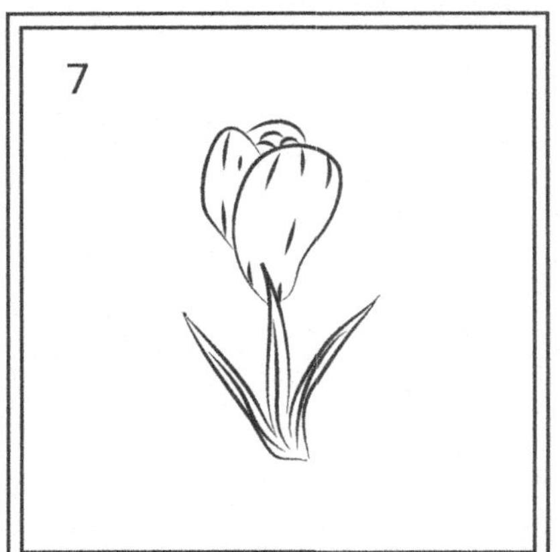

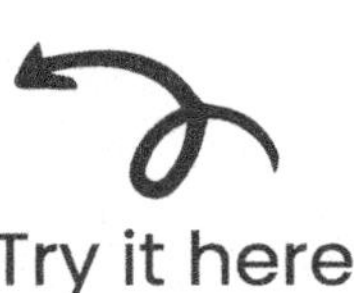

Try it here

Tulip

65

1

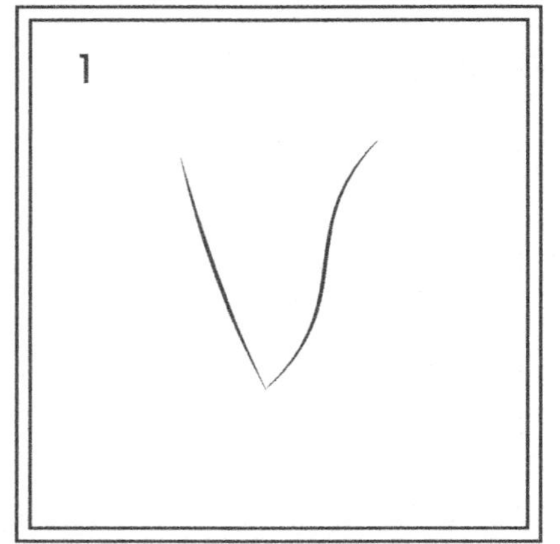

2

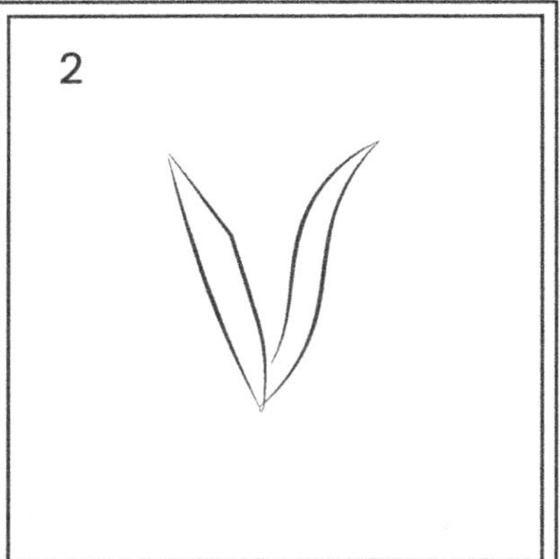

3

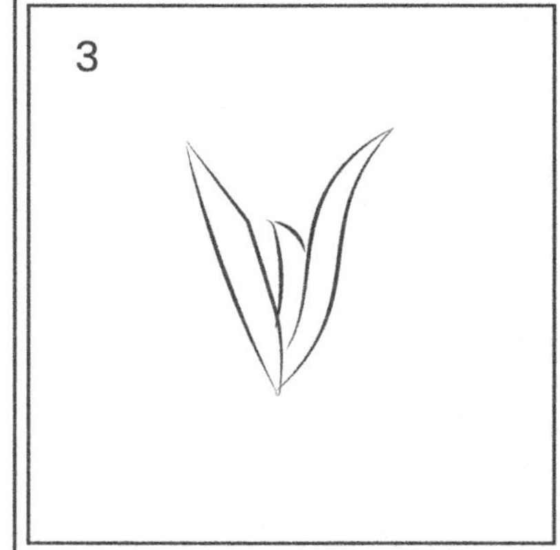

4

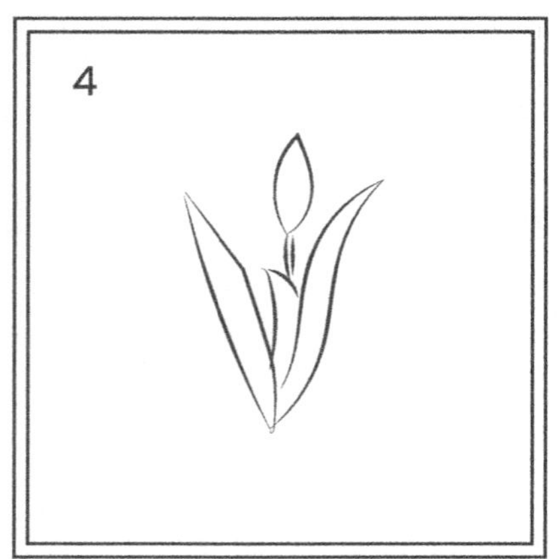

5

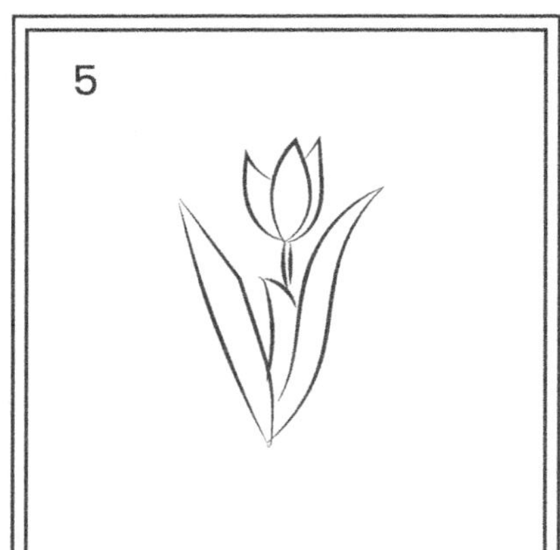

6

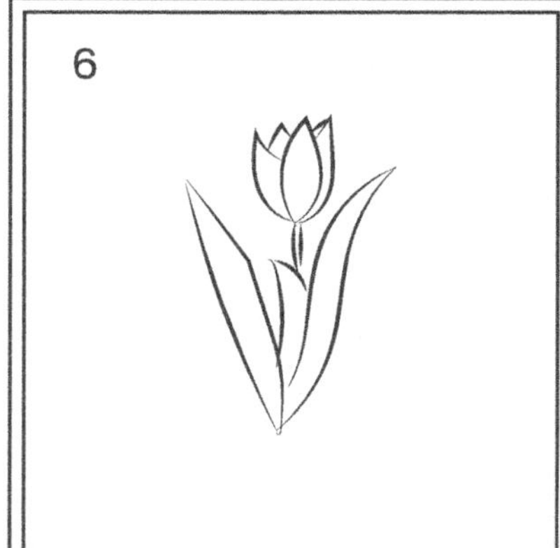

7

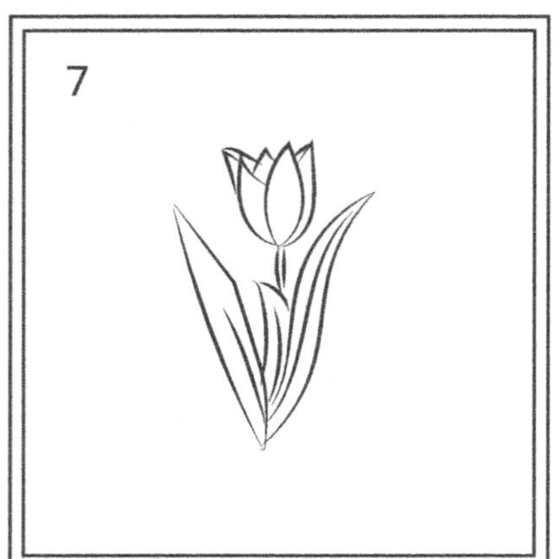

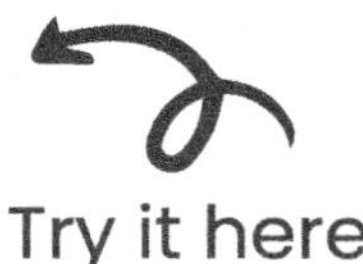

Try it here

Botanical Line Drawing 1

Blue Flax

66

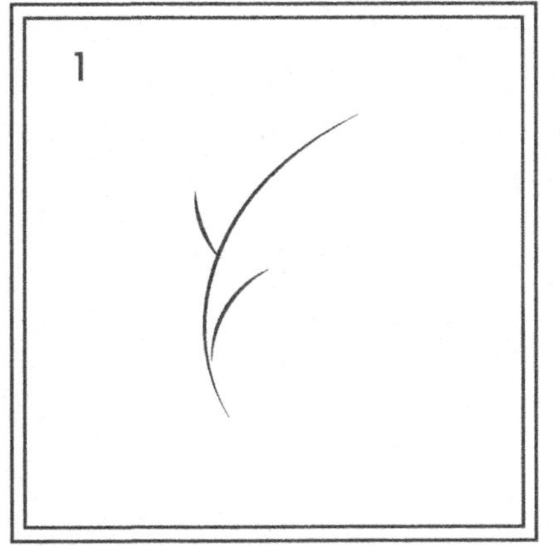

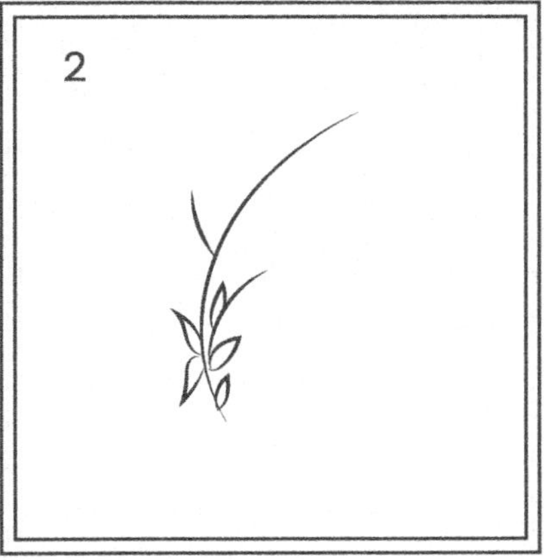

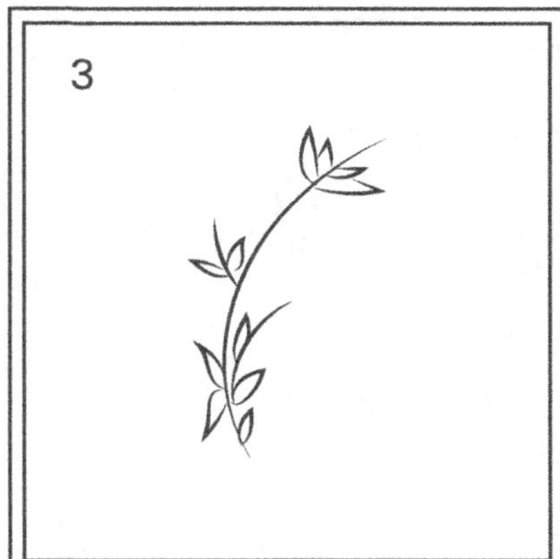

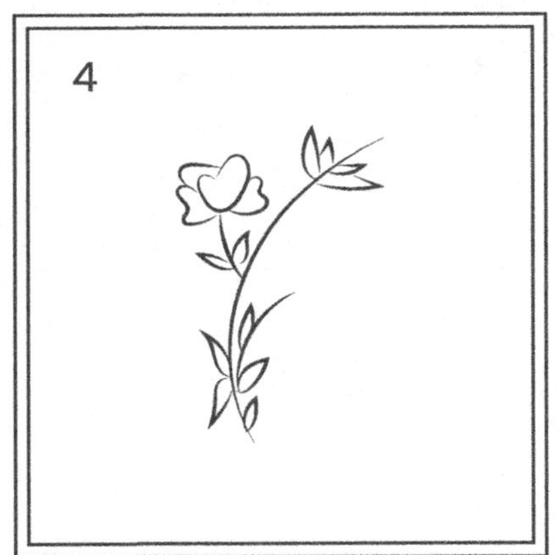

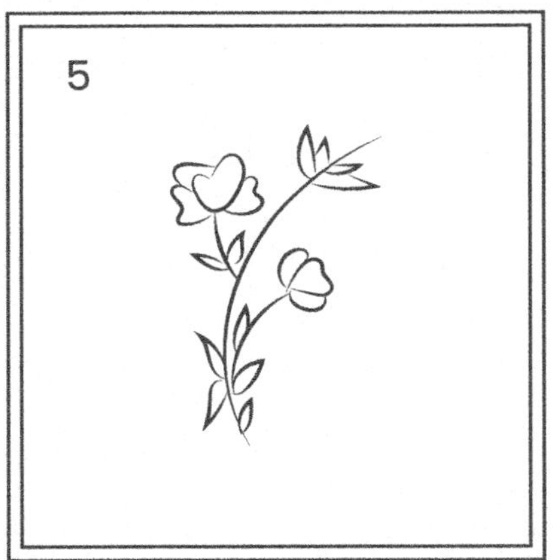

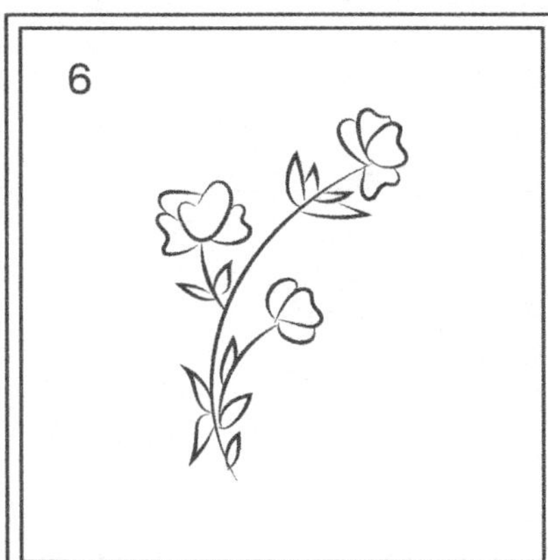

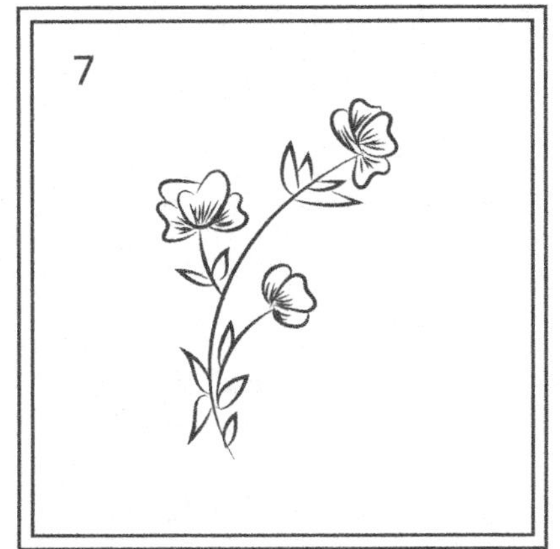

Try it here

Botanical Line Drawing 1

Rose 2

67

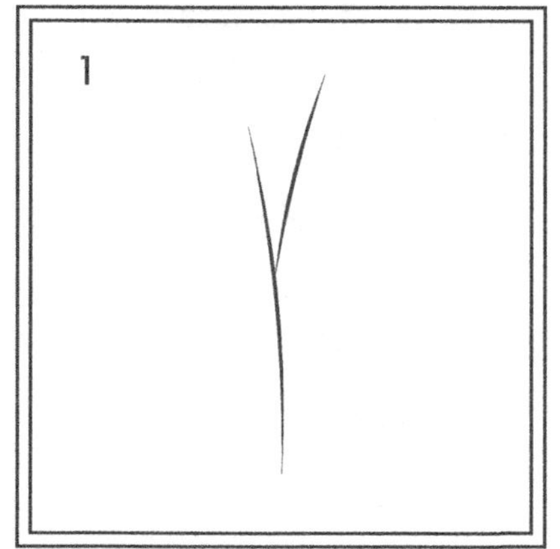

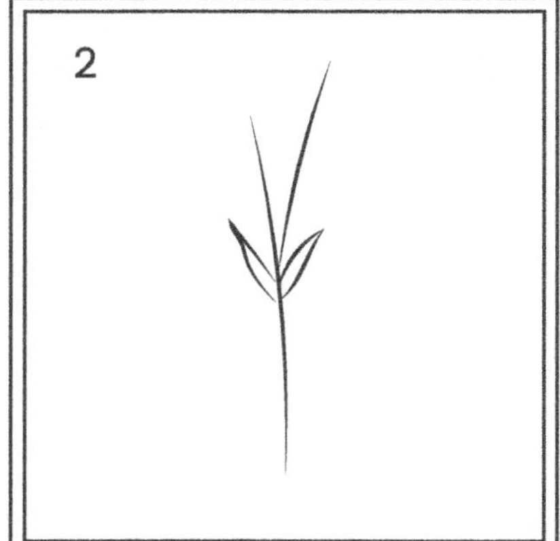

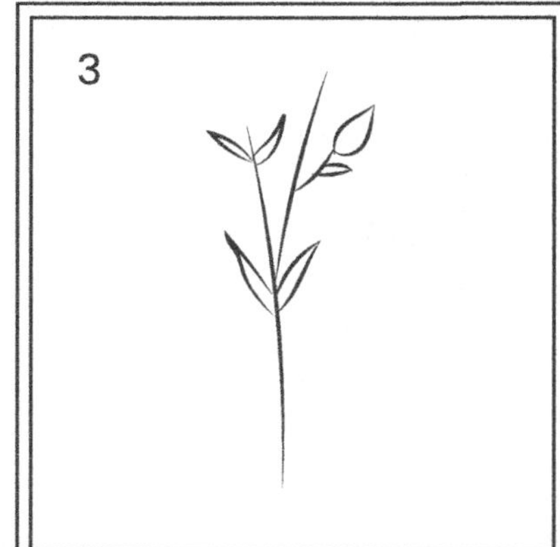

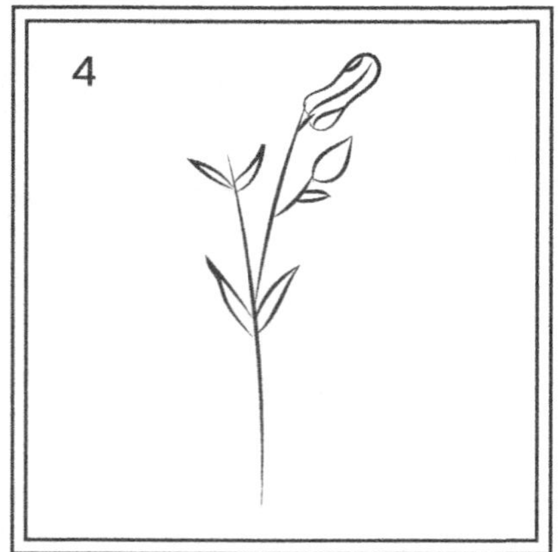

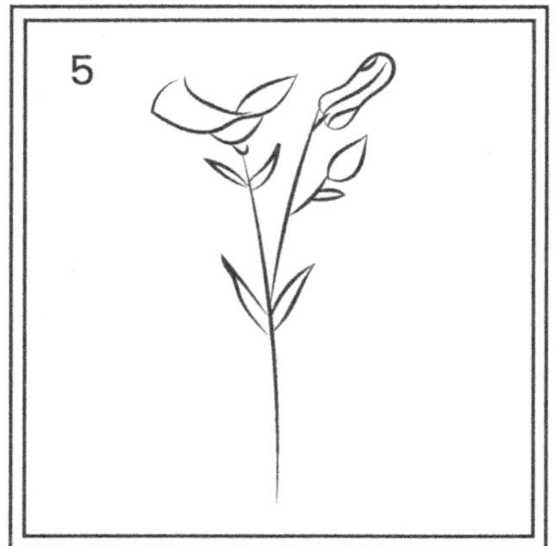

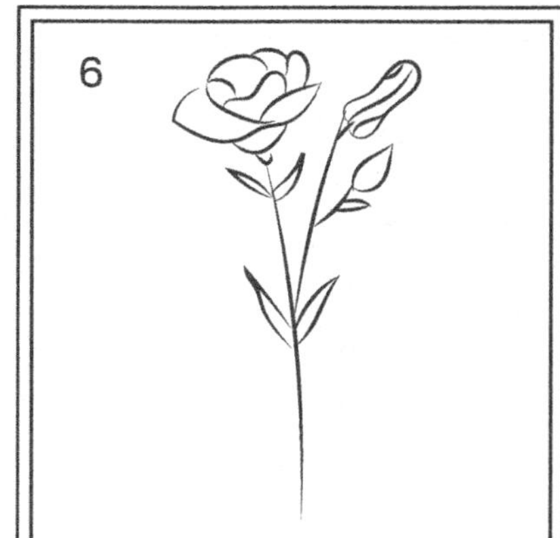

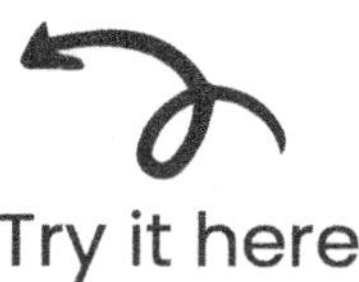

Try it here

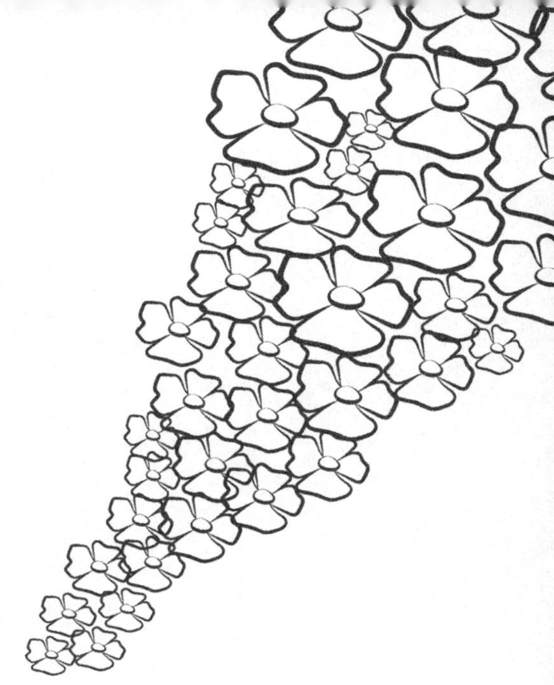

I sometimes think there is nothing so delightful as drawing.

Vincent Van Gogh

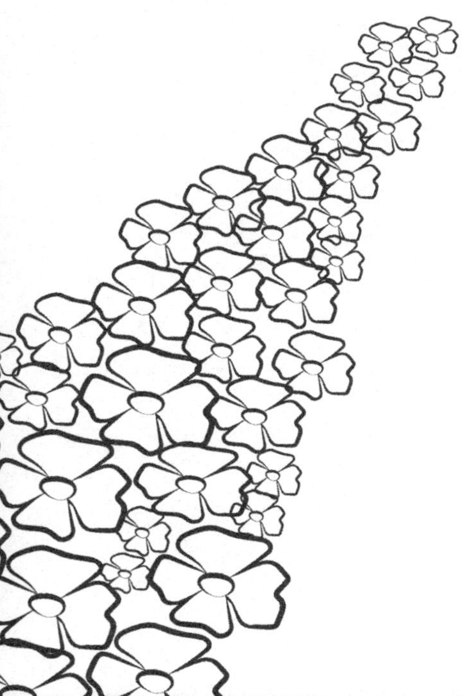

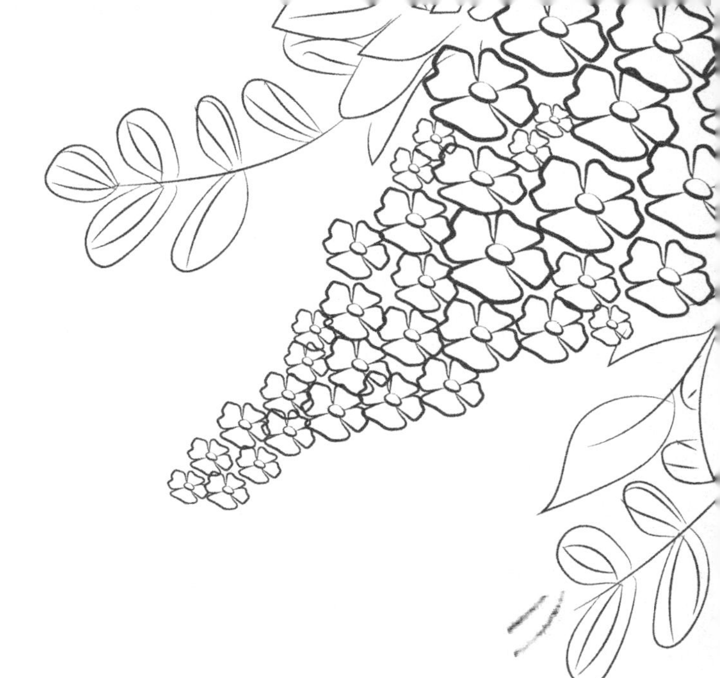

VARIATIONS

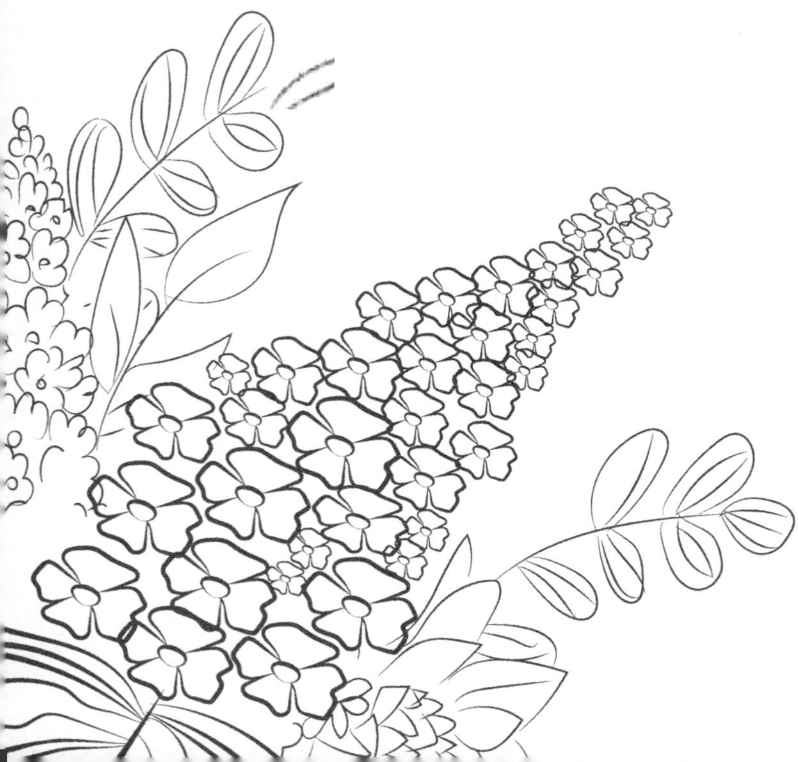

Once you have a few botanical drawings in your repertoire, you can start playing with different methods and come up with many, many variations.

You can add color, you can try white pens on black paper, you can draw in gold instead of black, or you could just add some gold touches to a black and white drawing. You could scan your images and use them to create art prints, mailing labels, bookplates, and so much more!

LINE WIDTHS

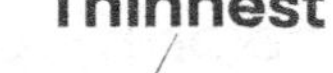

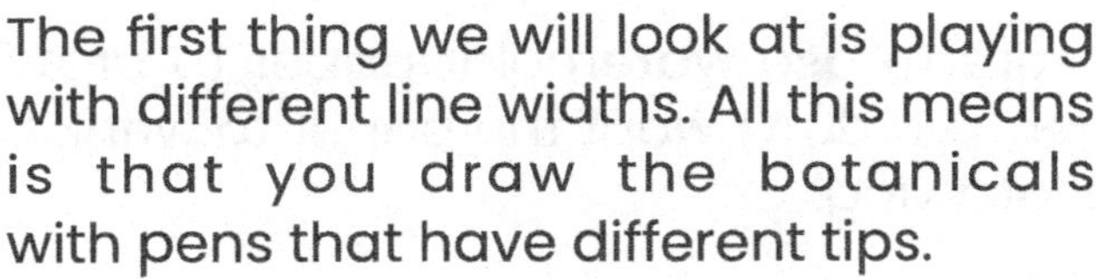

The first thing we will look at is playing with different line widths. All this means is that you draw the botanicals with pens that have different tips.

You can see a few examples on this page. Some of the drawings are done with a thicker line width, and some with a thinner one.

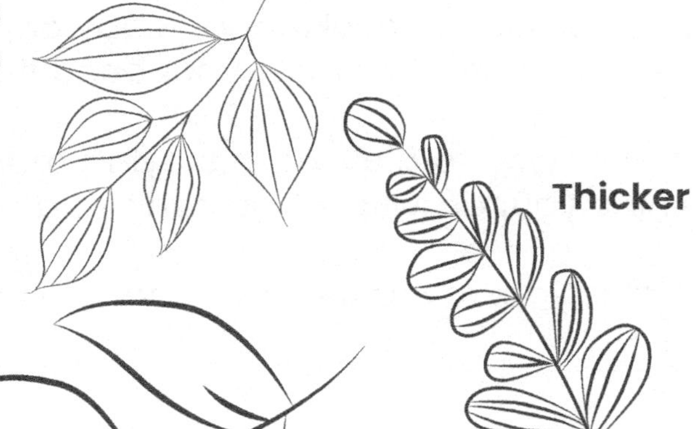

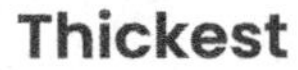

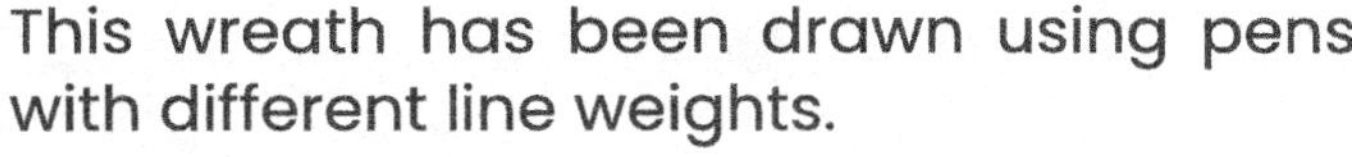

This wreath has been drawn using pens with different line weights.

The leaves are bolder than the flowers. You could play around with this technique and see if you like the way it looks!

ADDING COLORS

You can always add color to your botanical drawings. I prefer to leave them black and white or just add some highlights with a gold marker, but you can totally color them in using color pencils, crayons, markers, or watercolors, whatever your heart desires!

Colored pencils and watercolor pencils are both great for coloring botanical line drawings. Just make sure you use a waterproof pen for your drawings if you want to add any kind of water medium.

When using water color mediums, be sure to use watercolor paper to draw on or something thicker than copy paper. You don't want the paper to wrinkle beyond repair and waste your beautiful drawing.

Another way to play while staying monochromatic is by adding a grey wash behind your drawings. You can see an example of this below.

What is your favourite way of adding color to your drawings?

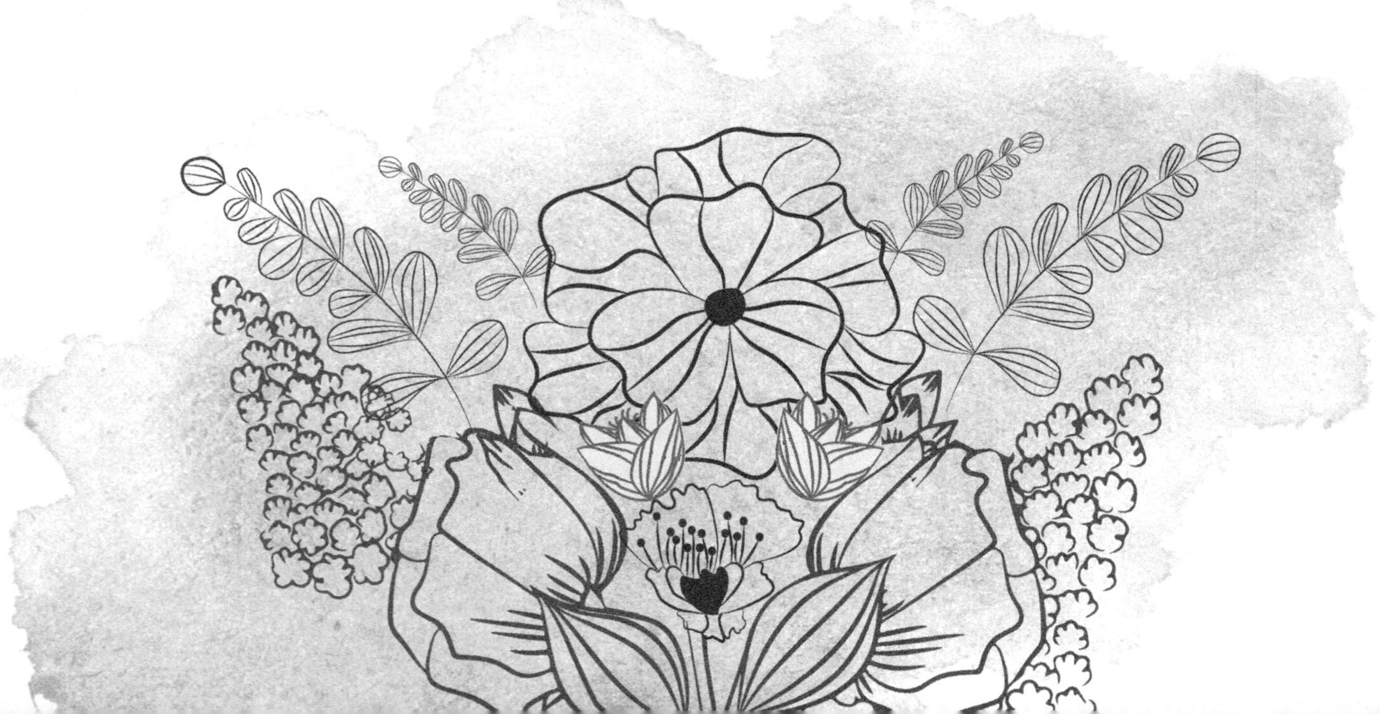

WHITE ON BLACK

This is my favourite technique! I love seeing the white line drawings on black paper. The effect is so dramatic that all you do is switch your black ink for white and your white paper for black.

The only challenging thing in this entire exercise is finding the right white pen for you. I've had good luck with Signo white gel pens; others love the Sakura ones. I suggest you go to your local art store and try a few out before you buy them.

This entire page is an example of how amazing white on black can look!

Another fun way to play with this technique is to add black ink splatters to white cardstock and do black line drawings on the white parts and white line drawings on the black parts.

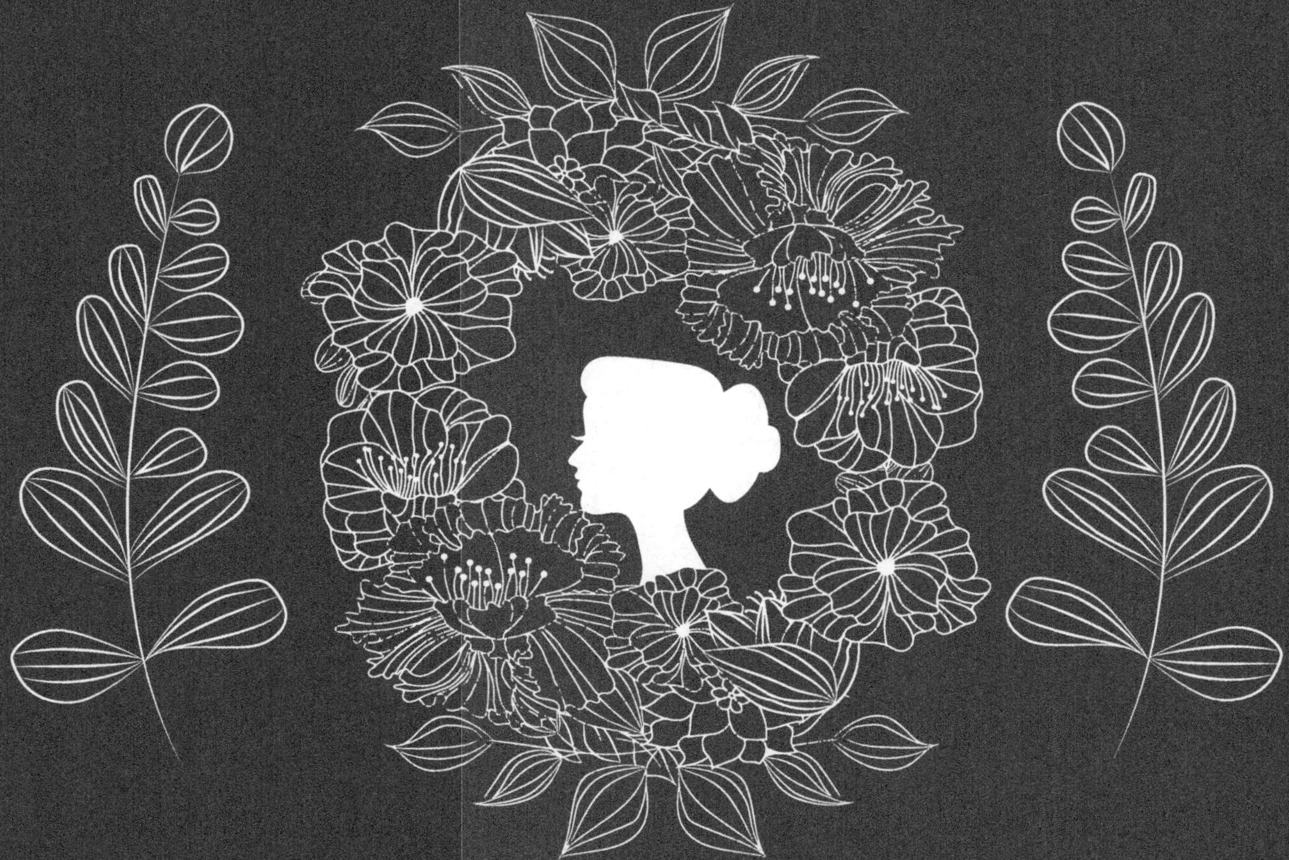

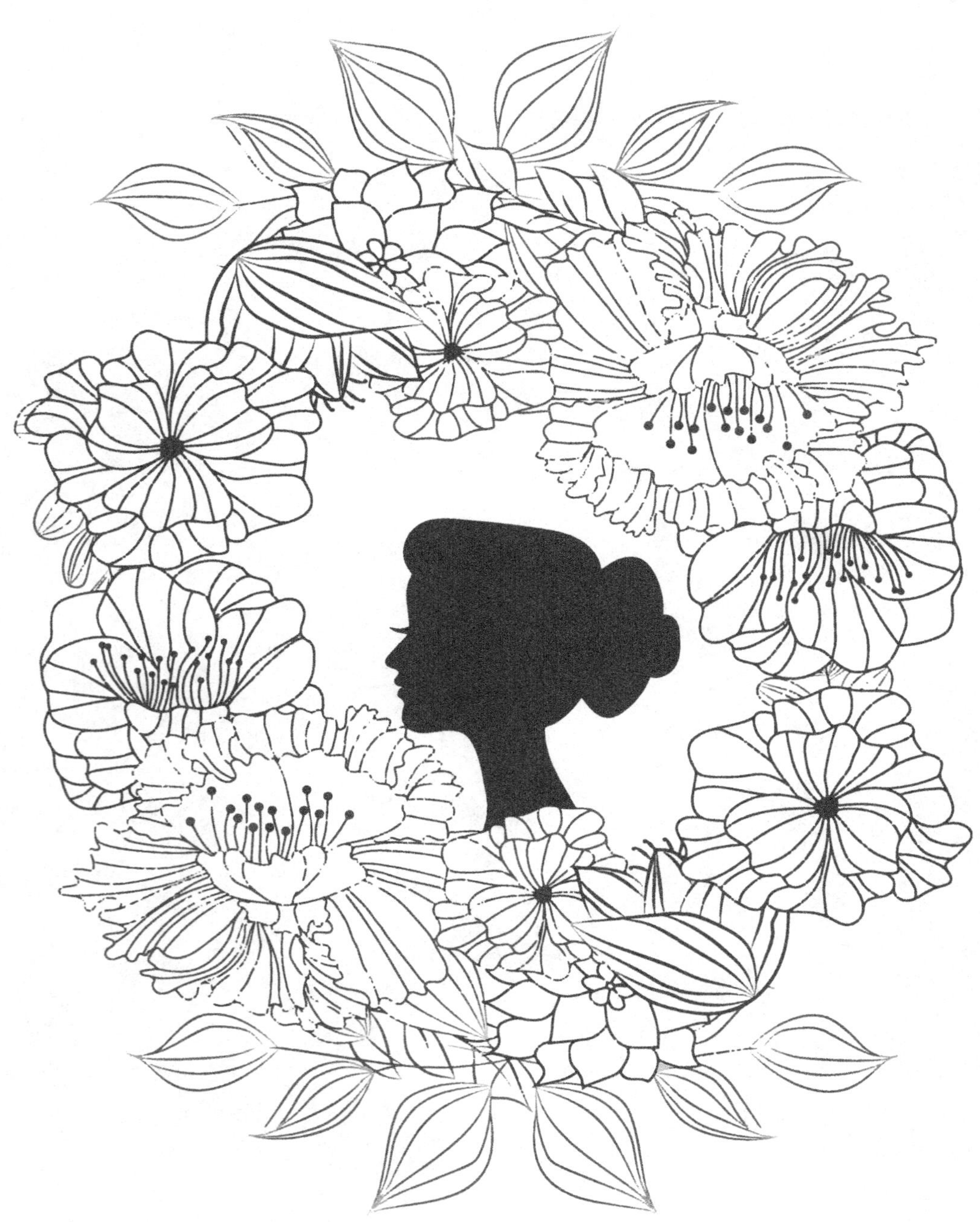

Look at a similar drawing on the page before this one; that was white on black, and this is black on white. Which do you like better?

PUTTING IT ALL TOGETHER

FLOWER BUNCHES

Now that we know how to draw many different botanical elements, we can move on to see some ways in which we can put them together.

Two of my favourite compositions are wreaths and bouquets. I like to do them by hand and digitally. Both ways are a lot of fun.

In digital art, it's easier to manipulate your scanned drawings into various combinations. Most of the bouquets and layout elements in this book were done digitally to ensure high print quality.

But in this section, I will go over how I construct a wreath step by step, and then we will move onto a bouquet in a mason jar.

Hopefully these instructions will give you some information to start with. The rest will come with practice.

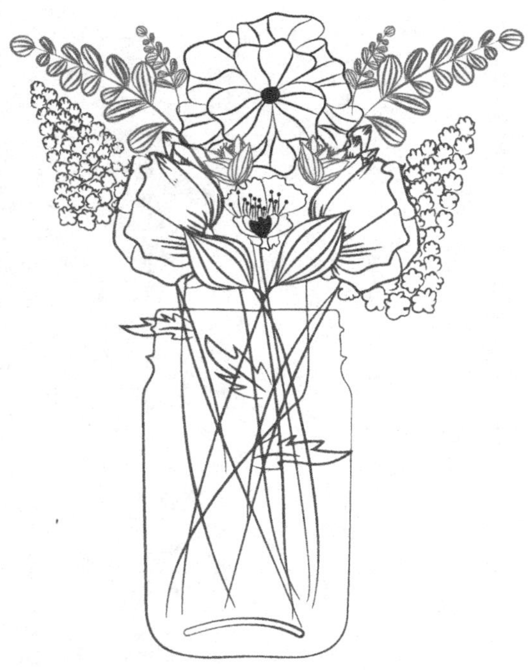

WREATH

Now that we know how to draw many different botanical elements, we can move on to see some ways in which we can put them together.

Two of my favourite compositions are wreaths and bouquets. I like to do them by hand and digitally. Both ways are a lot of fun.

In digital art, it's easier to manipulate your scanned drawings into various combinations. Most of the bouquets and layout elements in this book were done digitally to ensure high print quality.

But in this section, I will go over how I construct a wreath step by step, and then we will move onto a bouquet in a mason jar.

Hopefully these instructions will give you some information to start with. The rest will come with practice.

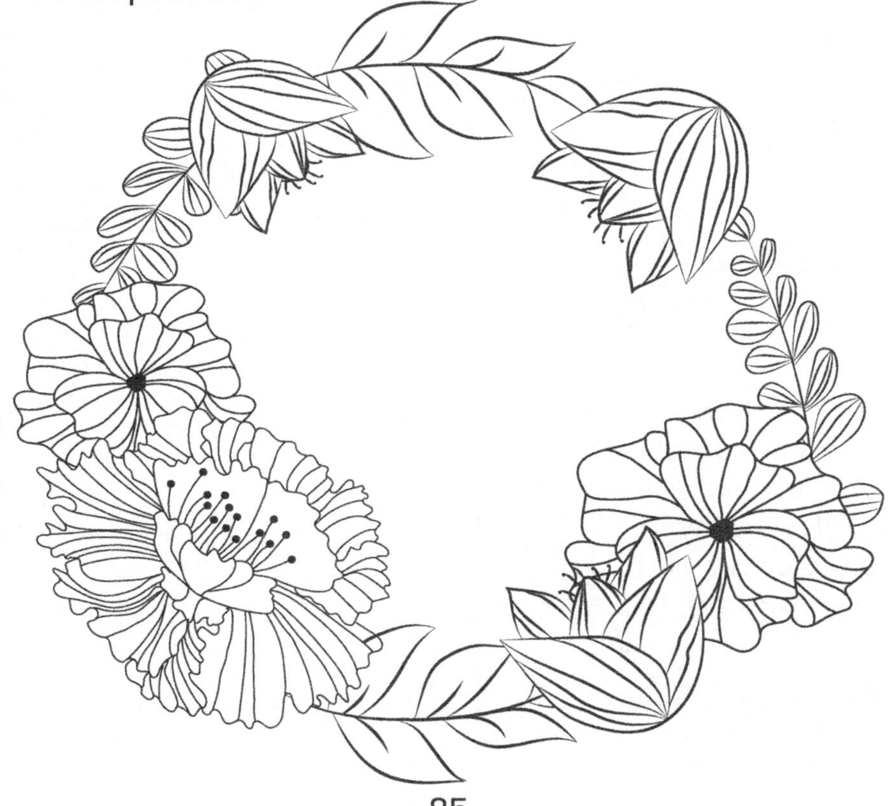

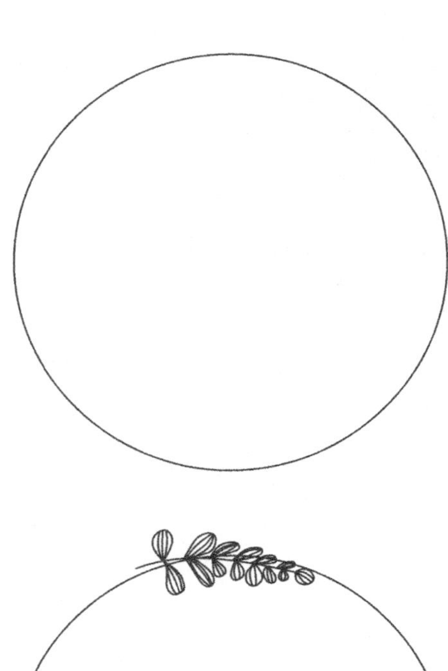

Always start with a basic circle sketched with a pencil on your paper.
This is your guide for the wreath you will create. In the following pages, I will leave the circle sketch in all the steps and remove it from the last step to show you the neatly finished wreath.

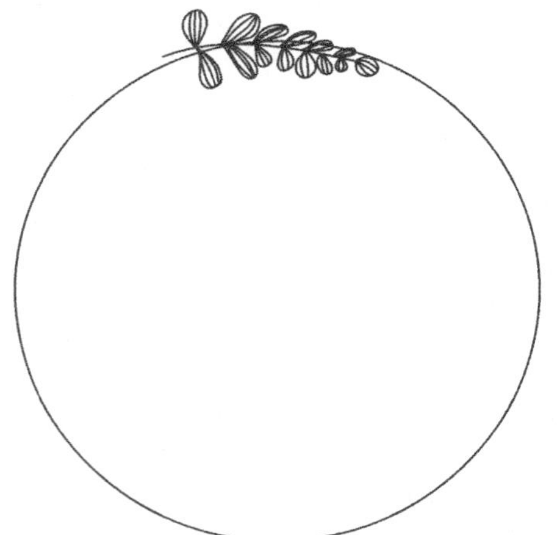

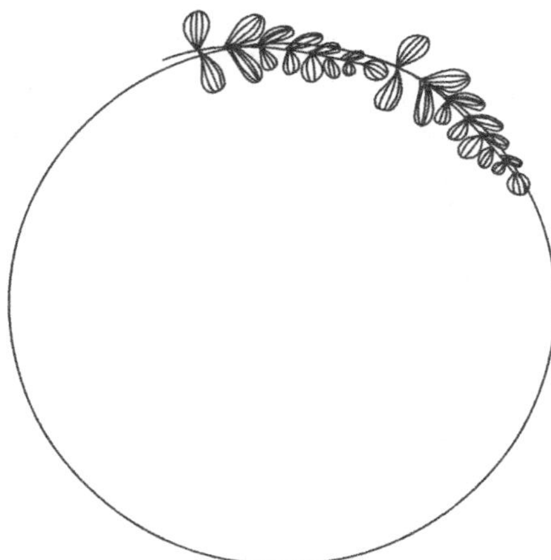

The pencil lines can be erased after you go over your drawing with a fine tip pen. Just make sure the ink is dry and won't smudge. A good eraser is a great tool to have!

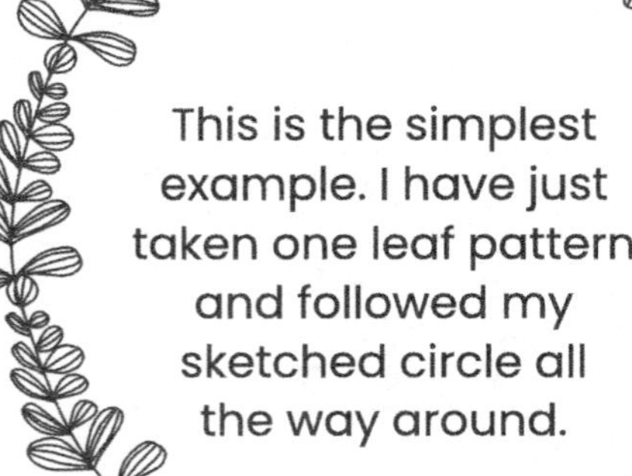

This is the simplest example. I have just taken one leaf pattern and followed my sketched circle all the way around.

Try it here

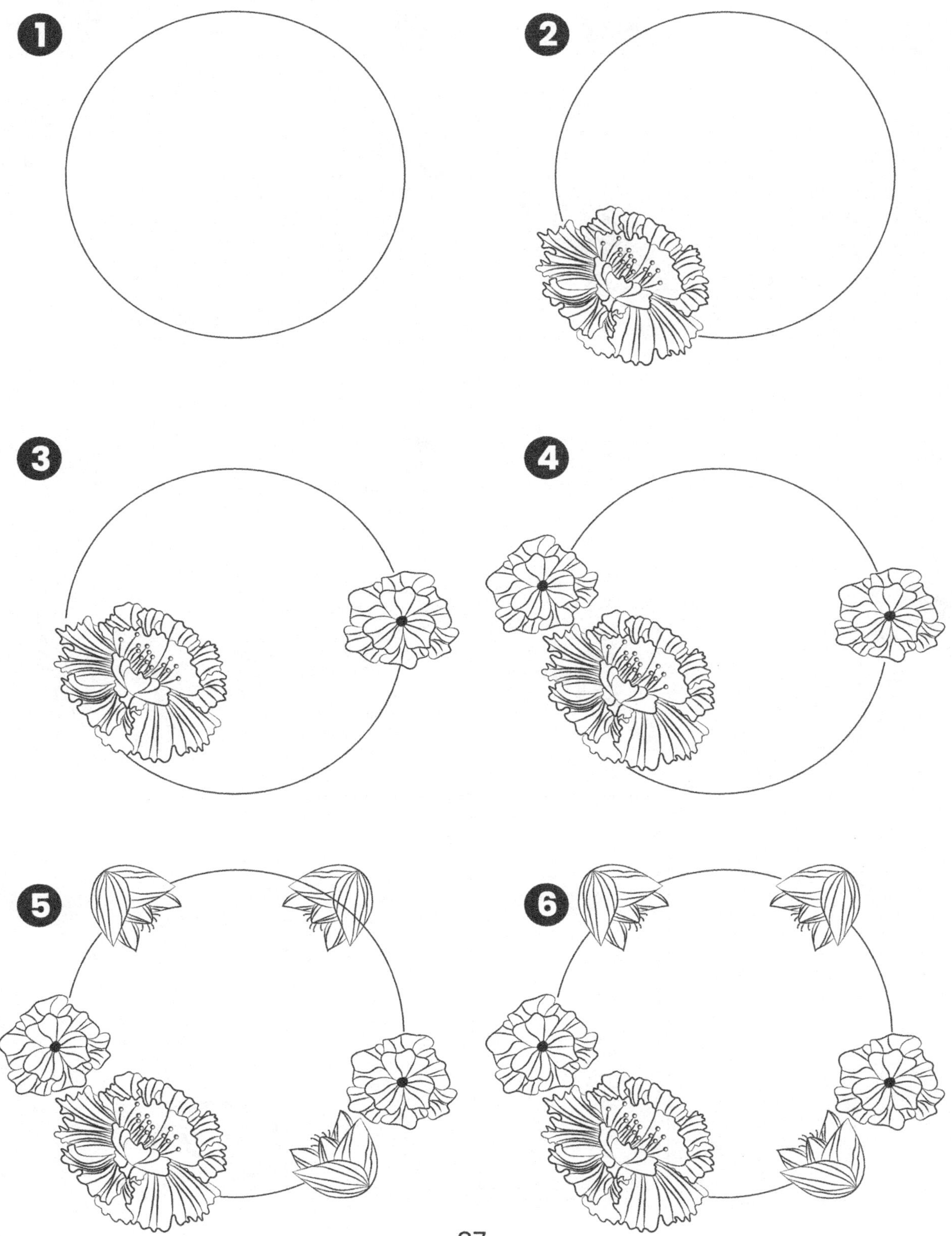
1
2
3
4
5
6

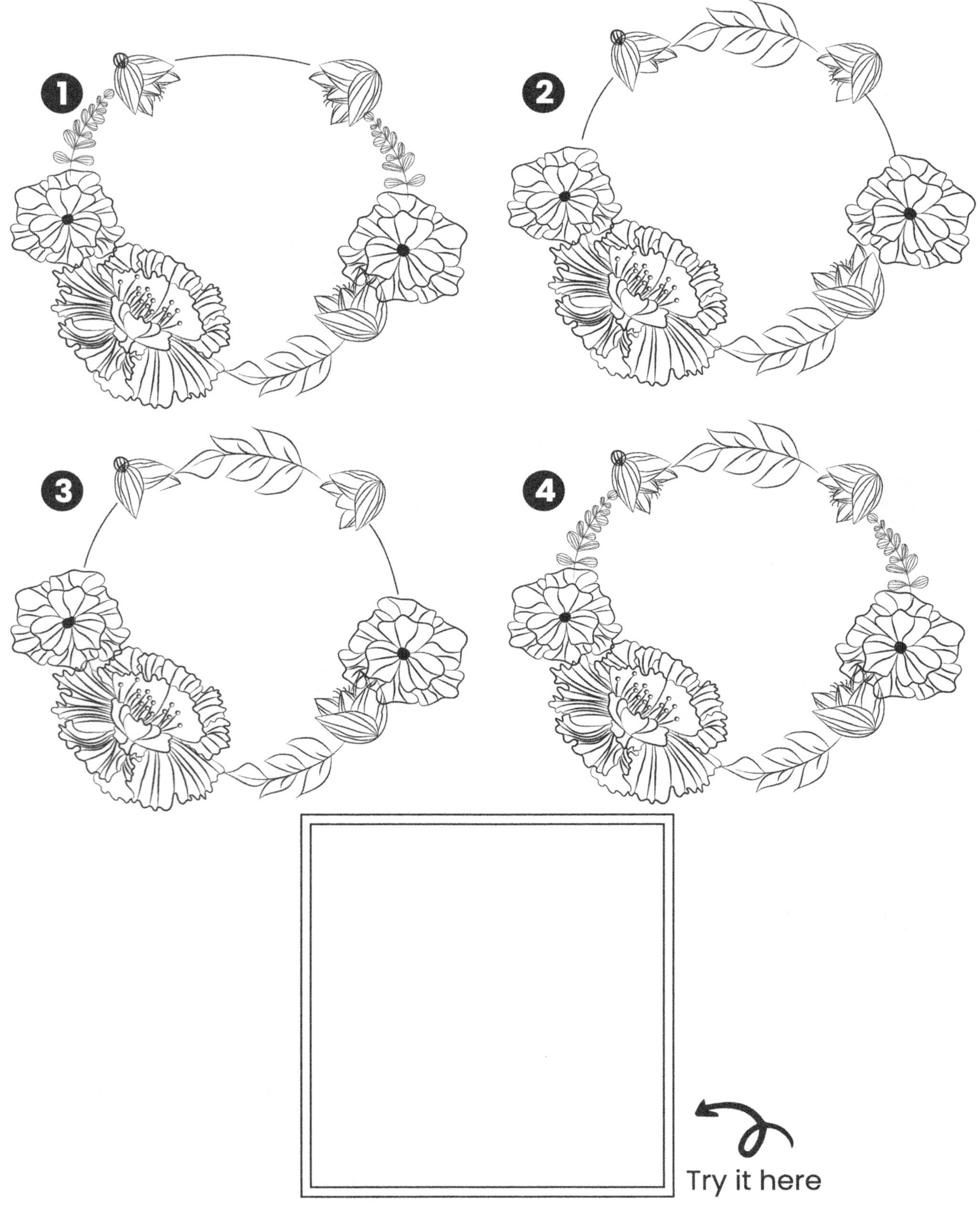
1
2
3
4
Try it here

1

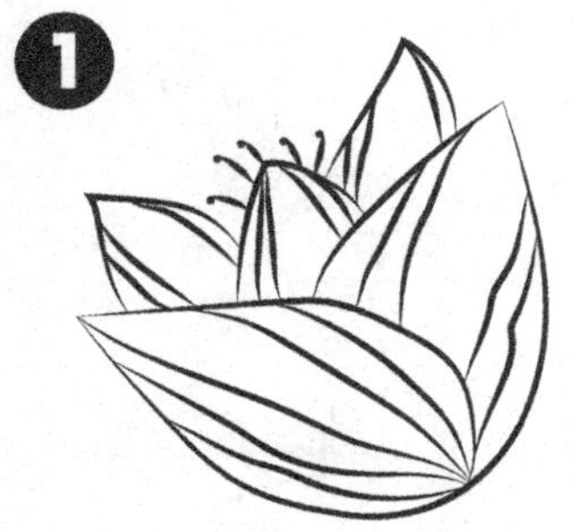

2

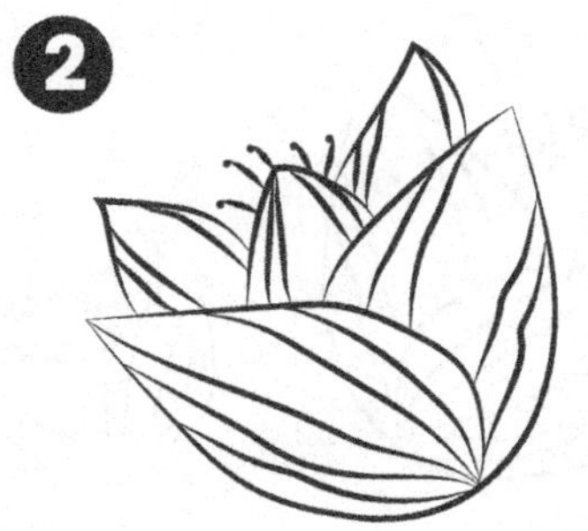

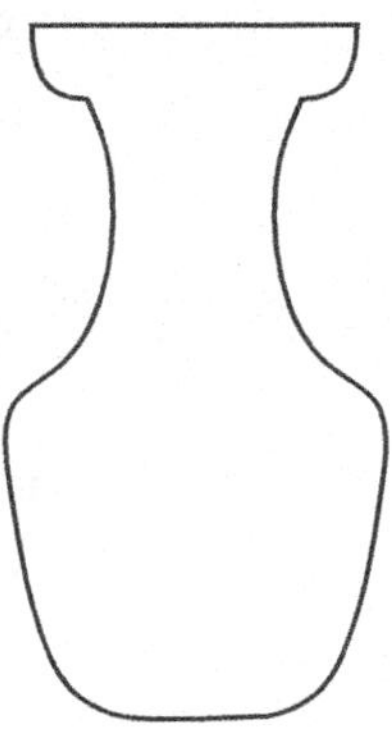

3

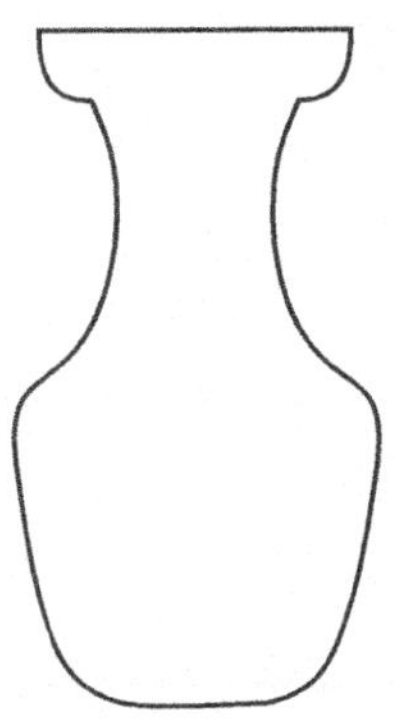

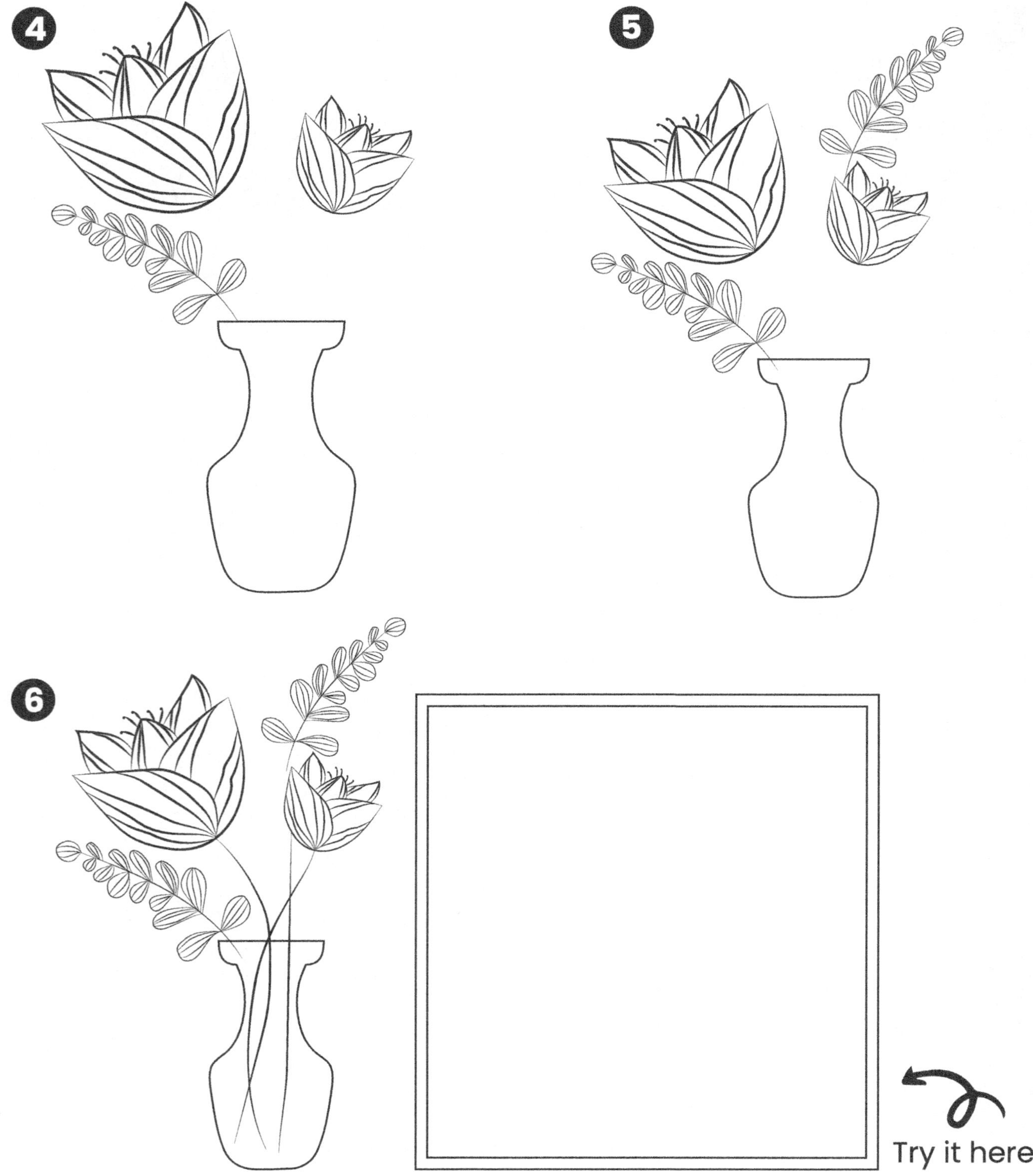
4
5
6
Try it here

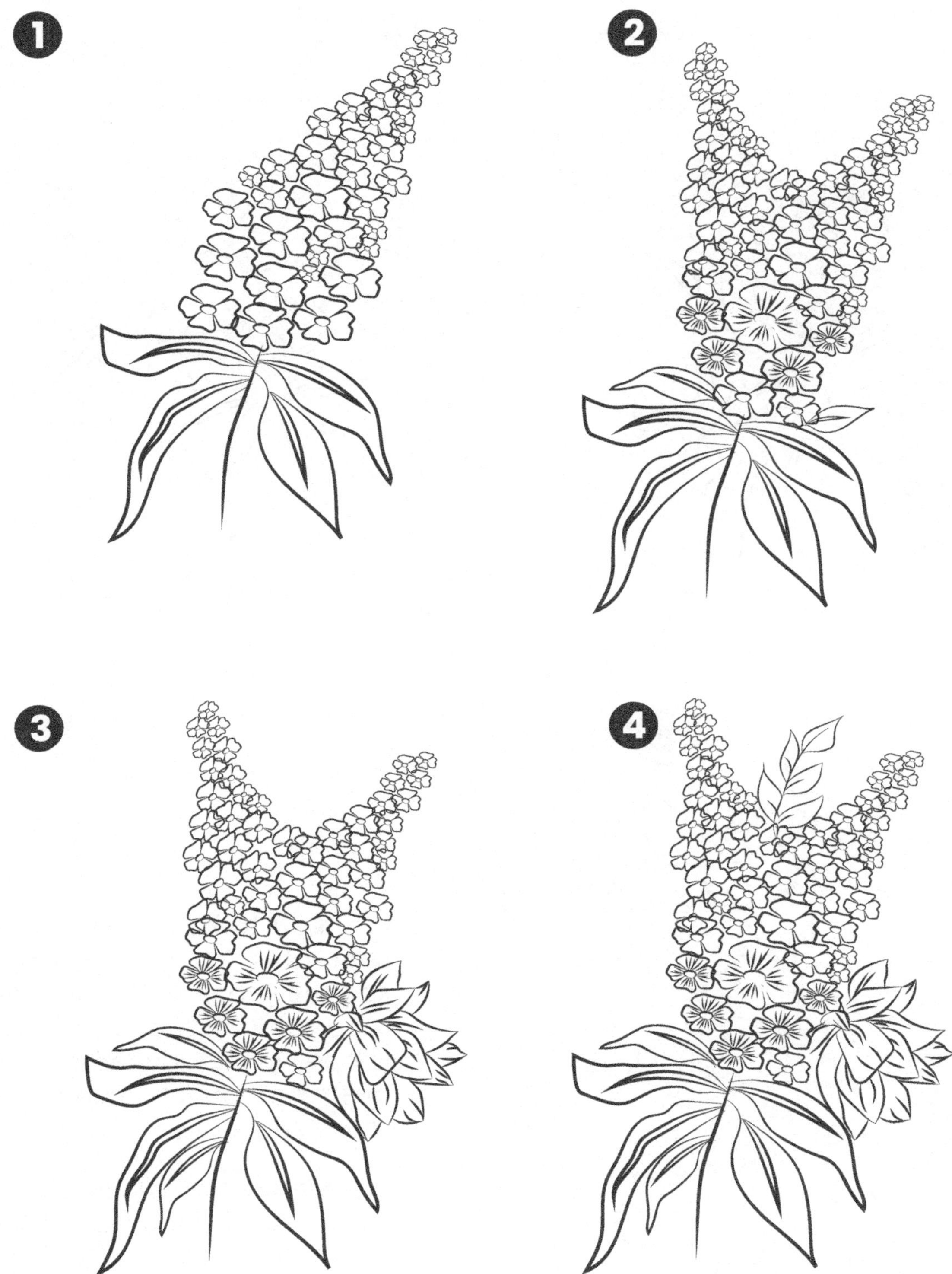
1
2
3
4

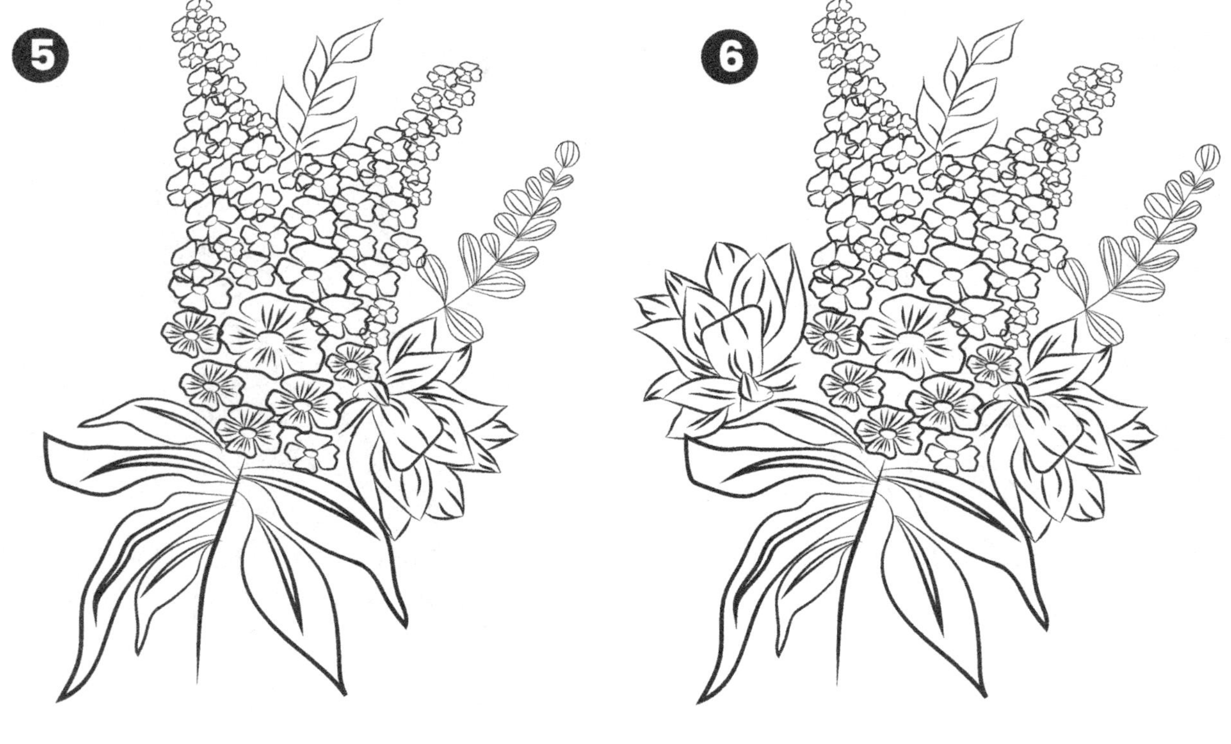

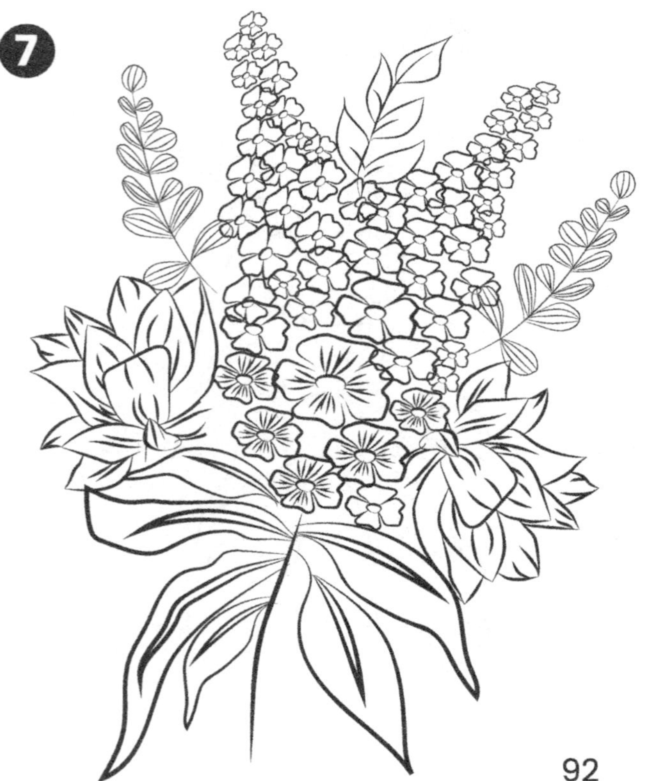

I've tried to add each flower separately so that you can see the process. This is a bit hard to do in a book, and so I hope you'll study these bouquets and bunches and then make some of your own.

I can leave this bunch the way it is or position it over a mason jar and add some lines showing the stems going down.

Drawing is an escape from all the unnecessary things in life that get in the way of being free.

Jamie Hewlett

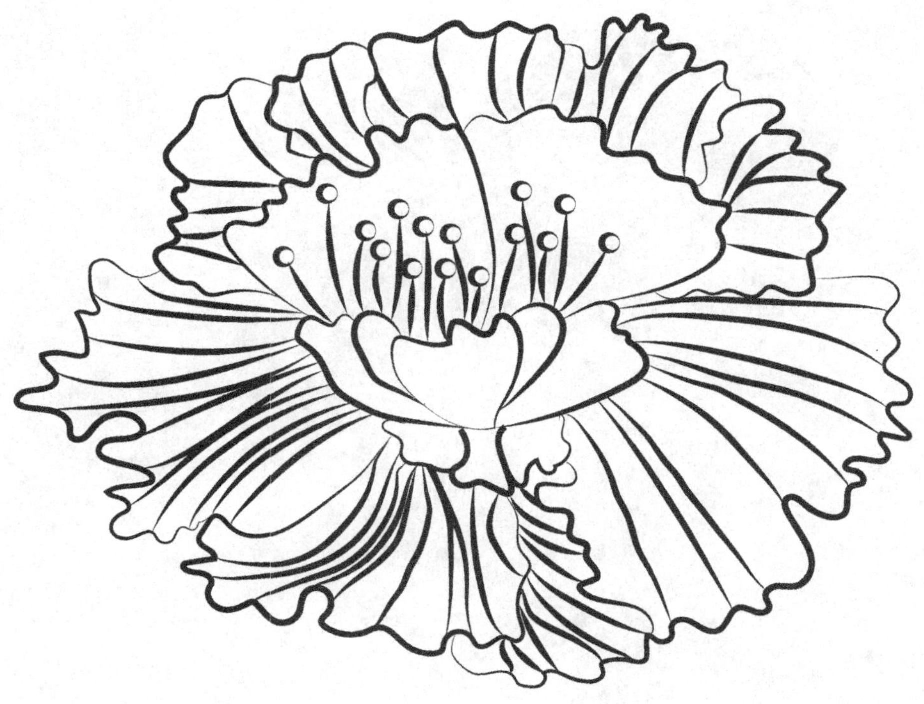

PROJECT IDEAS

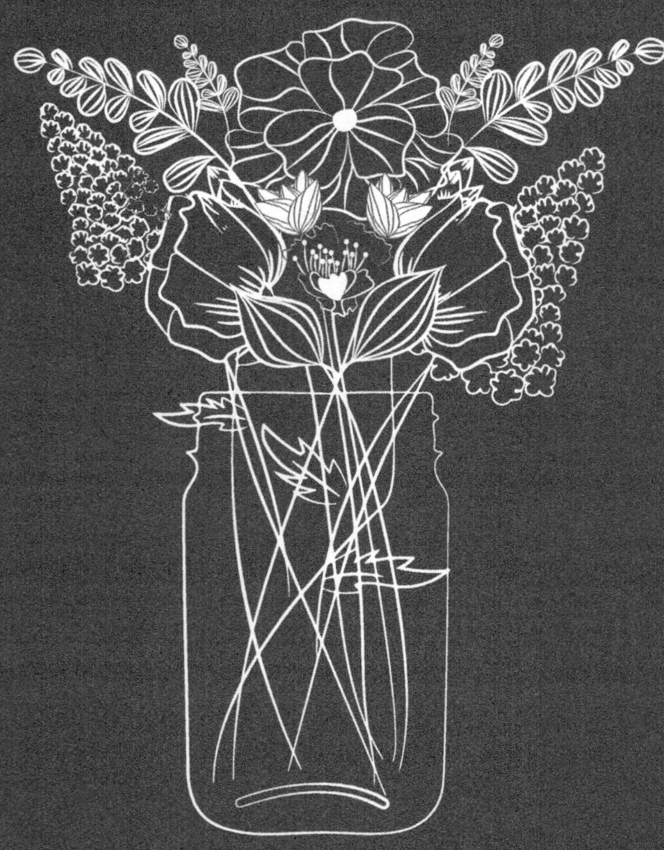

She turned her Can'ts into Cans and her Dreams into Plans.

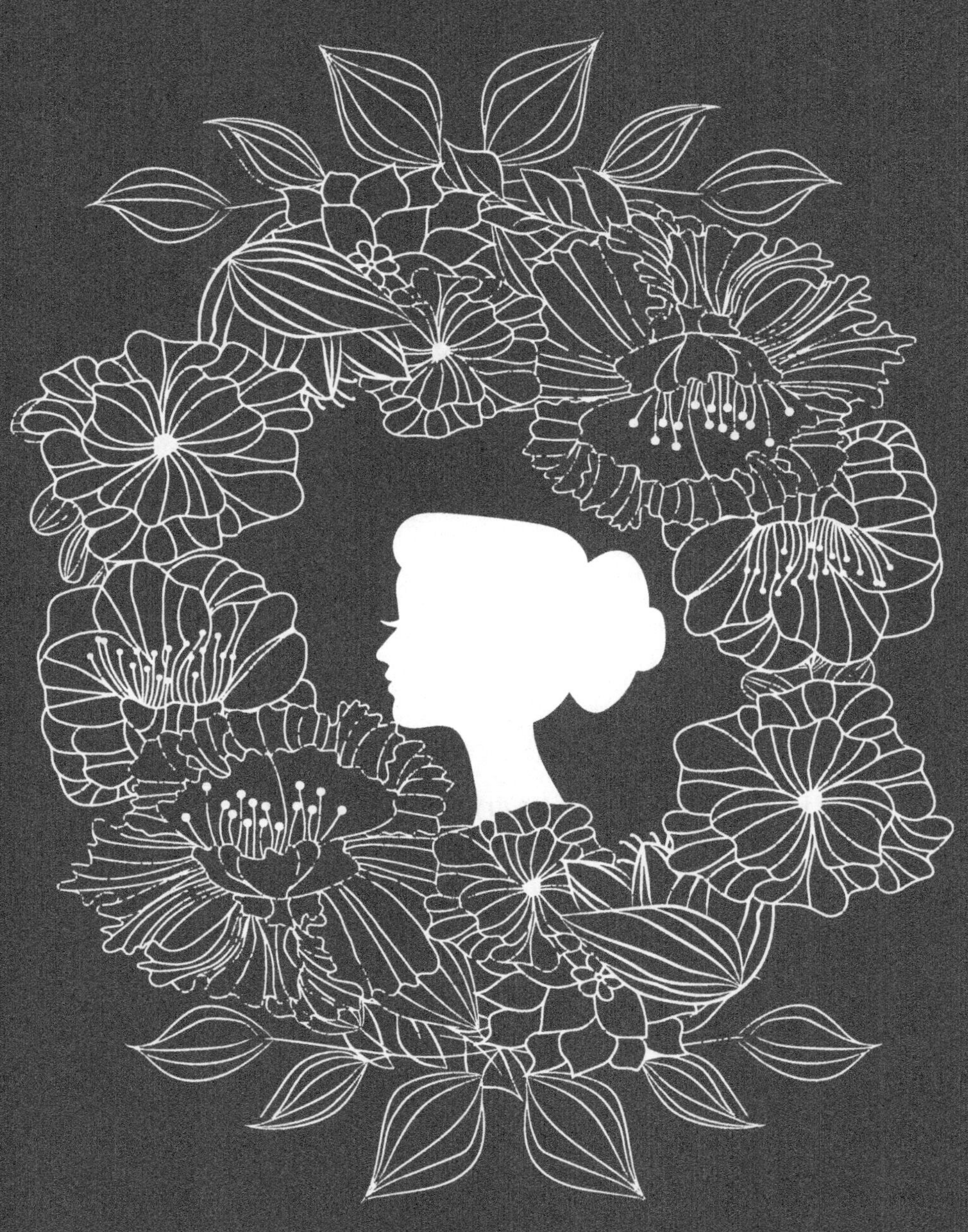

PROJECT IDEAS

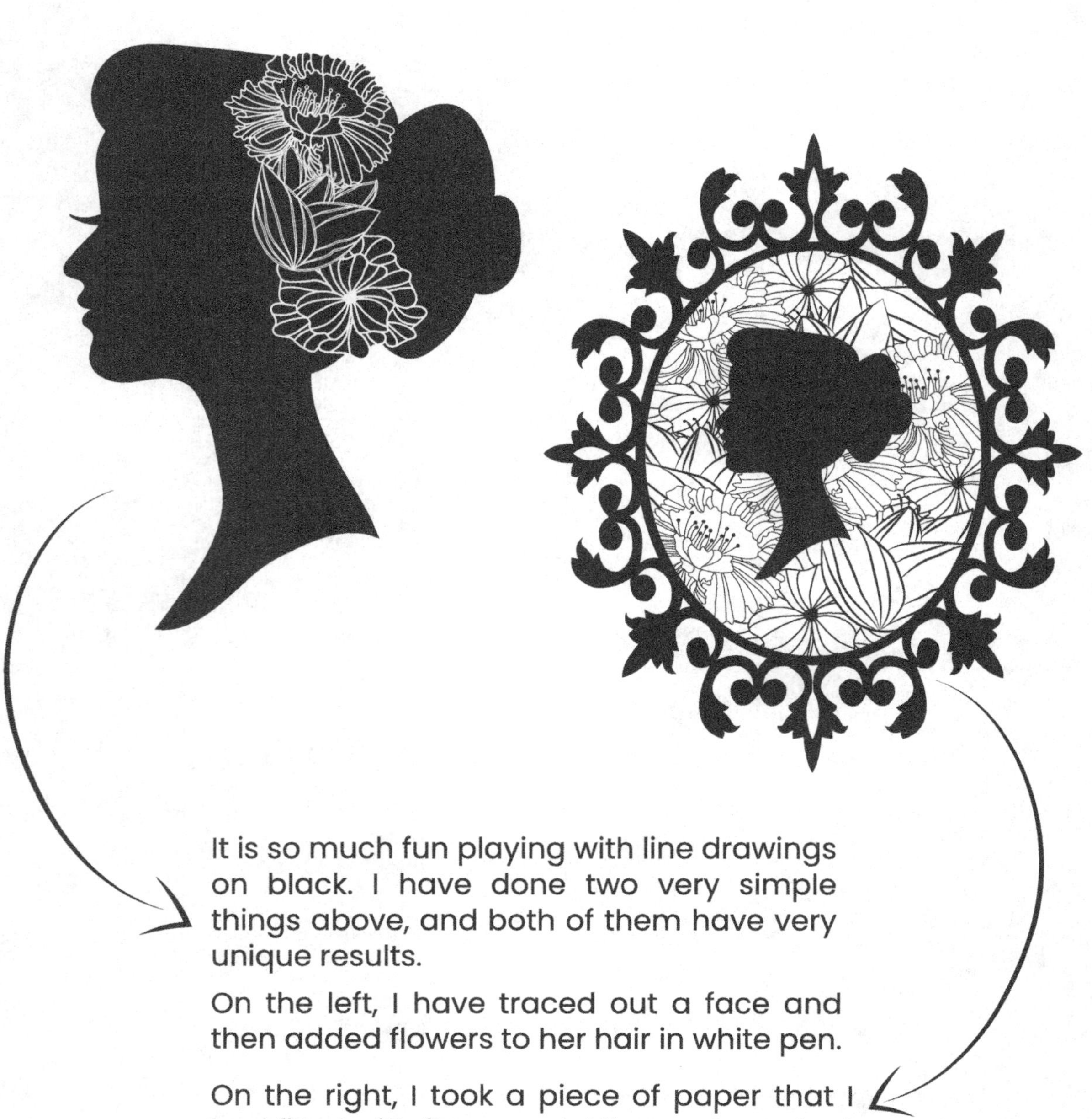

It is so much fun playing with line drawings on black. I have done two very simple things above, and both of them have very unique results.

On the left, I have traced out a face and then added flowers to her hair in white pen.

On the right, I took a piece of paper that I had filled with flowers and then put a cutout on top and added a frame around it.

Use your line drawings to add the wow factor to your planner spreads.

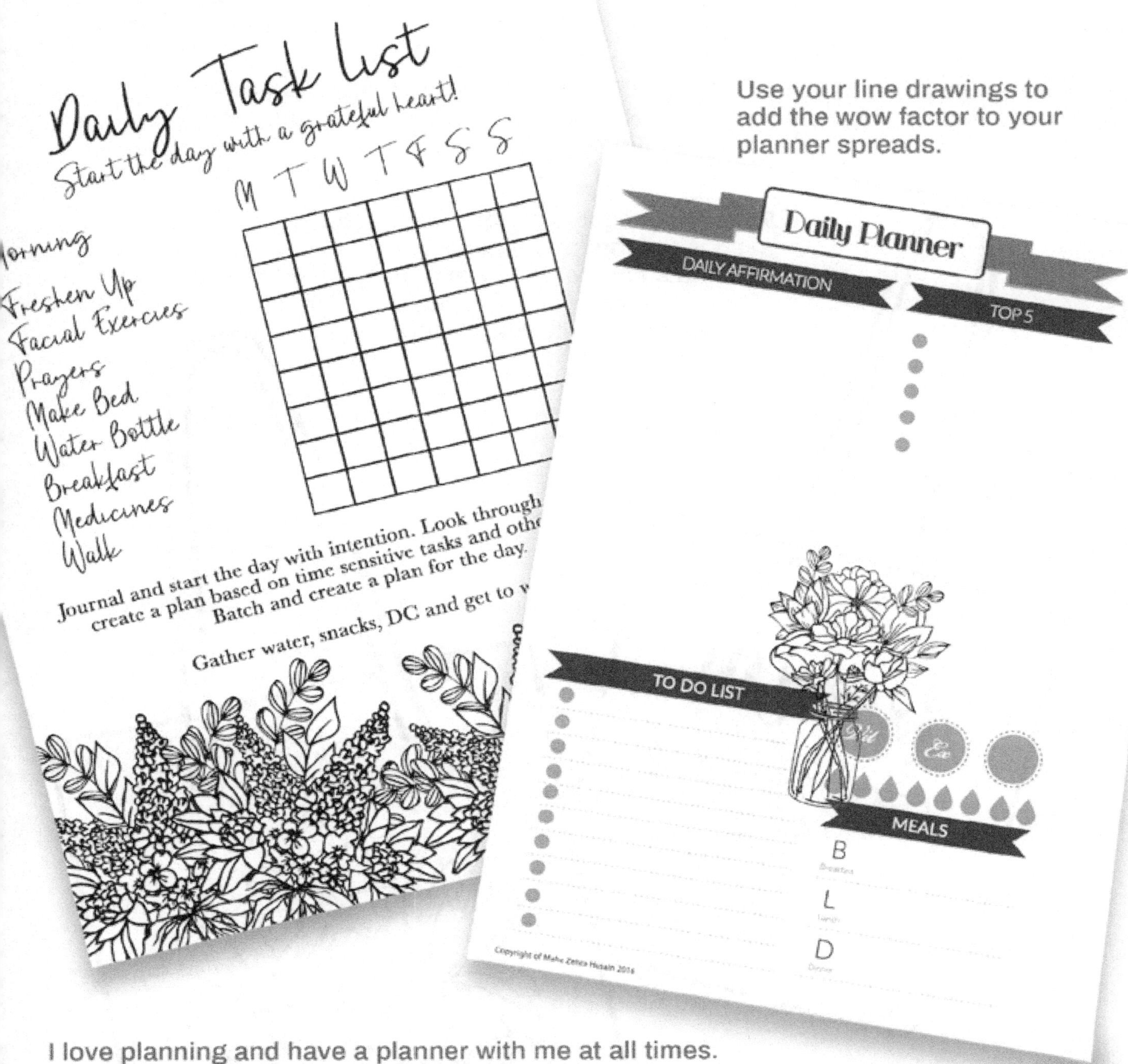

I love planning and have a planner with me at all times. That is the only way I can keep my life organized.

The two images you see on this page are actual planner layouts I have designed and use on a daily basis. Often, I turn my drawings into scanned digital images so that I can create something that can be replicated.

But in my bullet journal, I stick to my drawings. It has such a calming effect on me to draw while I am thinking of things I want to write.

Another project I love to do, especially with the kids in my life, is create tote bags. We are really trying as a family to reduce the amount of waste and packaging we use, so these tote bags are very handy for short market runs.

Plain canvas totes are available at most craft stores. All you need is the tote and a good-quality black fabric marker. Try and find a couple of different markers with varying line widths. You can make the outlines with a heavier line weight and the details with the fine marker.

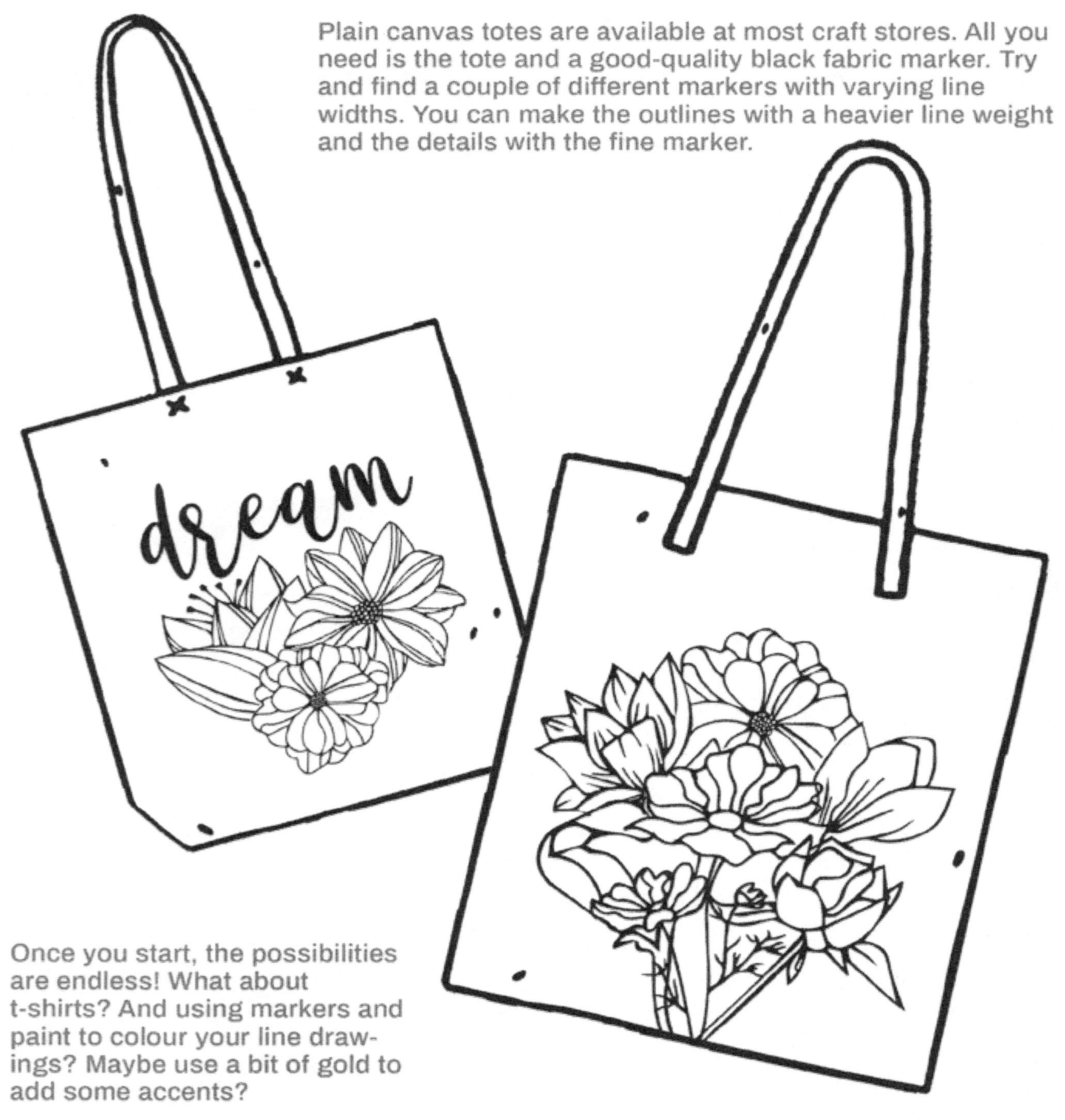

Once you start, the possibilities are endless! What about t-shirts? And using markers and paint to colour your line drawings? Maybe use a bit of gold to add some accents?

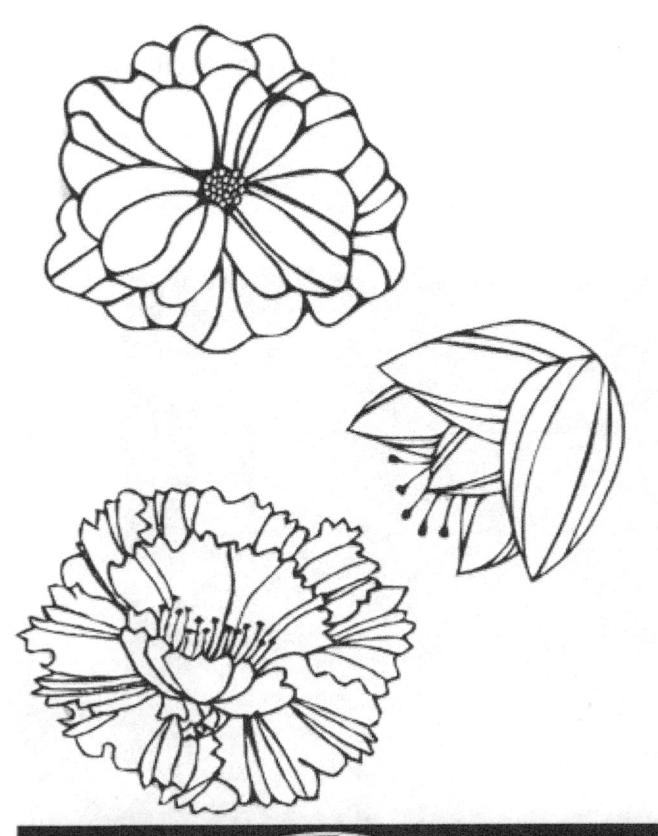

You can use your practise drawings in a really fun way.

Cut them up, leaving a little bit of a white border around them, and use them as embellishments for cards and crafts. journals, covers, and much more!

You can cut out a few and keep them handy; pull them out when you want to do some colouring to de-stress. Voila! You have handmade coloured embellishments.

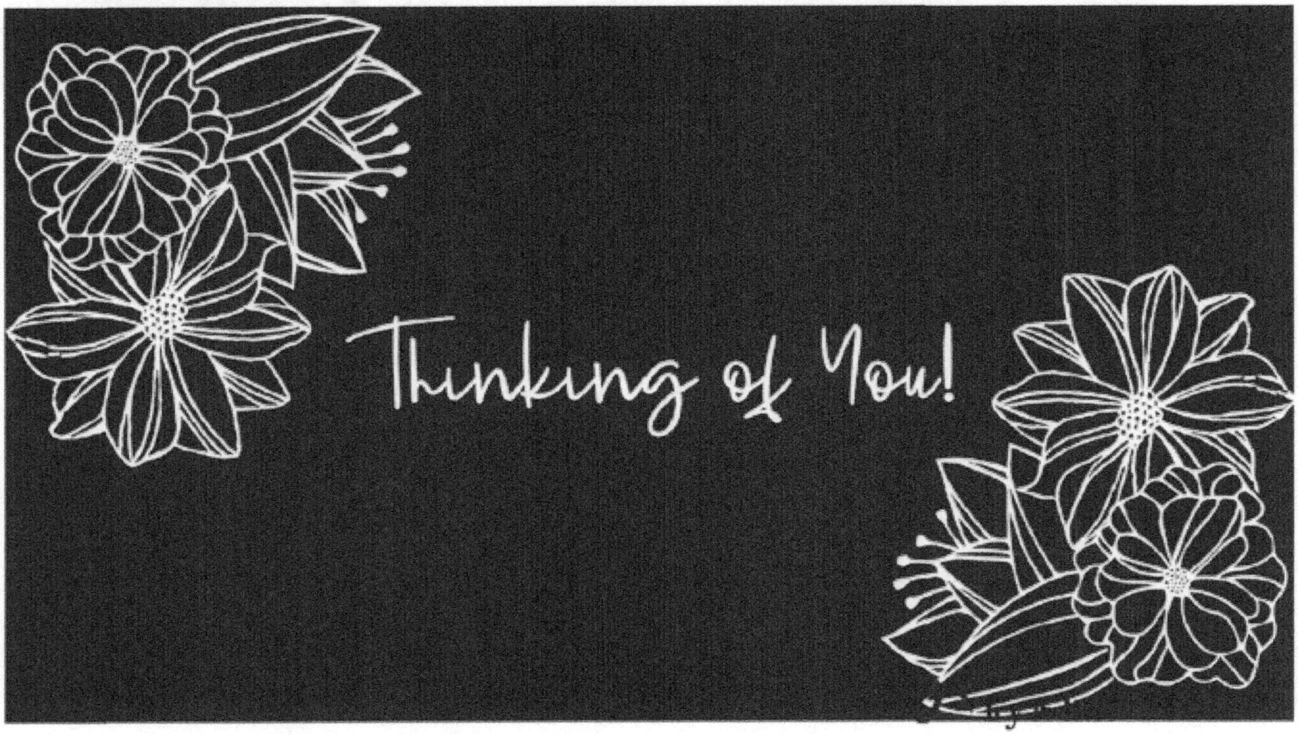

Thinking of You!

Black and white pictures make an amazing canvas for white botanical line drawings!

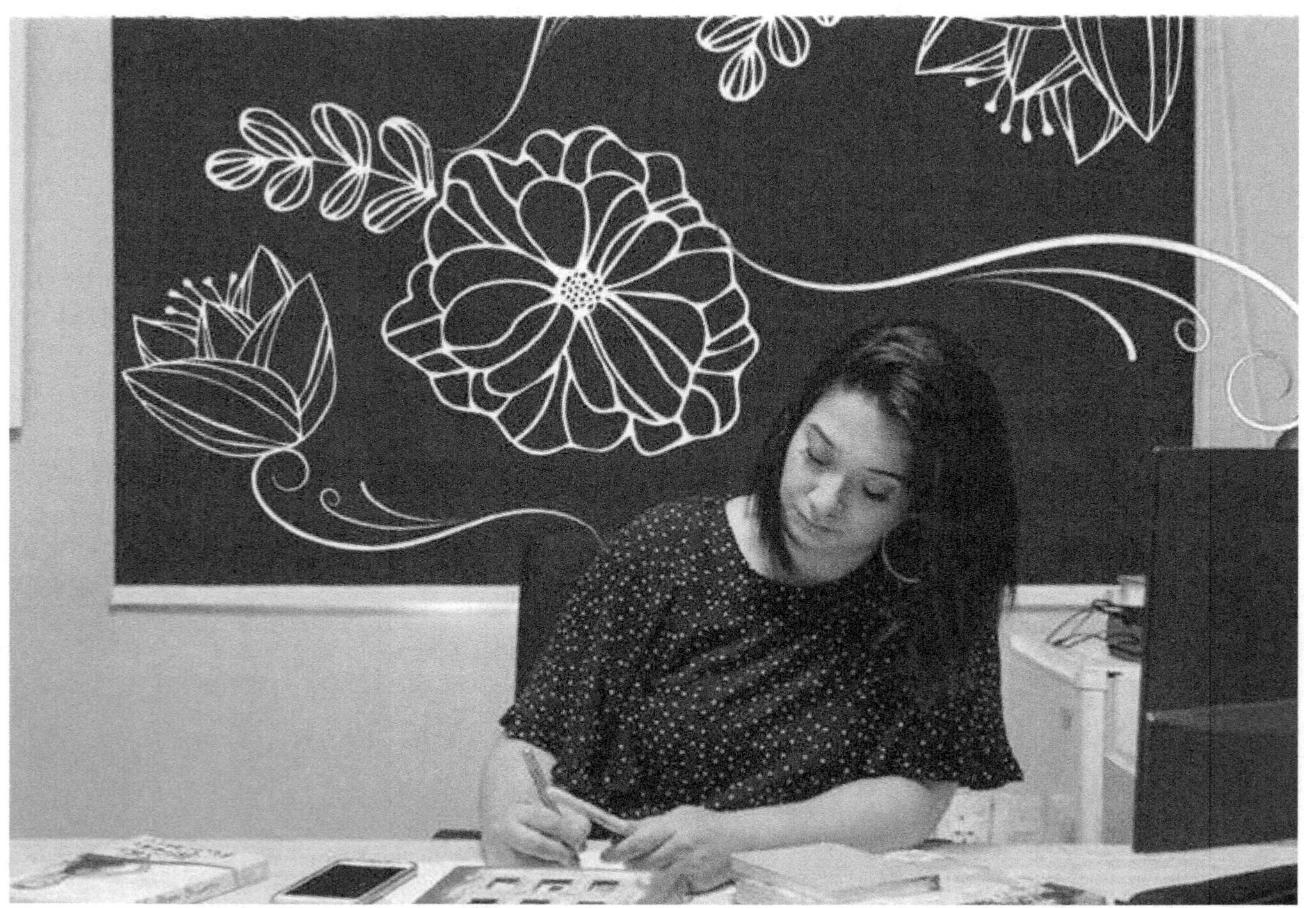

I like using my photographs in art journals and planners. I don't like them living just on my phone. I like to have them in book form so I can flip through them and relive beautiful moments.

Another way in which I have been using my line-drawing skills is to add some life and movement to black-and-white photographs. Images with large areas of black like the one above are the best.

You can use a white paint pen to try this technique and see if you like the way it looks!

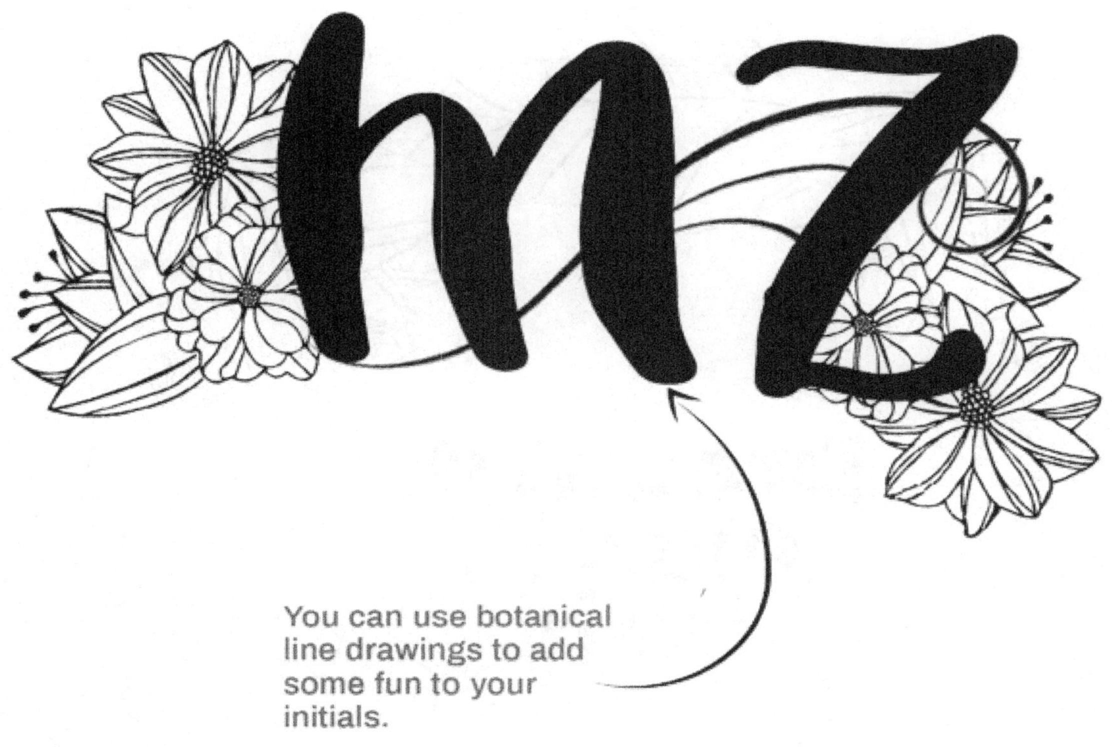

You can use botanical line drawings to add some fun to your initials.

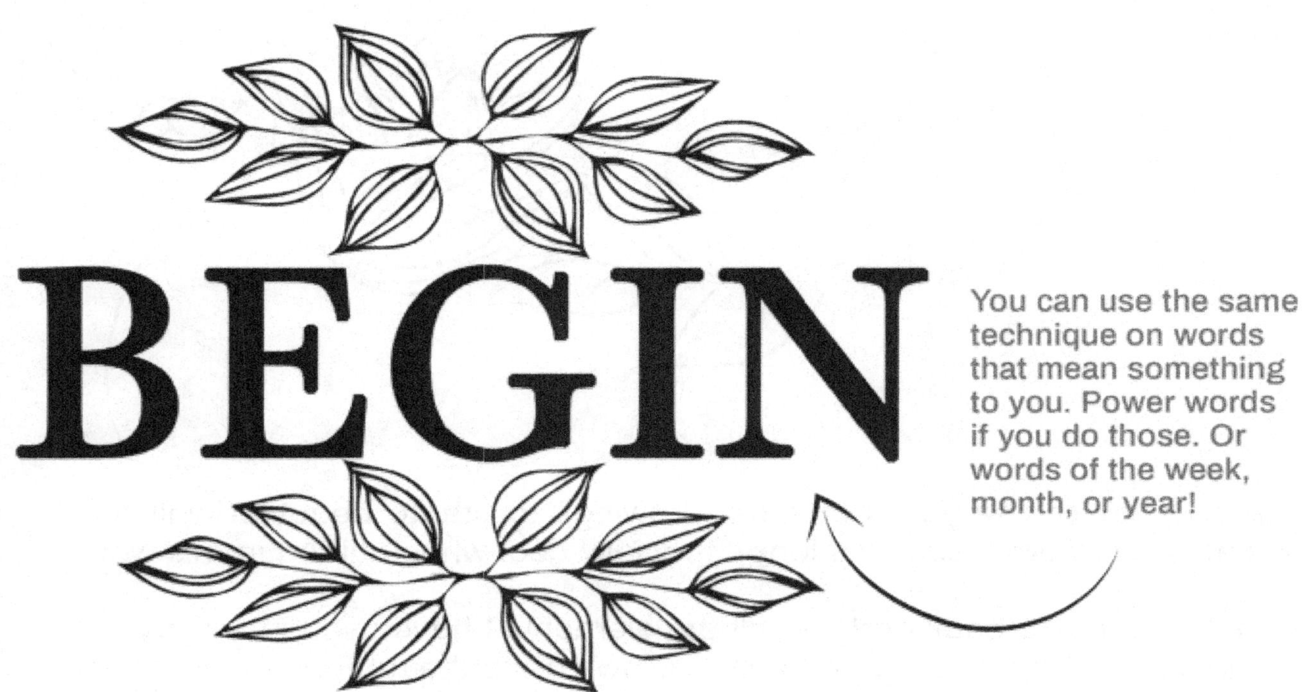

You can use the same technique on words that mean something to you. Power words if you do those. Or words of the week, month, or year!

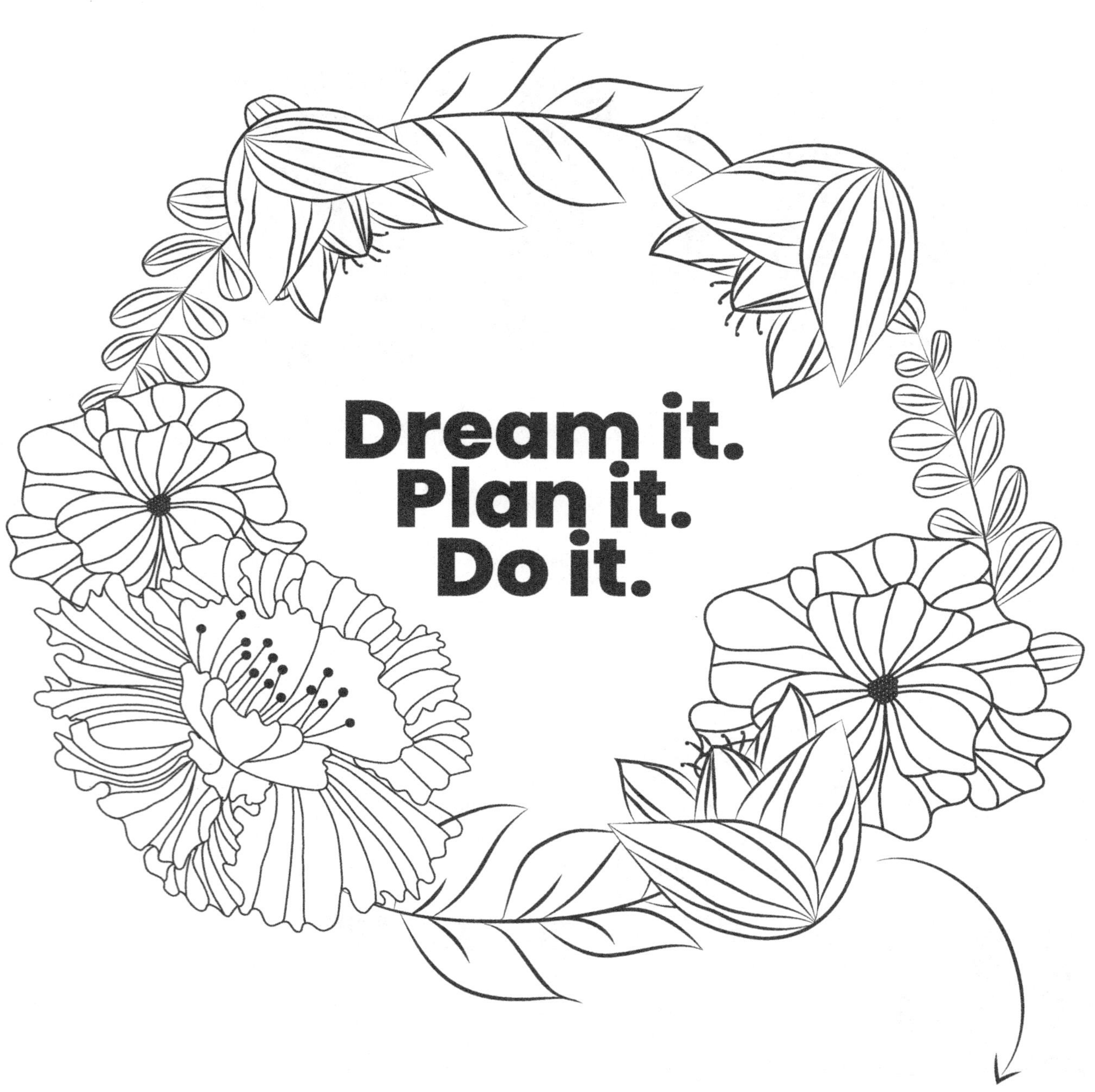

It is so easy to use your botanical drawings to create beautiful wall art. Wreaths and flower bunches look especially cool when utilized in this way.

Look through this book and see all the elements I have used in the layout of the book. All of these elements were drawn using the tutorials in this book.

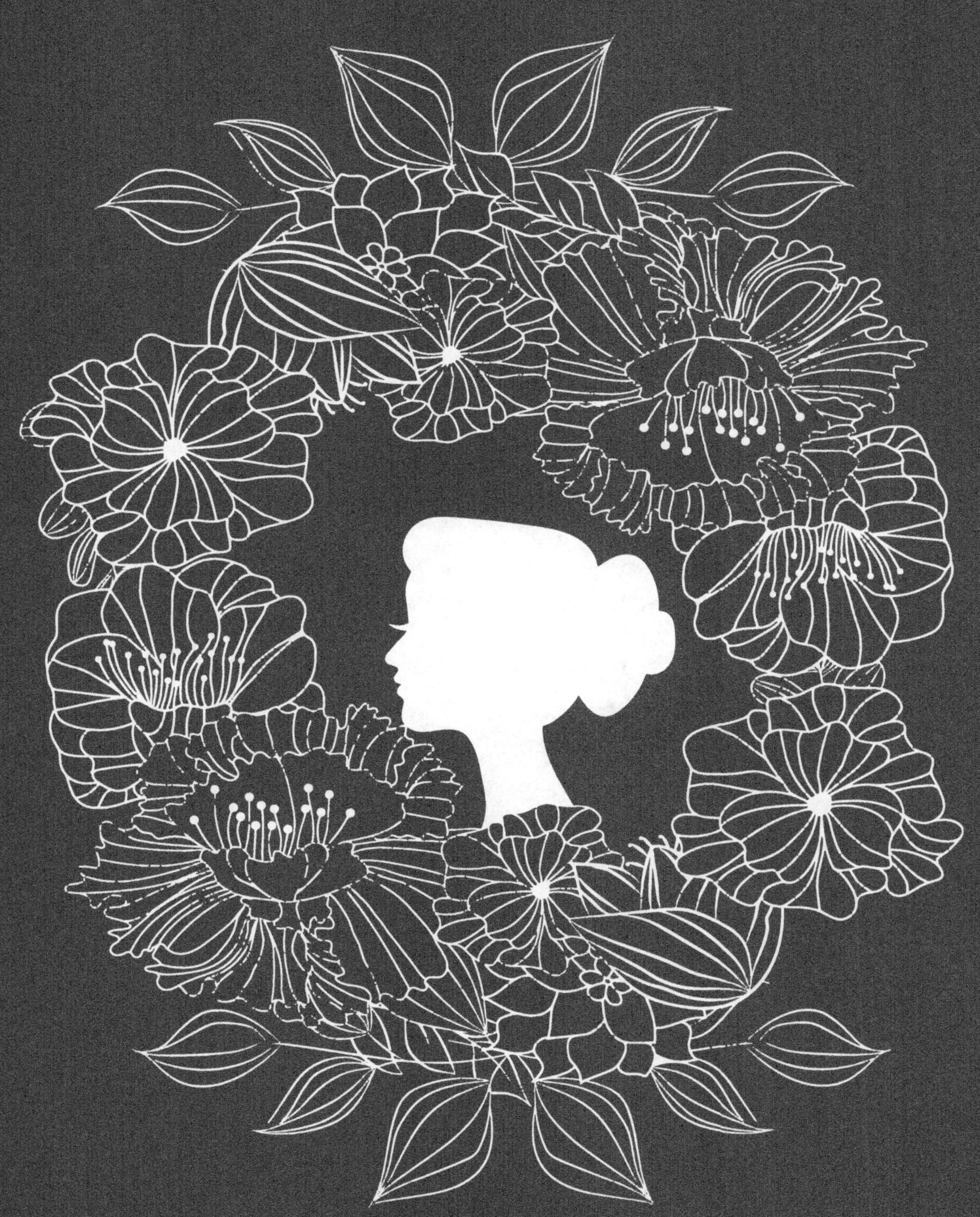

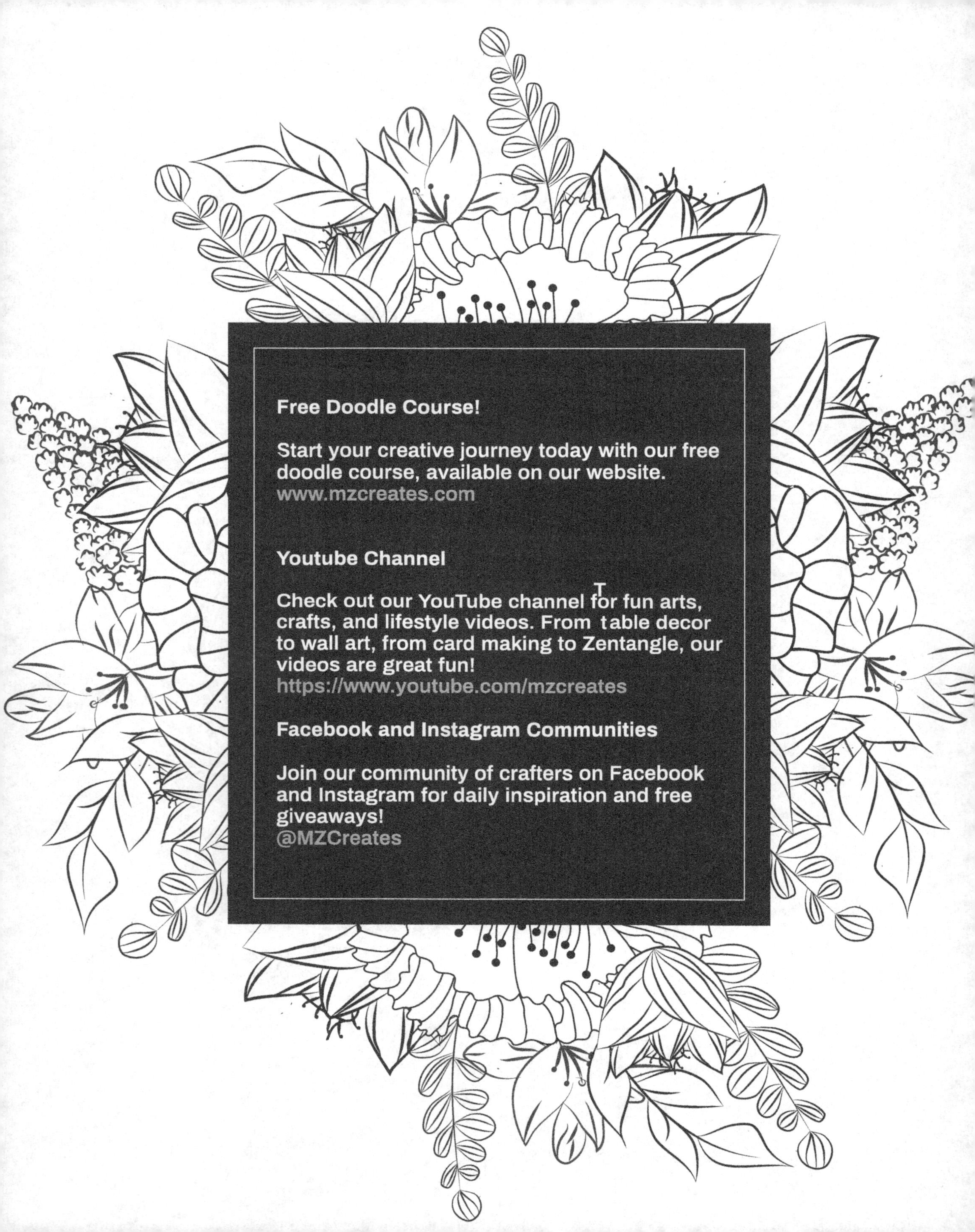
Free Doodle Course!
Start your creative journey today with our free doodle course, available on our website.
www.mzcreates.com
Youtube Channel
Check out our YouTube channel for fun arts, crafts, and lifestyle videos. From table decor to wall art, from card making to Zentangle, our videos are great fun!
https://www.youtube.com/mzcreates
Facebook and Instagram Communities
Join our community of crafters on Facebook and Instagram for daily inspiration and free giveaways!
@MZCreates

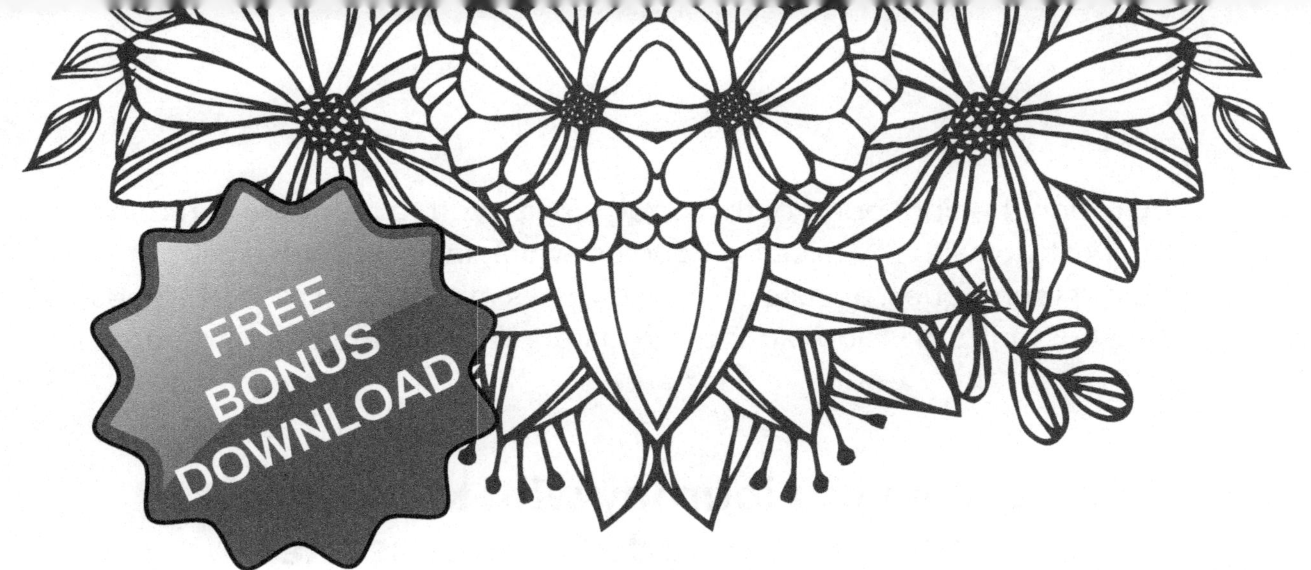

Discover a blooming surprise!

Delve deeper into the enchanting world of flowers with our exclusive bonus content. Downloadable and printable pages include additional floral line drawings, innovative project ideas, and captivating coloring pages.

To download follow this link:

https://mzcreates.com/botanical-line-drawing-bonus-pages/

Enter your email and recieve the download link!

As you reach the final page of this book, I invite you to continue exploring your creativity with my exciting courses, which include Zentangle®, Art Journaling techniques, transforming old books into altered masterpieces, crafting customized vision planners, mastering lettering skills, and much more!

Continue your journey with MZCreates, just scan the QR code to access these exciting courses to keep the spark going.

As a token of appreciation, my readers will get a special discount!

Scan QR Code and enter **Promo Code** for exclusive **40% off**

Planner Bootcamp:	RAKSS7B
Vision Planner:	8RQMCYY
Lettering Class:	SA4TASE

So don't stop here.
Let's keep creating together!

Hugs,
MZ

If you enjoyed this book please consider leaving a review on amazon. That helps us to bring you more drawing and art books.

If you have any questions, concerns or comments please reach out to us via ***www.mzcreates.com*** and we'll get back to you ASAP.

Search for **MZ Creates** on **amazon** for more fun, creative books and activity books!

ABOUT MZ CREATES

Ever since I can remember, I've been obsessed with numbers and creating. It could be any kind of project—beading, stitching, papercrafts, painting—it really didn't matter. I would take to any new craft like a fish to water. The same was true for anything related to mathematics and numbers. I spent hours on end listening to music and making my way through numerous math problems.
This is the way I've always been; I know of no other way to be, and I don't think I could change.
As time passed, I got my graduate degrees in mathematics and operations research, but at the same time, I started a creative blog and wrote several books for the Amazon Kindle. These books ranged from cardmaking to mixed media and more.

Today, when I would like to place myself in a neat little box and write a simple paragraph 'about me," I'm getting stuck. I can't define myself as just an artist or just a mathematician; I've always been both and feel life without one would be quite dull.

So now I run a software company and my creative blog. I'm a multi-passionate entrepreneur with an education in mathematics and a passion to create. I love pretty things, beautiful spaces, happy colors, and elegant proofs. I hope you'll join me on my journey as I DIY my way through this precious and beautiful thing called life!

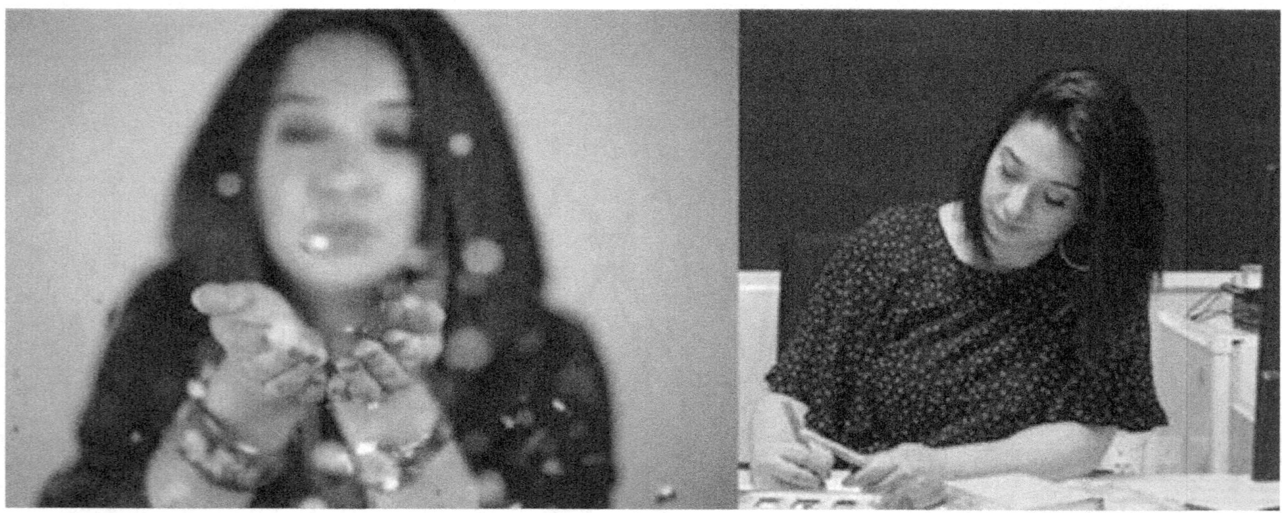

On my blog, I stick to the workings of my right brain. All my creative DIYs, product reviews, book crushes, and travel diaries are hosted there.

I love to create all sorts of things, so you will find art journaling, mixed media, Zentangle® (I am a Certified Zentangle Teacher), drawing, watercolor tutorials, and DIYs here. I love hosting fun parties with beautiful tablescapes, decor, and fun and yummy eats. I also enjoy creating beautiful spaces. I feel that if we are in a happy environment, we tend to be our best selves, and so you will find some home decor tips and DIYs here as well.

Most of all, though, I just love sharing the joy of creating something beautiful on a budget—yes, I am super conscious of the budget aspect—and I hope you'll enjoy your visit with me!

If you're looking for a place to start, maybe you would like to: Try my Free Zentangle® Art Class series on my blog.
Check out my YouTube videos: MZ Creates
Follow me on Instagram @mzcreates

Love,
MZ

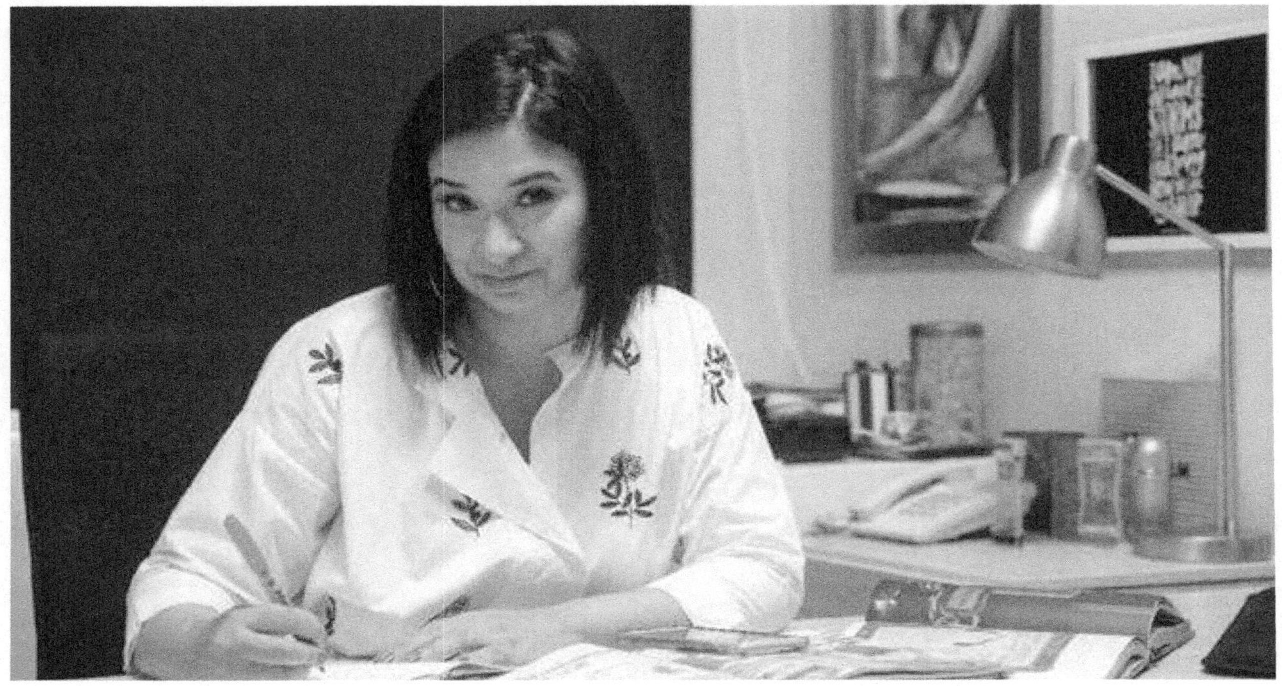

Made in United States
North Haven, CT
14 May 2025